DISCARD

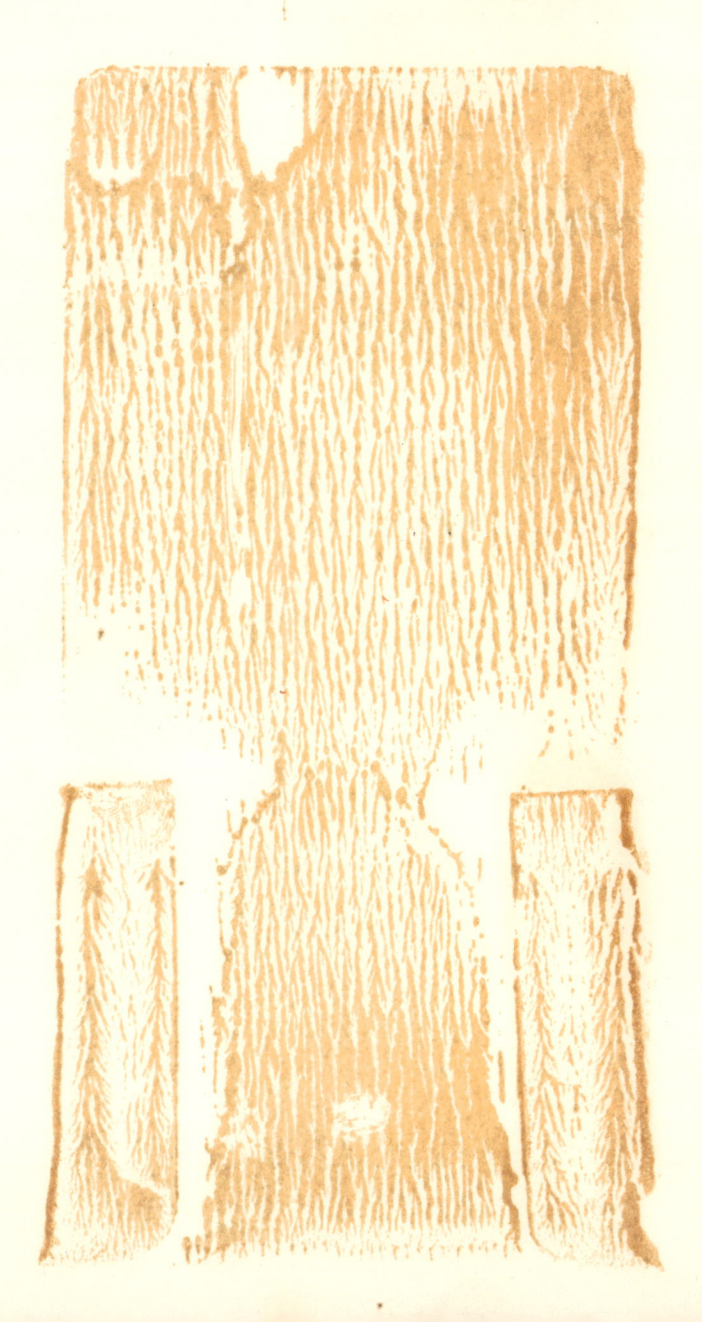

SOCIAL CHANGE

SOCIAL CHANGE
WITH RESPECT TO CULTURE AND ORIGINAL NATURE

BY
WILLIAM FIELDING OGBURN
Professor of Sociology at the University of Chicago

NEW 1950 EDITION
WITH SUPPLEMENTARY CHAPTER

GLOUCESTER, MASS.
PETER SMITH
1964

Copyright 1950 by William Fielding Ogburn
Copyright 1922 by B. W. Huebsch, Inc.
Reprinted 1964 by Permission of The Viking Press, Inc.

PREFACE

The vast social changes which characterize our age raise to a plane of great importance for sociology theories of social evolution and practical programmes. Our interest in the pages which follow is not primarily with specific programmes but rather with the more general and perhaps more fundamental aspects of social change, which are not, of course, without bearing on particular issues. The treatment deals with inquiries concerning the nature of these changes, why social changes occur, why certain conditions apparently resist change, how culture grows, how civilization has come to be what it is. These questions involve considerations of the nature and frequency of inventions, and of the part will power and human nature play in producing these processes. Are these changes solely in man's social heritage or are they changes in the biological nature of man? Could the great progress that has taken place since the last ice age have occurred without changes in mental ability and human nature? We are also interested in inquiring how satisfactorily human nature fares amidst these many changes, whether the inherent nature of man is better adapted to the new conditions than to the old, and how serious and frequent are the social maladjustments. To discuss these questions means that we must draw somewhat on researches in several different sciences, namely, biology, anthropology, psychology and economics, as well as on prior researches in sociology.

The reader naturally wishes to know how scientific consideration of such broad questions can be made. The most widely current conception of scientific method stresses the verification by data. That the collection of data is of the greatest importance is not denied. But the data must be relevant to some inquiry; there must be something to verify. Therefore the construction of hypotheses must take its place along with the accumulation of evidence; the random collection and study of facts are not indeed the sole factors in formulation of theories. There is always something that the human being wants to know; there is thus a demand for knowledge as truly as there is an economic demand. Particularly in the early development of a science the demand is much greater than the supply of material; and the demand is often not specific and over-simplified. Thus the inquiries demanded are often broad, and later it is found that they break down into a series of special inquiries. In the early history of a particular science there is therefore a wide field to be surveyed preliminary to the verification of special hypotheses.

The analysis of complex issues depends somewhat on facts and the more complete the data the better will be the analysis. With the available facts incomplete, however, good analysis demands that special hypotheses be formulated in such a way that they can be later proved or disproved by facts. The merit of the formulation depends upon a number of factors, especially a certain sagacity for the significant and a knowledge of the trend of the development of the sciences as well as the popular demand. The greatest source of error in valuations and in conclusions is probably prejudice or emotional bias. In the absence of complete data, it is thought that the most effective check against error is an examination of the sources of one's own prejudices.

The reader may be annoyed because the conclusions which follow are less emphatic than he customarily finds and because a good many suppositions and probabilities are involved. It seems to the writer that while such inconclusiveness as is found is regrettable, yet it is imposed by the magnitude of the inquiries and the scarcity of data. Despite these limitations there is value in the critical estimates of the various theories.

Suspended judgment is quite as necessary in the development of knowledge as bold theories, and should accompany them.

It has not been the purpose, particularly, to formulate a treatment of the sociological questions which would show them in their proper perspective or according to their relative importance as a set of general sociological principles. The work may therefore seem somewhat uneven. The emphasis has been of course, to a certain extent, according to importance, but it has also been the aim to present, if not new material and original considerations, at least formulations that are not widely known among sociological readers.

It has unfortunately not been possible to give credit to all sources for the information and conclusions found in the text. No one indeed ever honestly knows the origin of his ideas. They come as a result of a body of information gathered from innumerable sources during years of study. However, to many readers the current stock of sociological knowledge will be familiar and it will be known when such a stock of information has been drawn on.

W. F. O.

CONTENTS

PART I

THE SOCIAL HERITAGE AND THE ORIGINAL NATURE OF MAN

		PAGE
1.	SOCIAL HERITAGE	3
2.	THE ORIGINAL NATURE OF MAN	7
3.	THE CONFUSION OF CULTURE AND THE PSYCHOLOGICAL NATURE OF MAN	11
4.	DIFFERENTIATION OF CULTURAL AND PSYCHOLOGICAL FACTORS	16
5.	THE OVEREMPHASIS OF THE BIOLOGICAL FACTOR	29
6.	SOME SOCIOLOGICAL CONCEPTS REËXAMINED	40

PART II

SOCIAL EVOLUTION

1.	CONCEPTIONS OF SOCIAL EVOLUTION	56
2.	THE BIOLOGICAL FACTOR AND THE CULTURAL FACTOR IN SOCIAL CHANGE	61
3.	EARLY RECORDS OF CULTURAL DEVELOPMENT	66
4.	THE CUMULATIVE NATURE OF MATERIAL CULTURE AND ITS DIVERSIFICATION	73
5.	INVENTIONS, MENTAL ABILITY AND CULTURE	80

		PAGE
	A List of Some Inventions and Discoveries Made Independently by Two or More Persons	90
6.	The Rate of Cultural Growth	103
7.	Biological Change in Man	118
8.	The Correlation of Cultural and Biological Change	130

PART III

Cultural Inertia and Conservatism

1.	Various Conceptions of the Persistence of Culture	146
2.	Survivals	150
3.	The Utility of Culture	154
4.	Difficulties of Invention and of Diffusion	159
5.	Vested Interests	166
6.	The Power of Tradition	170
7.	Habit	173
8.	Social Pressure	180
9.	Forgetting the Unpleasant	186
10.	Psychological Traits and Conservatism	190

PART IV

Social Maladjustments

1.	The Hypothesis of Cultural Lag	200
2.	Verification by the Facts of Workmen's Compensation for Accidents	213
3.	Illustrations: Taxation, Family, International Relations, Trade Unions, Representative Government, Pueblo Dwellers	237
4.	Reasons for Cultural Lag	256

5. Correlation between Parts of Culture 265
6. Material Culture as a Source of Modern Social Changes 268

PART V

Adjustment between Human Nature and Culture

1. The Theory of the Cave Man in the Modern City 284
2. Evidence of Lack of Adjustment: Nervousness and Insanity 312
3. Evidence of Lack of Adjustment: Social Problems 331
4. Changing Human Nature versus Controlling Social Evolution . . . 336
5. Suggestions for Better Adjustments . 346

PART VI

Social Evolution, Reconsidered

1.   369
2.   377
3.   392

PART I

THE SOCIAL HERITAGE AND THE ORIGINAL NATURE OF MAN

I

SOCIAL HERITAGE

When a child is born into the world he is born into a natural environment, a heritage of nature. This is true of all animals. But man is born also into a social heritage.[1] This is a heritage that does not devolve upon a particular individual, in the manner in which a man inherits a piece of property. This heritage is social and is common in general to all the children born into a particular group. It is also called social heritage because it is the product of human society, the results of many social achievements during the ages that man has been on the earth. It differs from a heritage from nature such as land, water, air, vegetation, animals, in that the social heritage is the product of human social endeavor and is not the gift of nature, untouched by the hand of man. A group of new-born infants on an island uninhabited by man would be without a social heritage, although, like the lower animals, they would

[1] Graham Wallas, *Our Social Heritage.*

be born into a natural environment. The social heritage is therefore not coextensive with environment. The environment of man may be said to consist of two parts: natural environment, including air, heat, land, water, soil, moisture, vegetation and minerals; and the social heritage, consisting of buildings, technological equipment, social organization, language, the arts, philosophies, science, religions, morals and customs.

The social heritage is very similar in meaning to the word, culture, as used by sociologists and anthropologists. Culture has been defined by Tylor as "that complex whole which includes knowledge, belief, art, morals, law, custom and any other capabilities and habits acquired by man as a member of society."[2] In this definition of culture the use of material objects is not particularly emphasized, and there is a tendency to think of culture as somewhat removed from material objects. However, the use of material things is a very important part of the culture of any people. A special term, material culture, is frequently used, giving particular emphasis to the material features of culture. The word, culture, properly includes, as does the term, social heritage, both the material culture and also such parts of culture as knowledge, belief, morals, law, and custom. To enumerate in detail the

[2] E. B. Tylor, *Primitive Culture,* Vol. I, p. 1.

variegated subject matter of culture or the social heritage would include a very long list indeed; such an enumeration would comprise all the diverse parts of "that complex whole" of which Tylor speaks. The social institutions or organizations are very important parts of culture, as truly as the other parts that have been specially mentioned.

The concept, civilization, is very closely related in meaning to the concept, culture. Civilization is used in a number of different ways. To some it means certain finer, choicer, and more spiritual or moral achievements of mankind and is thus contrasted with barbarism or savagery. Civilization is also used by some writers to refer to the conditions of society where it is organized on a civil basis as contrasted to a kinship basis. Civilization may also be thought of as "that complex whole" in its recent stage of development. If culture be looked at historically then civilization is the late phase of culture, in other words, modern culture.

This conception has been further described by Herbert Spencer as the superorganic. Spencer conceived of a time when there was no life on the earth; all was inorganic.[3] Then followed the inorganic and based upon it came the organic, and this organic developed through an evolutionary

[3] Herbert Spencer, *Principles of Sociology,* Vol. I, Chap. I.

process to its highest product, man. Finally, following man and based upon man came the superorganic, and this superorganic is also developing, he said, through the process of evolution. These processes, the inorganic, the organic and the superorganic, are all interrelated and based one upon the other. Very probably the superorganic began with man or shortly after man evolved. It may be that some of the higher animals have something like the beginnings of a superorganic. For instance, certain learned tendencies may be passed down from one generation to another by animals as a sort of rudimentary social heritage. Thus birds may learn to sing a certain note from another bird. The question as to the time of origin of the superorganic, or whether the higher animals other than man possess it, may be of great importance for some problems of science, but the solution of this question is not of great significance for the purposes of the present analysis. The terms, the superorganic, social heritage, and culture, have all been used interchangeably.

The social heritage is different in different localities, with different peoples and in different eras. It also grows or decays, and no doubt there are definite processes describing its change. The causes of this variation and growth are of greatest interest, but our first purpose must be to differentiate certain concepts.

2

THE ORIGINAL NATURE OF MAN

Man as we see him and know him is always a product of two factors, heredity and environment. The contribution of heredity to this product we call original nature. The fertilized ovum carries the determinants of what will later be his original nature. The germ cell develops into an individual with definite anatomical and physiological characteristics. It determines, for example, whether the individual will be blond or brunette, male or female, large-boned or small-boned. But of the total biological equipment developed from the fertilized cell, we are interested primarily in that part of his endowment which is the subject matter of the study of psychology. The line of demarcation between physiological and psychological behavior is not clear-cut, but certain parts of the body, such as certain glands and the nervous system appear to be more intimately and conspicuously related to the behavior found in social phenomena. So we shall use the term original nature as relating to man's psychological equipment.

The orginal nature of man is described in detail in the textbooks on psychology, but these descriptions are too long for summarization here. However, in general the contribution of heredity to human nature is an organization of mechanisms that responds to stimuli in part or as a whole along specific channels. The conception of original nature is therefore that of a responding mechanism, living matter which has properties of activity as truly as gunpowder has the property of exploding or hydrogen and oxygen have the property of uniting.

The mechanisms active in reactions are sense organs, nerve centres, motor nerves, dendrites, axons, synapses, cerebellum and cortex, that, with other parts, make up the nervous system which is connected in its functioning with muscles, blood, glandular secretions, etc. The behavior of these structures is quite varied and complex. But classifications have been attempted with more or less success. The psychological properties of man are usually spoken of as reflexes, instincts, impulses, sensations, emotions and feelings. The varied reflexes and instinctive tendencies are types of responses differing in degree. The more simple, prompt and automatic responses are called reflexes. The instincts are somewhat more complex, involving many parts of the organism.

The instinctive responses are also more delayed than reflexes involving a series of bodily preparations and adjustments. Many of what we call motives are thought to spring from the mechanism of instincts. The drives which impel the behavior of man and the activity of the personality are said to come from the various mechanisms, such as the glands and nerves, that are a part of the machinery of instinct. The wishes, which have sources, too, in instinctive equipment, affect also attention, choice, judgment, habit and thought. While the capacities of man to behave are varied and complex, the theory is that these reactions can be analyzed into a few constituent elements, very much as matter may be analyzed into a few chemical elements. It is the combinations of the elements that give the variety.

In trying to see social phenomena in terms of culture and original nature, it is the behavior of man's mechanism as a whole that is particularly important, rather than such a detailed response as the reflex. It is rather what are called the motives of human beings that are important for social behavior. The original nature of man, in addition to the capacity to act, has the capacity to feel. Emotion, feeling and sensation also are a part of the equipment, and are found accompanying various responses. Emotions are usually thought of as part of that response which we have called instinctive. The behavior seen in social life can be fully accounted for, no doubt, only by the whole of man's psychological nature, but, it is thought, emotion and instinct are quantitatively and relatively the more important part of this equipment for social behavior.

Human nature is generally conceived by psychologists, fundamentally, as the nature of behaving of organized living matter of human beings possessing capacities for definite reactions. This has not always been the view of human nature. Primitive man thought of the human body as animated by spirits. Emotion, feeling, and behavior during emotion suggested the body as a dwelling place of mysterious spirits which suddenly came and went. Later the spirit of man was thought to be peculiar to man. Human nature was greatly different from animal nature.

The work of such evolutionists as Darwin, Huxley and Spencer and the study of animal psychology threw a flood of light on the emotions and instincts. The nature of man was seen to be very much like the nature of animals. The survival value of instincts was appreciated. The knowledge of the origin and development of the emotions took away much of the mystery surrounding these qualities of man. Researches in physiology, and experimental work in psychological laboratories further strengthened the idea of mechanism and response. Animal psychology and physiological psychology have added greatly to our knowledge of human nature, yet left much of our curiosity about human motives and human spirit unsatisfied. The work of students of abnormal behavior as seen in neuroses and psychoses is uncovering a wealth of material on distinctly human motives and desires. From all of these sources, then, we are learning much more about our original nature and how it behaves.

3

THE CONFUSION OF CULTURE AND THE PSYCHOLOGICAL NATURE OF MAN

The presentation just made of the two factors, the social heritage and the psychological nature of man, indicates quite clearly that they are two distinct and separate things. In fact, to the reader they doubtless appear so distinct that he wonders why they should be thus differentiated, contrasted and compared. They seem to be on two different levels, one the organic and the other the superorganic. The objects of material culture are certainly clearly differentiated from biological man. A house will never be confused with a human being; and factories, boats, machines, vehicles, clothing, food, are clearly marked off from muscles, glands, bones. The material objects of the social inheritance are distinct from the material organs and parts of man. But the social heritage is not wholly made up of material objects, nor does the nature of man consist wholly of material organs. A part of the social heritage consists of ways of doing things, methods of making material objects, ways of reacting to nature and material culture, and habits of organizing socially. So also a part of the nature of man consists of methods of reacting to stimuli, reflex activities, instinctive drives, habits, and various ways of behaving.

It is the activities required by culture and the activities occasioned by the original nature of man where the planes of the superorganic and the organic meet. Confusion resides where these two factors affecting behavior occur together, and it is in this meeting that there is necessity for differentiation. The communication of animals by instinctive and untaught sounds may be called biological-activity, whereas the communication of men by a spoken language may be called a cultural-biological-activity. Language is a feature of culture, and communication by language could not occur without a culture. It is possible to imagine at least the material objects of culture as existing for a time without man and it is possible though difficult to imagine men existing without any culture, but actually the two factors occur jointly. Some individual acts, particularly of special organs, such as breathing, occur often without influence from culture, but a great deal of individual behavior and particularly social behavior takes place in a cultural environment. The factor, social heritage, and the factor, the biological nature of man, make a resultant, behavior in culture. From the point of view of analysis, it is a case of a third variable determined by the two other variables. There may of course be still other variables, as for instance, climate, or natural environment. But for the present, the analysis concerns the two variables, the psychological nature of man and culture.

It is sometimes desirable to know how much the behavior of biological man in a cultural environment is determined by activities of the biological equipment and how much it is shaped by culture. It has been said that civilization is simply a veneer, that if you scratch the back of a civilized man you discover a barbarian. This is simply a crude way of stating the desirability of keeping clearly in mind the distinction between the cultural and the biological. The traits of nations and peoples differ, and one wonders how much the differences in national traits are due to the variable, culture, and how much to the variable, the biological nature of man.

The psychologists have worked for many years trying to segregate from the environmental influences the original traits of human nature. The difficulty of distinguishing original nature is indicated by Woodworth in the following passage:

John Doe is a strongly built man, over six feet high with big bones and muscles, erect, vigorous, with plenty of color in his face, dark-haired, blue-eyed, clean-shaven with a scar on his cheek, broad face and large ears. He is easy-going, even-tempered, fond of children and also of women, rather slangy and even profane in his talk, has a deep, sonorous voice and can carry the bass in a chorus. He is handy with tools, can drive or repair an automobile, is a fairly good carpet salesman, but much prefers out-of-door work. Rather free in spending his money, he has never run into debt except on one occasion, which turned out badly for him. Which of these traits of John Doe are native and which are acquired? How far are his physical, mental and moral traits the result of his 'original nature' and how far have they been ingrained in him or imposed upon him by his training and his environment?[4]

John Doe's big muscles are partly the gift of

[4] Robert S. Woodworth, *Psychology, A Study of Mental Life,* p. 89.

his inherited endowment, but part of the size of these muscles may have come from work in his youth on the farm or in the blacksmith's shop. While it is difficult to measure these respective influences, we know each influence has a limit. His fondness for children is due in part to an inherited parental instinct. But it may be influenced by experiences in his own childhood or with his own offspring.

Psychologists have been accustomed to using several tests for determining what are the traits of original nature, as contrasted with traits due to culture, training, experience or habit. The traits that the individual shows at birth are very likely to be original nature, because of the limited influence of environment on the fœtus. The newly born infant is a fruitful object of study in the search for original nature. But, of course, just as all traits are not developed in the fertilized ovum, so they are not all developed in the infant. Certain traits and features do not appear until later, as, for instance, at puberty. The longer the period of development, presumably the greater the possibilities of environmental influence. Another rough criterion of original as contrasted with acquired traits is the learning process. Traits that are learned show a large cultural influence, while many that are not learned are native.

Thus a bird flies without being taught to fly. Man vocalizes but learns to talk. Still another test that is sometimes used is the universality of the trait. All men or women are attracted by the opposite sex; we say the sex instincts are part of the original nature. Culture, however, is universal among human beings also, so some traits common to all men are not wholly native but partly cultural, as, for instance, talking. But when traits are found among all peoples and the higher animals as well, the presumption is that they are inherited and part of original nature. The tests for original nature are not, however, always definitive and infallible.

4

DIFFERENTIATION OF CULTURAL AND PSYCHOLOGICAL FACTORS

The concept, culture, and the concept, the original nature of man, have been set forth and it has been claimed that there is a confusion of these two factors in social behavior. It seems desirable therefore to consider some instances where such confusion exists, and we shall set forth several illustrations and at least one in some detail. Let us consider types of reaction of the French and the

Americans, as the illustration is fairly simple in analysis. For instance, Americans consider the French as thrifty and the French consider Americans as wasteful. Such an observation is probably true despite the fact that the comparisons are often made between wealthy tourists and poor peasants. But what are these traits due to? To differences in the biological natures of the peoples or to differences in their cultures? Theoretically, it is possible that such behavior as practicing thrift or being extravagant may be determined by the biological nature of man or by a cultural environment. In approaching this problem in this particular instance we examine the cultural factor first.

In many ways the cultures of these two peoples are similar, particularly when contrasted with the cultures of earlier eras. There are, however, some striking differences, two of which may be noted as affecting these traits. One concerns the development of the steam industry. The factory system is highly developed in the United States. Coal and iron are abundant. There is a great deal of manufacturing. Whereas in France there is, or was, not very much coal and iron. The factory system is not very widespread. The effect of the use of artificial power in making objects of use contrasts markedly with the use of the hands. Wealth and riches multiply with astounding rapidity under the influence of steam power in manufacturing as compared with the handicrafts, or as compared with agriculture, particularly where the large, power-driven agricultural implements are not extensively used. In other words, in the countries where the industrial revolution has gone far there is a good deal more wealth than in countries which have not been thus affected. There is more wealth to consume and the purchasing power per individual is greater. There is, in short, less occasion to be thrifty and more opportunity to gratify the various cravings that can be answered by the expenditure of money. The rapidity with which wealth is created also has much to do with the habit of spending. In the United States the development and spread of manufacturing have been very rapid, particularly since 1865. Also, the extent of the use of advertising, which is rather great in the United States, is not without point in the argument, as advertising is a great incentive to spending.

Another difference between French culture and American culture is the presence of a great amount of natural resources in the United States, as compared to the population. While natural resources, such as minerals, forests, soil, and water power, have not been classed as a part of the social heritage, nevertheless their presence in greater or lesser amount is not without effect upon the social heritage. Certainly the wealth of a nation is determined in large part by the abundance of its natural resources. The rapid coming into use of vast natural resources is not a situation to encourage thrift, but rather tends to produce recklessness and waste. The phenomenon of exploitation occurs all through recent American history.

The wealth of the United States in comparison to population is a good deal greater than the wealth of France. Comparable statistics of real wages are difficult to find, but the money income per capita is nearly twice as great in the United States as in France; the ratio in 1914 was $335 a year to $185 a year.[5] The comparison under discussion could be presented much more exhaustively and measurements could be made with some degree of completeness and accuracy. The situation in other nations where there is variation in these factors could be brought in. An analysis of the French settlement in Quebec could be made. But a further consideration would tax the patience of the reader. The observations made have probably been sufficiently sound and full to demonstrate that differences in culture can account for much difference in a trait like thrift.

[5] Mitchell, King, Macaulay and Knauth, *Income in the United States*, p. 85.

Turning to the biological factor, there is of course a basis for thrift in the mechanism of the human body. Some psychologists claim there is an instinct of acquisition and it has been said that there is a hoarding instinct. So variations in the original equipment of men may account for variations in a trait like thrift. But thrift may be much more complicated on its psychological side than the operation of a single hoarding tendency. It may involve conceptions of self, or love of display, or a valuing of future goods more than present goods. It may indeed be determined largely by the ability to repress many other instincts. Very probably it is quite a complicated type of behavior. To make even a first approximation of what thrift is psychologically is difficult.

But even if some sort of an approximation is made, a satisfactory account is difficult to obtain due to the present lack of agreement as to the nature of the instincts and the ignorance in specific cases of the physiological mechanism of the instincts. That is to say, the measurement of the biological factor in thrift depends to a certain extent on the analysis of its mechanism. Experiments have been made, though, on the relative strength of instincts without knowing much about their mechanisms, and the relative strength of desires may be known, with little being understood as to their nature of origin. Psychological tests might be made on French and on American children, while very young before cultural influences have operated much, should the practical or the theoretical importance of any problem warrant it.

But however difficult it may be to measure a biological trait free from cultural influences and however inadequate the present state of information on the instincts may be, it is not to be implied from these remarks, or from the fact that the cultural influences can be somewhat more easily analyzed, that the cultural explanation is the only true one. Indeed, while all human beings seem to possess the same general equipment of instincts, they no doubt vary in their strength, just as there is hereditary variation in stature. And if individuals vary in the strength of instincts, so collections of individuals might conceivably vary. Such variation by groups should not be assumed as a fact, but needs special investigation in each case. The general question of racial traits, about which there is so much feeling, is greatly complicated by the phenomenon of culture. But with reference to the particular question of French and American traits, these two peoples belong to the same white race. The northern French are of the same general subdivision of the white race as the old American stock. This conclusion is based on certain measurements used in classifying groups, such as stature, hair color, eye color, cephalic index, width of face and certain other general bodily features. From such measurements it is seen that the northern French and the earlier native-born Americans belong to the tall racial type found in northern Europe whose centre of dispersion was probably the Baltic sea. There is a great deal of intermixture among the racial types of Europe and purity of type is rare. But there are striking resemblances in the measurements of physical traits of the peoples of northern Europe. It would therefore seem from a consideration of the biological factor and the cultural factor that the differences between French and Americans in regard to thrift are more probably due to cultural influence.

In some instances differences can be traced with great certainty to the cultural factor as there appears to be no variation in the biological factor. Such is true, for instance, in the manifestations of hospitality in different parts of the United States. The southerners are traditionally hospitable and so are those of the pioneer west. The phenomenon of hospitality is certainly more prominent in these agricultural regions than in the cities and towns of the east. The culture of the south and of the west, a few generations ago, was certainly conducive to hospitality. Food was plentiful, there was sufficient room in the houses; there was no overcrowding. The distances between farm settlements was great. Travel was not heavy and inns were few. Furthermore, visitors meant "company" and associations and news. In the towns and cities of the east the conditions were different in all these regards and hence hospitality would not be quite so strikingly manifested. It can very readily be seen how a type of behavior called hospitality can be determined by social conditions.

Of course, there may be physiological structures determining such a type of behavior also. Some persons are by nature, we say, penurious, while others are generous and these traits are not always determined by the size of the pocketbook. Such differences may be occasioned by variations in instinctive tendencies, as hoarding or gregariousness, or by sentiments of sociability. But in the United States the people were of the same racial type, that is at least until the immigration from southeastern Europe set in. The New Englanders migrated west; and the south and the east were settled in the main from England. In other words the racial factor appears to be constant; the variation is more probably in the cultural factor.

Some types of behavior that seem largely biological and little cultural may nevertheless upon examination be found to be largely determined by the social conditions. Pugnacity and fighting seem to suggest immediately the original nature of man. Yet the social conditions determine in large part the frequency and nature of its manifestations. The same peoples will at one age settle their quarrels by duels, and at another time by a different method, the custom of dueling having become obsolete. The development of the police system, of business and of the law courts causes the instinct of pugnacity to find other outlets. And war itself while it certainly has a psychological basis manifests itself in particular social and economic settings. If war were dictated purely by the instincts no doubt there would be a certain regularity and continuity as in the functioning of hunger. Head-hunting in Melanesia has been customarily interpreted as due to blood revenge, that is, a rather simple and direct manifestation of the original nature of man. Yet Rivers,[6] as a result of a careful study, finds that the idea of revenge does not enter into the practices at all. Head-hunting is the result of a rather elaborate social ritual; it is to be explained culturally rather than biologically.

Illustrations might be presented in great numbers, if the method were statistical or descriptive. But the foregoing illustrations may be considered

[6] W. H. R. Rivers, "Sociology and Psychology," *Sociological Review*, Vol. IX (1916), pp. 1–13.

as representative of the type of analysis which it is desirable to carry in mind, namely, that social behavior is shaped both by the physical heredity and by social heritage. Further illustrations, however, of the great power of the social heritage to cause variations in manifestations of human behavior are found in great numbers in books on customs, such as Sumner's *Folkways*. In this book the analysis is not made with particular consideration of the biological element, but from such a treatise one is greatly impressed by the great variability in culture as a way of doing things, and particularly of the power of culture to select and magnify for special display, as it were, here one type of biological reaction and there another type.

This problem from the point of view of analysis is similar in several respects to the problem of heredity and environment. In fact, the psychological nature of man and culture is part of heredity and environment. The stature of an individual is certainly affected by forces of heredity. Yet it is also affected by the food one eats and by the diseases of one's childhood. Each of these influences operates to effect a permanent result, a stature which is permanent for a lifetime, subject to only slight diminution after the maximum growth is reached. The influences of environment are not passed on to the next generation through heredity. In like manner human behavior is in part the result of the influence of the original nature of man and in part the result of the influence of culture. The influence known as the original nature of man is passed on through heredity, but this is not true of the influence of culture. The influence of culture tends towards a certain permanency of result on the individual as does the influence of food on stature. Culture in early life has a good deal to do with shaping personality, which it is difficult to change very much in later life, and culture does tend to produce even in the adult habits which resist change. Just as it is desirable to segregate the factor of environment from heredity, so it is desirable to differentiate the influences on behavior of the psychological nature of man and of culture.

In discussing the variability in the biological factor and the variability in culture, it has been said that quite frequently the cultural factor varies but the biological nature of man is constant. It should be remembered that the variation in the biological nature may be conceived from two different positions, as regards individuals within a sample population and as regards samples of population in different periods or in different areas. It is the variation according to the samples and not according to individuals that is meant when it is said that the biological factor is constant. It should certainly be remembered that individuals vary in regard to any particular trait in any sample population, though the average trait of a sample does not vary from one sample to another, except as such variations are due to the smallness of the sample. Unless this point is remembered confusion may arise in such illustrations as the following. In modern civilization, individuals are found to vary in their mathematical ability. One individual can not count above ten whereas another individual is able to handle a tool like calculus. Such a difference may be due to innate capacity, that is, the individual who can not count above ten may have a mental defect. Such an individual may be at the low end of the scale on a curve of distribution of mental traits. In some primitive cultures, however, an individual can not count above ten not because he is at the lower end of the curve, but because the culture of these peoples does not have a system of counting that goes further than ten in number. In another and higher culture the same individual might be able to solve problems by the use of calculus. Theoretically, it is conceivable that samples of these two peoples might not vary biologically, although their cultures do. So in thinking of comparisons of peoples, it is the samples of the peoples as a whole, thought of as averages or frequency distributions, that should be compared; or else if individuals be compared, they should be drawn from the same relative positions in the curve of distribution. The illustration just presented is of course an extreme one. Another illustration is that an Eskimo and a civilized European may be equally uncleanly in their habits; but in the case of the Eskimo it may be due to lack of cultural provisions for cleanliness while in the European it may be due to an inferior psychological equipment. In this case individuals compared are not from the same relative position on the scale of variation. The psychological basis for cleanliness of the Eskimo may be the same as that of the European, but the cultural difficulties of keeping clean are much greater among the Eskimo.

It is therefore seen that individuals or populations may differ biologically and that cultures may also differ. In cases where cultural-biological-behavior differs and the biological factor is constant, the differences are cultural and the differences may be characterized as differences in cultural traits. On the other hand where the differences cannot be accounted for as being due to culture, they may be characterized as due to variation in psychological traits. The term, cultural trait, does not refer so much to the material features of culture as to such parts of culture as knowledge, custom, belief, art and the various ways of doing things; and of course does not mean that the material objects of culture have traits in the same manner in which the material organs and substances integrated into the human body have traits. Nevertheless the term is a useful descriptive term, as for instance, in the statement that in a particular situation cleanliness is a cultural trait not a racial trait, or in the case where the people of a nation who do not change biologically over a period of time, at different periods during this time display quite different cultural traits.

5

THE OVEREMPHASIS OF THE BIOLOGICAL FACTOR

Popular tendency to confuse the cultural and the psychological or, as Kroeber phrases it, the social and the mental, probably results in an overemphasis of the psychological and an underemphasis of the cultural. This is particularly noticeable in accounting for the traits of the sexes. Women, for instance, are supposed to have an absorbing interest in purely personal affairs and relationships while men are more interested in objective discussions of movements and events. This difference is frequently commented upon in considering the entrance of women into politics and into business. The somewhat intimate relationship between women and children is supposed to account for this difference on biological grounds. As a biological explanation it is a bit mystical. It seems more plausible to seek the explanation in the differences in daily activities of men and women. The work of men takes them more into the world of events, social movements and business. Whereas woman's restricted sphere of the family, centring around husband and children and social friendships, seems more personal. So that while women may be more interested in the personal than men, this difference is either wholly due to culture or else is greatly accentuated by culture. Women are said also not to be averse to methods involving slight deceptions, at least apparently they resort more readily than men to subterfuge or other less direct but ingenious ways of obtaining their ends. This observation, if true, may be intended to apply to the fields of the more purely personal relationships and not for instance to the spheres of business activity. This is popularly supposed to be a feminine trait, meaning a hereditary biological trait, yet close observers have attributed its origin to a cultural situation where men hold economic and social power. Men are thus more direct and frank in their actions, while with women there is a more or less variable pressure to be indirect in the pursuit of their aims. And even such a trait as modesty which seems so closely identified with the distinctive biological characteristics of women is certainly greatly emphasized by social conditions.

A great many of these so-called feminine traits are analyzed and their cultural aspects explained by Mrs. Coolidge in her most interesting book, *Why Women are So.* Such a study as Mrs. Coolidge has made, while it does not segregate and measure the influence of original nature and of culture, certainly does demonstrate quite satisfactorily that there is a popular tendency to attribute much that is cultural to hereditary biological factors. Popular opinion describes a large assortment of traits as feminine, perhaps a slightly smaller number as masculine, and a more or less vague list as common to both the sexes. If these traits were considered from the purely biological point of view, the list of feminine and of masculine traits would probably be much smaller and certainly much less prominent, or if plotted in curves there would be great overlapping of the curves. The great division of labor along sex lines found all through society, while perhaps in part occasioned by biological differences, certainly results in an exaggeration in the popular mind of the biological differences between the sexes. The point under consideration is not an inquiry as to what biological differences do exist. There are morphological differences, quite probably emotional differences, and there may be indeed some intellectual differences. But what should be pointed out is that these emotional and intellectual differences are popularly exaggerated by reading the psychological into the cultural influences, a confusion of the two factors.

There are several reasons why cultural traits tend to be popularly interpreted as biological traits. The effect of culture on an individual is carried around by that individual in the forms of habit, training, education, technique, conditioned reflexes. These acquired ways of doing things are seen as part of an individual as truly as his physiognomy is. The association is almost as close. They become a part of his psychological self and are generally more or less permanently descriptive of the personality. The concept of the original nature of man does not frequently appear in the ordinary judgments of life. It takes some special training and imagination to see the original nature of man beneath his cultural exterior, for it is only in special situations in life where such penetrating observation is called for. Man as nature plus nurture is thus popularly seen as nature. Acquired characteristics are thought to be so integral a part of an individual as to be hereditary.

Indeed it required special research to disprove this. So it seems very natural to interpret cultural traits as psychological traits.

In attempting to formulate the concepts of the social heritage and the biological nature of man, it has been seen that a difficulty lies in the confusion of these two ideas due to the general tendency to consider the cultural influence on behavior as biological. There is also another source of confusion. This does not concern behavior so much as the products of behavior. But the results are similar in that the cultural influence is obscured and the biological influence is magnified. Consider, for instance, the appearance of some hitherto undeveloped object of material culture, say, a steam engine. What are the factors that operated to make the steam engine? Obviously one factor is mental ability. Also the formerly invented and prepared materials that go to make up the steam engine, and the existing state of knowledge, are another factor. These two factors are quite different in nature but are quite definitely two general factors operating to produce the steam engine. It could not be produced without the mental ability, nor could it be produced without scientific knowledge and without materials in a certain degree of previous preparation. The factor of mental ability is always recognized. But very often one does not appreciate the cultural factor, that is, one does not think how dependent an invention is on previous inventions and on the previously developed state of knowledge. The steam engine could not have been invented, for instance, without a knowledge of fire, combustion, vaporization, the metals, the wheel, the piston, valves, the screw and numerous other inventions and processes. The existing state of the social heritage is thus a very important factor in the invention of a particular cultural object. The cave man, had he the ability of a modern genius, could not have invented the steam engine, living as he did on the plane of culture existing during the last ice age. Presented in this manner, it is readily seen that the cultural factor is necessary and as important as is the factor of mental ability. But popularly there is full recognition of mental ability but a neglect of cultural influence. When Edison makes an invention, credit is given to his ability and rightly so because the social heritage is the heritage of many, yet only a few utilize it to make discoveries and inventions. The variable factor is the individual and is therefore thought of as the causative factor. He is not thought of as original nature plus the social heritage.

In a somewhat similar way the culture of Great Britain and her colonies is seen as the product of the ability of the Anglo-Saxon peoples. The dependence of British culture upon the inventions and achievements of other peoples is not called to the attention. To think of this implies a certain historical and cultural knowledge, not possessed by many. Indeed the total knowledge on the origin and diffusion of inventions is quite limited. But many peoples of various periods from different parts of the world have been associated with the development of the modern culture possessed by the British. It has been quite customary to attribute the Greek civilization in a somewhat complete fashion to the genius of the Greek people. Indeed it is only recently that research is establishing how much Greece borrowed from the peoples to the north, the east and the south. Great Britain has borrowed many times as much as she has invented. But even admitting a differentiation between what a people has invented and what borrowed, the concept of cultural evolution is not conceived in any full sense. That is to say, it is not seen that culture would have changed and increased from the time of the Angles and the Saxons until now, more or less irrespective of the particular peoples that may have been associated with this culture. Such an idea is not common, and indeed it is seldom noted in intellectual circles, very largely for the reason that at the present state of our knowledge the laws governing the growth and change of culture are not clearly and quantitatively formulated. Culture grows because of mental ability, but the existing basis of culture is a very important factor in determining the nature and rate of growth of culture.

The prevailing status of general opinion is seen from the fairly complete identification of the state of culture of a people with their abilities. The Egyptians produced the Egyptian culture, the Indian culture is a product of Indian ability, as the European culture is a product of European ability. And the Hottentot culture is an index of the ability of that people. So popular opinion runs. There may be variation in the abilities of peoples but the state of culture is not a good index. The varying social inheritances may be correlated with the abilities of peoples, but the proof is not clear and certainly the correlation is not very close, for the very reason that purely cultural or historical causes are such an important factor in determining a particular culture. These questions of the relations of culture to mental ability and of the causes and laws of the growth and change of culture are far-reaching and will be considered further later on. But enough has been said to show that the purely cultural influence tends to be obscured and overshadowed by the biological factor.

The overemphasis of the biological influence as contrasted to the cultural influence has certain roots in the facts of everyday life. The results of the training are seen through the eyes of youth very much in terms of personal achievement. Honors, prizes, grades, diplomas, emphasize this fact. In the classroom the same culture is presented to all, the variations in results are variations in personal abilities. Honors or diplomas are not given to the textbooks or the teacher. Variations in social opportunity are seen as something to be grasped. And this utilization of opportunity for a greater culture is interpreted in terms of personal ability. Moral training of the young is a matter of doing right or wrong, of praise or blame, an emphasis of the personal and a neglect of the cultural. Achievement reflects the glory of the ego and the hero is given full credit. There is no particular occasion to give the credit to so impersonal a factor as culture. The particular political party in power claims credit for a period of prosperity even though it be a matter of crops and rainfall. And failure, particularly in the other fellow, is a matter of personal inefficiency. Especially among the wealthy classes is it customary to attribute their position almost solely to ability and to make the converse interpretation for those not at the top— a very comfortable theory. In many such simple daily estimations the influence of culture is not appreciated. Thus a mental pattern is ready-made, prepared since youth, and one brings such a ready-made pattern to the study of sociology or to the reading of history, which it may be remarked is also usually written from this same mental pattern.

In intellectual centres, the overemphasis of the biological is in part occasioned by the prevailing status of the various sciences; the prestige of biology among the social sciences has been very great, because of the extraordinary significance of the discovery of natural selection and the emphasis on evolution due to the researches of Darwin and Wallace. The significance was so overshadowing that it seemed to cast something like a hypnotic spell over others doing research. The biological terminology was borrowed quite widely; and it became almost a fad to refer to biological causes and to make biological interpretations for many social phenomena. Of recent years the tendency to get away from this spell is noticeable but the rise of the eugenists has given added emphasis to the importance of biology for sociology.

Eugenics centres attention on biological variation, with the purpose of improving biological ability and eliminating biological inferiority. The eugenists are so impressed with the importance of racial stock that scant attention is given to the social heritage and there is very little understanding of its nature. All through the writings of the eugenists is found the implication that a particular culture is quite simply and directly the ability of the racial stock. They do not seem to realize that cultural growth is caused largely by purely cultural causes. They see inventions and improvement chiefly in terms of mental ability, failing to appreciate the extent of the dependence of future change on existing cultural elements. The result of the spread of the eugenics idea is, like the discovery of natural selection, an overemphasis of the significance of the biological factor in social progress.

The discussion has gone sufficiently far to show something of the concepts of the original nature of man and of the social heritage, and of the significance of such a delineation for sociology. Human behavior never occurs except in a cultural *milieu* and the social heritage could not grow except by the group activities of biological men. For this reason, to some an attempt to segregate these factors may not seem necessary. But such an attempted segregation is quite necessary, for the two factors meet in all social phenomena and are indeed the occasion of it. An understanding of social phenomena and the handling of modern social problems makes desirable a consideration of these two factors, in very much the same way as there is occasion to know something of the relative influence of heredity and environment. In describing these conceptions it has been shown that popularly and in intellectual centres the tendency is to confuse these factors, obscuring the cultural and exaggerating the biological, an overemphasis of biology and a neglect of sociology.

6

SOME SOCIOLOGICAL CONCEPTS REËXAMINED

The concepts of the social heritage and the inherited nature of man are of such theoretical importance, that it is desirable to examine some of the definitions in sociology which are generally recognized as important, to see whether these two concepts throw any light on these definitions. It is realized that the discussions of the scope and function of sociology, the definitions of society, social evolution, social mind, etc., are a field of considerable magnitude about which there has been much controversy for many years. To enter at all comprehensively into this field would involve an extensive consideration of terminology and the discussion of many writers. There will be no attempt here to settle these moot points.

The purpose is rather to examine some of these more important sociological conceptions, as formulated by certain representative sociologists, to see what they mean in terms of the social heritage and of the original nature of man, and particularly to see if this differentiation helps to clarify these problems.

Of the founders of sociology, Comte was freer from the confusion of the biological with the sociological factors than some writers who followed him. The prestige of biological science was at that time not so great, and Comte [7] conceived of sociology a good deal in terms of what has been called culture, and the influences he considered were in large part cultural. He speaks of the constancy of the human factor, the influence of former generations as a source of modification of the social movement, and the preponderant importance of historical analysis and the auxiliary aspect of biological considerations.

To Spencer is due the conception of the fundamental types of evolution, the organic and the superorganic. In the organization of his system of the sciences he recognized the difference in nature of these two fields of evolution; but when he came to work out the development of the superorganic in his *Principles of Sociology*, he con-

[7] A. Comte, *The Positive Philosophy,* Vol. II, Chap. IV.

cerned himself very largely with a consideration of the influence of the biological factor on the superorganic. At this time the development of biology was far-reaching in significance. Spencer had worked a great deal in the biological field before writing his *Principles of Sociology* and biology is certainly most prominent throughout his sociological writings. Customs, organizations and institutions are seen as the result of man, physical, emotional and intellectual. There is comparatively little account of such cultural phenomena in terms of culture itself.

Giddings has not been concerned particularly with culture as such. He has studied the psychological nature of society and association. To him sociology is the study of society and society is the result of such psychological activities as like response to stimuli, interstimulation and response, concerted activities and consciousness of kind. The shift in recent years has been somewhat away from culture and history in the direction of the psychological nature of society. However, these excellently laid psychological foundations of sociology do not alone explain a particular type of social heritage. It is quite necessary to consider the historical process entirely apart from the psychological nature of collective behavior.

What then is the relation of society and the social heritage? Giddings defines society "as any plural number of sentient creatures more or less continuously subjected to common stimuli, to differing stimuli, and to interstimulation, and responding thereto in like behavior, concerted activity or coöperation, as well as in unlike or competitive activity; and becoming therefore with developing intelligence coherent through a dominating consciousness of kind, while always sufficiently conscious of differences to insure a measure of individual liberty."[8]

According to this definition, society is a plural number of individuals manifesting group behavior. Other definitions similarly emphasize the group and group behavior. Society is therefore different from the social heritage. The social heritage may affect the group and group behavior but it is probably often thought of as the product of society. The social heritage, however, is not solely the product of human association occurring at a particular period, of course, but is a certain surviving product over a very long period of time. The existing social heritage plays an important part in creating newer forms of culture as truly as does collective behavior. It may be claimed that the social heritage is not only the

[8] F. H. Giddings, *Descriptive and Historical Sociology*, p. 9.

product of collective activity but also of individual activity, particularly as certain objects of the material culture appear to be the result of individual activity; but in such cases the individual functions because of his life in society. The social heritage, especially some of these learned ways of doing things, such as social organization and rules of collective procedure, quite directly concern such psychological activities as response to stimuli, concerted activity and consciousness of kind, as truly as does the psychological nature inherent in man.

Conceptions of society should therefore not neglect the factor of social heritage. Society is, according to Giddings' definition, a plural number of psychological human beings acting in certain variously defined collective ways. But this definition of collective behavior says nothing with reference to the cultural media. It describes rather the nature of social human behavior either with or without a culture. The particular nature of the culture, however, determines the forms of the concerted activity and to a certain extent the amount. For instance, within or between societies the amount and nature of the fighting that occurs will depend on the type of culture. Culture certainly conditions the response to stimuli. Giddings has therefore emphasized the psychological nature of society and his account of society tends to be in terms of the original nature of man.

It is interesting to observe how some of the organismic theories of the state and some of the earlier conceptions of the social mind attempted to deal with the superorganic. The writers of these theories did not confuse the cultural and the biological in the manner discussed in preceding paragraphs, that is, by interpreting a particular social phenomenon through the psychological activity of man. Instead they confounded the nature of the whole superorganic of a particular organized people with the biological nature of man. This they did by distinctly naïve analogies such as likening the transportation system to the circulatory system of the human body. These attempts seem fantastic but they did truly imply an idea of the superorganic as such. The reaction away from these organismic theories swung far away from the purely cultural influences and in the direction of the psychological influences which were becoming better understood through the rise of the biological and psychological sciences.

What does the social mind mean in terms of the psychological nature of man and in terms of culture? It is very difficult to get a clear idea of the social mind in any terms. The idea of the social mind seems to have arisen from notions of society as an organism. Spencer has likened the deliberative assemblies of modern society to the cerebellum. In popular conceptions the social judgments show the operation of the social mind. Mob activity has likewise been characterized as a manifestation of the mob mind. Giddings has defined the social mind "as the like responsiveness to stimulation, the concurrent feeling and intelligence, the consciousness of kind and the concerted volition of two or more individuals." [9] He thus eliminates the idea that the social mind is a separate entity possessed by a group but not by the individual, to which most modern writers are agreed. But, it is observed, the innate psychological traits are particularly emphasized in this definition. These psychological traits function, however, in cultural media and are affected by cultural experiences, as is true of the individual mind. The mind of the individual is generally thought of as the inherited mental equipment as modified by learning and training; indeed the knowledge and education as aspects of the mind are sometimes emphasized more than the inherited factor. So at times that part of our social heritage known as knowledge, science and the like is thought of as a part of the

[9] F. H. Giddings, *Descriptive and Historical Sociology*, p. 185.

mind of the race, perhaps the social mind. In any case, in referring to the social mind, it should be remembered that the purely psychological manifestations which are an important factor of what is called the social mind are much affected by that inherited portion of our culture known as knowledge, science, belief, custom, etc.

Are "social problems" to be explained in terms of culture, of the original nature of man or of both? Many courses in universities and colleges and many textbooks in sociology deal with what are called social problems, such as problems of industry, labor, the family, immigration, the woman's movement, and crime. These problems are often problems of adjustment between the social heritage and the original nature of man. Sometimes the emphasis is rather largely on the cultural side, as for instance, in an issue concerning the compensation of workmen for injuries because of industrial accidents, and sometimes the considerations are markedly on the side of the original nature of man as in the divorce problem and in the treatment of mental defect. While often these problems arise from interrelations between the two planes, the organic and the superorganic, the term, social conditions, can be used interchangeably with culture; thus when the social conditions of two sections are said to be different, what is probably meant is that the cultures are different, leading of course to different cultural manifestations of social behavior.

Kroeber [10] has recently made an attempt to show that the subject matter of sociology is culture, apparently relatively free from any consideration of the organic factor. His attempt is quite bold considering the agreement existing as to the nature of society and the acceptance of society as the subject matter of sociology, and is also significant because of his logical and consistent analysis which sets forth the importance of culture as a subject of science. Briefly his thesis flows from his classification of sciences according to planes, the inorganic, the vital organic, the mental organic, and the superorganic. The inorganic, including chemistry and physics, is on quite a different plane from the vital organic, including biology. Thus the biologist accepts life and "inquires into its forms and processes as such." That is, he expresses organic life in organic terms as on the organic planes. It may be possible to express life in terms of chemistry, "but that is not the first task of the biologist, else his biology would be pure physics and chemistry." The chemist and the physicist may be on one plane and

---

[10] A. L. Kroeber, "The Possibility of a Social Psychology," *American Journal of Sociology*, Vol. XXIII (1913), No. 5, p. 633.

the biologist on another, but it does not follow by analogy that the planes of psychology and of culture are similarly separated. It is indeed possible to exaggerate the planar separations of biology and of physics and chemistry. Heredity may be classified by a charting in organic terms but a knowledge of the effect of chemical substances on mutations would not be without interest for biology. Certainly there is tremendous demand for an understanding of the interrelations of culture and the psychological behavior of man, the effect of culture on behavior and the effect of behavior on culture. This is testified by the great body of writing and the number of courses of study on these interrelations, both in sociology and in the special social sciences. Consider, for instance, criminology. The cause of crime may be economic or due to mental defect; and prison reform, probation systems, indeterminate sentences, prison discipline and self-government in prisons all involve interrelations of culture and behavior. Neither can it be maintained that the study of crime is the domain solely of psychology by practice or by theory. And even on the most strict theoretical grounds, particular cultural forms are not determined solely by cultural forces flowing out of previous or contemporaneous cultural stages; a very important creative factor is the psychological nature of man.

It is also a distinctly limiting factor to cultural forms. It is true, that in the study of society, social phenomena, social problems, social organization, and social processes, the cultural and historical factors have been neglected and there has been an over-interpretation in terms of the psychological and the biological factors; but such a condition does not justify a swing completely away from the psychological and wholly to the cultural.

In conclusion, then, two factors in social phenomena have been recognized and their significance for analysis shown. Usually the cause of the phenomenon is inaccurately thought to be largely biological or psychological and only slightly cultural. The cause of unemployment, for instance, was thought by many to be due to human nature, that is, to laziness, to unwillingness to work, to a desire to loaf, to lack of ambition or to many other psychological traits of the unemployed. The cultural causes of unemployment are not the first to be seen. But as a result of investigation it is found that a vast amount of unemployment is due to the cyclical and seasonal nature of industrial life, and to a particular organization of business which could be greatly improved by a good system of employment agencies. While it is a fact that the general tendency is to overemphasize human nature as a cause in the whole field, still the preceding analyses do not warrant any dogmatic doctrines. The dogma of the pure environmentalist is as untrue as the dogma of the biologist as previously indicated in the study of crime. The investigation should concern both factors and the facts in each case will determine the relative significance of each factor. There are perhaps several reasons why good methodology should sanction as a first step a consideration of the cultural factor. In the first place the cultural factor is directly connected with a description of the phenomenon; a description being necessary before an analysis of causes is undertaken. An account of the cultural factor is in part a history and an account of contemporary cultural relationships. Furthermore, it is frequently possible to make such an account with a fair degree of accuracy. It is usually much more difficult to describe the factor of human nature. Human nature is very elusive; our ignorance of its laws is great; measurement is difficult; and prejudices are strong. Furthermore the influence of the factor, human nature, can be seen usually much more clearly after the cultural factor is understood. These remarks, while applying specifically to analyses of particular social phenomena, are also applicable to accounts of cultural development in general.

PART II

SOCIAL EVOLUTION

In Part II the discussion will concern some of the ways in which culture has grown and changed. There was a time when culture was very small. Now it is very great and wonderful. We call it civilization. How has civilization grown to be what it is? Has the psychological development of the race been the cause of its growth? Can the nature of its growth and change be described in a few simple processes? Can we deduce a few leading causes or laws of its evolution? What of its future development? Can it be consciously directed and effectively controlled? These questions naturally occur to the mind thinking of social evolution. In a general way the questions suggest the nature of the inquiries which follow. They have been the subject matter of investigation of sociologists and other students of the social sciences for many years, and are listed here not so much with the idea of giving a satisfactory answer to them, but rather as suggesting the general nature of the topic under discussion. More particularly we shall raise the question whether the biological evolution of man is an essential factor in the growth of civilization, that is, whether culture may not develop when there is no biological change. We shall also try to describe in broad outline some of the processes by which civilization has come about.

I

CONCEPTIONS OF SOCIAL EVOLUTION

The topics referred to in the preceding paragraph have been the theme of a study known as social evolution. The publication of the *Origin of Species,* setting forth a theory of evolution of species in terms of natural selection, heredity and variation, created a deep impression on the anthropologists and sociologists. The conception of evolution was so profound that the changes in society were seen as a manifestation of evolution and there was an attempt to seek the causes of these social changes in terms of variation and selection, very much as changes in species had been accounted for. History had formerly been largely descriptive of events of a political, militaristic, economic or personal nature. But following Darwin there was a great impetus to sociologists to seek causes, in terms of processes and laws, of more generalized social changes such as the origin and development of social institutions. The tedious task of recording facts and collecting data was not abandoned but greater emphasis was laid on the search for causes. Preliminary to the search for causes, however, attempts were made to establish the development of particular social institutions in successive stages, an evolutionary series, a particular stage necessarily preceding another. The search for laws led to many hypotheses regarding factors such as geographical location, climate, migration, group conflict, racial ability, the evolution of mental ability, and such principles as variation, natural selection, and survival of the fit. A half-century or more of investigations on such theories has yielded some results, but the achievements have not been up to the high hopes entertained shortly after the publication of Darwin's theory of natural selection.

The inevitable series of stages in the development of social institutions has not only not been proven but has been disproven. For illustration, the history of a particular social institution among a particular people may show a series of forms; among other peoples, though, no such similar series of forms has appeared. The attempts to find laws of heredity, variation and selection in the evolution of social institutions have produced few results either vital or significant. These results are in the main only analogous and illustrative. Strong claims have been made for climate and race, but for many of the generalizations the evidence is not authoritatively conclusive. The field of psychological causes is in the stage of being opened up. Certainly the study of social evolution is still in the process of its early development and no such impressive conclusions have been as yet forthcoming, as the theory of evolution for biology.

The facts of social evolution will be recorded, however, in greater and greater number; some of the work that has already been done will serve as foundation for further researches; and eventually the processes, causes and laws will become clearer. It is hoped that the analyses which follow will add something to the knowledge of this field of investigation.

The following discussion is more accurately described as relating to the development of culture rather than of social evolution. Social evolution and cultural evolution are not the same, as society and culture are not the same. Culture may be thought of as the accumulated products of human society, and includes the use of material objects as well as social institutions and social ways of doing things. Hence cultural change is the change in these products. Social evolution is the evolution of society and society is usually described in psychological terms, such as sociability, gregariousness, association, response to stimuli and consciousness of kind, and not in cultural terms. If society be thus strictly defined, then social evolution would mean the evolution of such mechanisms of association. If these mechanisms of association be conceived in purely psychological terms, that is, as inherent psychological mechanisms, then it may be questioned whether there has been any social evolution in many centuries, for the inherited biological mechanisms of association may not have changed for a long time. There have been changes in response to stimuli, but it may very well be that such changes are in the cultural nature of the stimuli or responses and not in the inherited psychological nature of the responses. It may be that there has been change in the consciousness of kind, but the question is whether such change has been in the cultural nature of kind or in the inherited psychological nature of consciousness.

If social evolution be interpreted in this strict psychological conception of society, then the evolution in the psychological mechanisms of association becomes essentially biological evolution; and hence social evolution is merely a phase of biological evolution. But social evolution is usually not so narrowly understood. If social evolution means changes in the mechanisms of association then such changes may be quite truly cultural, for there are cultural mechanisms of association just as there are biological mechanisms of association. Social evolution, in such case, consists largely in the evolution of social organizations and social ways of behavior, as seen in religion, art, law, custom, etc. Social evolution thus includes a large part of the evolution of culture, virtually all but material culture. And if the objects of material culture are the products of social influence and behavior then the evolution of the whole of culture is a part of social evolution. Social evolution in addition includes the possible evolution of the inherited mechanisms of association which are not part of the field of cultural evolution.

However these definitions may be settled,[1] and irrespective of the overlapping of these fields, the subject matter under discussion in the pages which follow is the development of culture. Even from the point of view of social evolution it is thought that the study of changes in culture, rather than in society, is desirable methodology because the influence of the biological factor can be seen more clearly. In the previous chapter it has been pointed out that confusion has resulted from failure to segregate the cultural and the biological

[1] For further discussion, see Ellwood, "Theories of Cultural Evolution," *American Journal of Sociology,* Vol. XXIII, No. 6.

factors. The writers on social evolution have seldom attempted to differentiate these factors in explaining cultural changes. Frequently authors have seemed to assume that marked cultural changes have been due to a biological evolution of inherent mental ability, while a few others have recorded cultural changes without apparent concern as to whether these changes have been due to changes in the original nature of man or not.

2

THE BIOLOGICAL FACTOR AND THE CULTURAL FACTOR IN SOCIAL CHANGE

Theoretically, cultural changes may be accounted for in terms of changes in the biological nature of man or in purely cultural factors. Thus Lowie's explanation of the origins of the clan as the result of property rights and of modes of residence after marriage is a study of a purely cultural cause of a cultural change.[2] Such a change to a clan form of organization is not occasioned by a change in inherited human nature but may have come about as a result of the development of property and a change in residence habits. In

[2] Robert H. Lowie, "Family and Sib," *American Anthropologist*, New Series, Vol. XXI (1919), pp. 28-41.

this explanation nothing is said or implied regarding the change in the biological nature of man. Similarly the instability of the modern family and the recent changes in the family as a functioning organization may be explained wholly on a cultural basis. These changes are due largely to the discovery of the uses of steam and its application to mechanical industry, the rise of cities, the introduction of women into industry and the discovery of methods of birth control. Changes in the family may thus be explained without reference to causes due to changes in the biological nature of man. Man may remain biologically the same, yet important changes in a social organization occur.

On the other hand, the causes of changes in culture may be sought in changes in the biological nature of man. Thus Sollas [3] seems to assume a close correlation between biological evolution and cultural evolution, implying that the heights of cultural attainments of the various peoples are indications of the steps in their biological evolution. For instance, he tries to show that peoples to-day with cultures very similar to the cultures of the peoples living during the ice ages in Europe are of the same racial type as these earlier peoples. Thus, the Bushmen of modern times are the same

[3] W. J. Sollas, *Ancient Hunters*, Chapters VII, IX and XII, and pp. 302, 303.

peoples racially as the Aurignacians of the last ice age in Europe, the Aurignacians having migrated in early times to southern Africa, he thinks. His most important evidence seems to be that their cultures are much alike. So also the Australians are the Mousterians, and the Eskimo are the Magdalenians. Such reasoning leads to the conclusion that among the peoples possessing simpler cultures, the heights of cultural possibilities are limited by the stages of biological evolution of the various peoples. So we have an interpretation of cultural evolution in terms of biological evolution. In fact it is quite usually taken for granted that the civilized peoples are superior biologically, particularly in the inherited mental qualities, to our ancestors the cave men, because we have a superior culture. It seems to follow as a corollary that our superior culture is due to our higher mental evolution, i. e., biological evolution. In fact, it is quite generally assumed that the status of the culture of any people is an index of the stage of their inherent mental development as a race. For if a people had more inherent mental ability, then their culture would have been developed to a higher degree. This attitude is what is meant when it is said that the evolution of culture is interpreted in terms of the biological factor.

Another illustration may make the point

clearer. A number of anthropologists, particularly Lewis H. Morgan, held the following theory with regard to the origin of the clan.[4] In the clan, descent is reckoned through the mother only, kinship being counted among the relations on the mother's side only and marriage is exogamous. This peculiar method of tracing kinship was supposed to be a stage in an evolutionary series. Before the metronymic stage it was thought that there was no permanent marriage of pairs. There was promiscuity in sexual relations. Eventually man's sexual relations became more stable, and organized sexual relations emerged. Tracing descent through the mother was natural, since there was uncertainty about the father; hence kinship on the father's side was not counted. In so far as such a change from a state of promiscuous sexual relations to a family tracing descent through the mother occurred as a result of evolution in the inherent sexual nature of men and women, then we have a cultural change accounted for in biological terms. This theory is discredited now largely as a result of the accumulation of additional data. There is no evidence to show that a state of so-called sexual promiscuity ever existed and there are many primitive peoples with very crude cultures who count as kin the blood relatives of both parents, as we

[4] Lewis H. Morgan, *Ancient Society*, pp. 418, 433–

do. A change from promiscuity to the organized family could have occurred without any biological change in the inherent sexual nature of men and women. Culture may have brought about different habits without a change in the germ plasm.

Culture may therefore have changed possibly because of changes in the biological nature of man or possibly because of cultural processes. There is of course a psychological side to cultural changes, since culture could not change except through the medium of human beings. A consideration of the psychological side to cultural change unfolds the whole question of the relations of psychology and sociology. The psychological factor in social change is far-reaching, with many ramifications. We are not at this point concerned with this whole problem, but we are interested particularly in the relation of biological evolution to cultural evolution. We wish particularly to inquire whether biological evolution in man has occurred during the growth of our culture from its early beginnings in the glacial periods to its modern form which we call civilization. We are also interested in asking how, if cultural evolution does not depend on biological evolution, has culture grown, and particularly by what cultural processes. Both these questions will be considered in the pages which follow. The discussion of biological evolution will be postponed until we have considered the cultural factors in the growth of our civilization. We shall first review some of the actual facts of the early evolution of our culture. This is desirable in order to refresh the memory of the reader with certain records which will later serve as material for an attempt to chart some of the processes of cultural growth and also as material to be contrasted with biological evolution. Having made this review, we shall discuss some of the processes of cultural growth and then consider the possible relation to biological evolution. We will now pass in review some of the facts of the origin and development of our culture.

3

EARLY RECORDS OF CULTURAL DEVELOPMENT

The earliest evidences of material culture are eoliths or "dawn-stones." These eoliths are rough fragments of hard stones that might have been used as cutting implements or as scrapers. They have been found in considerable numbers over Europe, but so far no remains of early man have been found with them. It is not known positively that the eoliths were broken or fashioned by the hands of an animal. It is possible that these fragments may have been the result of forces of nature. They occur in deposits dating back to the early beginnings of the Pleistocene period and possibly well back into the Pliocene. The Pleistocene is the period of the four glacial and the corresponding interglacial and postglacial periods. Its beginning is a half-million or more years ago.

It is not until the third interglacial period, however, that stone implements are found which are definitely known to have been artificially chipped. These implements are made apparently from accidental forms by a few retouches. Five or six forms have been classified; planing tools, scrapers, drills or borers, knives, hammerstones and hand stones. This industry is called the Pre-Chellean and existed 125,000 years ago according to Osborn's estimate.[5] Others have dated it another 100,000 years further back. But certainly 125,000 years ago there was a material culture. Observations have been most frequent in Europe, and of course it cannot be said what future excavations may show. Only slight search has been made in Asia and the finding of remains of early culture is to a certain extent accidental.

The Chellean stone industry was fairly highly developed and quite extensive. Its date was around 100,000 years ago according to Osborn.

[5] Henry Fairfield Osborn, *Men of the Old Stone Age.*

The following references to the stone culture are from Osborn unless otherwise noted. The Chellean industry is in two phases, the early phase showing the appearance of the characteristic almond-shaped *"coup de poing"* made from a nodule of quartzite or flint, rather unsymmetrical, however, and with uneven edges. There were also improved scrapers, planes, and borers. In the late Chellean period, the *"coup de poing"* is more oval, longer and pointed, but flaked on both sides. The workers were still dependent on chance shapes of shattered fragments. A somewhat larger number of forms appear, disk forms, curved scrapers, "pointes," borers, pointed scrapers, knives, knives with coarse boring-point at one end, thick scrapers, and certain combination tools. Within another 25,000 years and towards the close of the warm interglacial period, the stone industry reached a high degree of development in the successive phases of the Acheulean industry. A number of new forms appeared: choppers, a chisel-like implement, points possibly used as darts or spearheads, thin and flat triangular pieces and the Levallois knife. There was an improvement in technique and a wider use of the flakes.

The stonework tells only what they did have in stone, but does not indicate very satisfactorily what they did not have. Of course it can be told that they did not have the metals, but regarding such items as clothing, dwellings, use of bone, art, types of food, the record is more or less blank. No definite inferences can be made either as to the status of their social organization, the family, rules of marriage, religious ideas, customs and law. It should be observed, however, that some considerable development of these features of culture at that time is quite possible. The aborigines of Australia, for instance, have a crude stone technique and the status of their material culture is low, yet their social organization is highly developed and their religious beliefs and practices are most elaborate.

Beginning with the last glacial period appeared the Mousterian culture, some 50,000 or more years ago, and with this culture there have been found a good many skeletal remains of man. The people of this time lived in caves and the climate of central Europe was quite cold. There were several changes in stone technique and some new forms Some bone anvils from the foot and leg of the bison and the horse have been found and also some few bone implements of the awl type. In contact with the Mousterian culture appeared the Aurignacian culture, 25,000 or 30,000 years ago. The Aurignacian culture included, in addition to the stone tools, a number of forms in bone and horn, such as blades, javelin points, smoothers, wedges, chisels, awls and needles. There was also that odd form, apparently a ceremonial staff, and usually called a *"baton de commandement."* Engraving and drawing were fairly well developed in this culture. These arts show a close observation of the animal form, the attainment of realism in a few lines, and a considerable ability to portray movement. Bas-reliefs of woman and a spear-thrower have been found, and a number of statuettes. In addition to the rather long list of stone implements used in industrial life and the somewhat short list, apparently used in the chase, there were found in this culture a number of different forms of stone implements which are used in art. Paint is used and crucibles for mixing red and yellow oxides of iron have been found. The burial positions and the presence in graves of objects useful in life suggest religious ideas. They lived in grottoes and many objects are found around the fire hearth. Much discussion has centred about the question of whether the Aurignacian culture as found in stations in Europe was autochthonous or was brought in from the south along the shores of the Mediterranean. There is a good deal of evidence to support the latter view.

With the Solutrean culture, possibly coming into Europe from west and south-central Asia, occurs the highly-developed new method of flaking stones by pressure rather than by blows. This method developed the fine laurel- and willow-leaf patterns, flaked all over with their smooth edges. Also the shouldered point and the barbed dart, for holding in the flesh, with a stem for attachment, is found. Animal sculpture began and also decorative art with geometric patterns.

The culture of the old stone age, as seen in the remains, reached the apex of its development in the Magdalenian period, which, according to Osborn, existed around 16,000 years ago. The work in flints was not, however, extraordinarily skilled, but work of an unusually high degree of skill in bone, ivory and horn existed, and particularly elaborate was the technique of the harpoon with double rows of barbs. There was an unprecedented variety of drills and borers. Many of the implements were richly adorned. The stone lamp was used and there is evidence of the throwing-stick and possibly of bows and arrows. Most spectacular was the art in drawing, etching, painting and sculpture. The somewhat lengthy treatises that have been written on the art of the Magdalenian period show it as an art culture quite comparable with later art periods in Greece and Italy. The material culture of the Magdalenian period is similar to that found among the Eskimo to-day. In fact, if the material culture found among the Eskimo had lain buried for so long a time, the remains would be very similar to those of the Magdalenian period, with not so high a record in painting and drawing. A great deal is known about the social organization, religious beliefs, literature, science, and customs of the Eskimo; but, of course, it does not follow that the Magdalenian culture was in these respects the same, for the material culture does not determine the status of the other features of culture.

Then comes the neolithic culture with polished flints, the axe, the hatchet, the pick, pottery, use of seeds and grains and knowledge of agriculture, the domestication of animals, the construction of houses. Later appear boats, the wheel, and the use of copper, bronze and iron.

From neolithic times the record of cultural advancement is generally known. At the dawn of the historical period, the material culture contained nearly all of the fundamentals of our own material culture; but since the beginnings of history the elaboration of such fundamentals as housing, agriculture, manufacturing, transportation, clothing, foods, and the like has been most striking. There have also been since the beginning of history a number of very important fundamental inventions. To-day the material culture is quite magnificent, consisting of the use of a great diversity of such objects and substances as factories, machines, agricultural tools, buildings, engineering accomplishments, means of transportation on land, on sea and in air, sanitation equipment, munitions for warfare, steam engines, gasoline engines, electrical plants and appliances, explosives, furniture, heating apparatus, clothing, foods, shoes, household utensils, objects of adornment, jewelry, medicines, drugs, chemicals, reading matter, printing, etc., etc.

4

THE CUMULATIVE NATURE OF MATERIAL CULTURE AND ITS DIVERSIFICATION

The foregoing pages have served the purpose of calling the attention of the reader to something of the origin and development of the superorganic, particularly on its material side. Looking at this growth of material culture from its beginnings there are several processes of its development that are seen at once but that require some consideration. The first point to be observed is that material culture accumulates. The use of bone is added to the use of stone. The use of bronze is added to the use of copper and the use of iron is added to the use of bronze. So that the stream of material culture grows bigger. The lives of material objects vary; some are much shorter than a human lifetime and others much longer. Indeed, there is no special relation between the life of material objects and the lifetime of human beings. Social inheritance differs from biological inheritance. We come into these two inheritances by quite different methods. It is remembered that acquired characteristics are not inherited and that each human life begins where its predecessor began unless there be mutations. The biological inheritance of each succeeding individual is more or less the same, with variations, but the social inheritance may be quite different and much greater in another generation, due to its cumulative nature. The cumulative nature of the process of material culture lies not in the life of the particular object but in the perpetuation of the knowledge of the method of making the object, which is passed on from generation to generation.

This cumulative aspect is due to two features of the cultural process, one is the persistence of cultural forms and the other is the addition of new forms. The persistence of cultural forms has been called cultural inertia and is so important a phenomenon as to warrant special consideration later. But in general a cultural object tends to persist because it has utility. The cultural object itself may wear out, be lost or destroyed, but the knowledge of how to create it continues and additional ones are made, because they possess utility. New forms may be created by means of inventions. The rate of accumulation of culture depends in part on the frequency of inventions. The rate of inventions, their cultural determinants and the dependence of inventions on ability make a most important feature of the cultural process. But at this point, we wish to point out only the cumulative nature of the growth of material culture which may be said to be one very important process of the evolution of material culture.

It should be observed, however, that not all material culture is accumulative and not all forms persist. The record indeed shows that the use of some objects declines and knowledge of making them is lost. For instance, we no longer chip flints to make stone implements for the chase, except in isolated spots. Chipping stones does of course occur in the various uses made of stone today. The bone culture of the Aurignacian and the Magdalenian periods probably replaced some use of stone and the perfection of bronze and iron almost wholly replaced it. The use of the domesticated horse is being replaced though not wholly by the use of motor-driven vehicles. The hunting cultures are being lost. It has been said that the canoe was lost by some of the island peoples of

Melanesia. The cultural forms may be lost for various reasons. A particular form may be lost because of the invention of a newer form which serves the purpose better. One invention may therefore not simply be added to the existing number but may replace a previous invention. Climatic changes or exhaustion of natural materials may cause a loss. The culture of a particular people may suffer a loss if they migrate to a new geographical location. Thus a people may give up their hunting culture and become herders of cattle.

It would be very desirable if we could form some quantitative estimate of the actual extent to which material culture is lost and to which it accumulates. It is quite possible that there may be a tendency to overemphasize its cumulative nature and to fail to recognize the amount that is lost. The material cultures possessed by a people in a particular location will, over a long period of time, show a large proportion actually lost. This would not be true to so great an extent for the world as a whole, though. However, it is certainly more accurate to refer to this particular cultural process as selectively cumulative; and by selective accumulation is meant the fact that new forms of material culture are added and some old ones discarded, there having been a selection. The additions have exceeded the discards, so that the stream of material culture of a particular people has widened with time. Material culture has very greatly accumulated if we add together all the cultures of the world.

The phenomenon of selective accumulation is certainly true of material culture, but it may not be true for other parts of culture, such as religion, science, art, law and custom. Customs may be only slightly accumulative. The selection or replacement aspect of the cultural process is very noticeable in the change of customs. In our modern civilization there is very little trace of the vast number of customs which are found among primitive peoples and which our ancestors may at one time have practised. Many customs are correlated with the material culture, since they are ways or habits of using the objects of material culture, so the accumulation of material culture means some accumulation of customs. Religion, indeed, as seen in its organized forms and practices may even have diminished. There certainly seems to be less organized expression of religion in modern civilization than occurs among most peoples with primitive cultures. It is difficult to make such generalizations regarding religion for the reason that there is disagreement as to just what type of behavior should be called religious behavior. But among peoples with primitive cultures what may be called religious practices seem to be much more prevalent in connection with such activities as medicine, warfare, festivals, recreations, social organizations and morals than with us. In general the cumulative aspect of culture is probably more noticeable with material culture than with those other parts of culture.

The selective nature of the accumulation of material culture does not always mean that old forms are wholly lost; but rather that they are discarded by a particular group or part of a group. They may continue to exist elsewhere. Peoples take up the use of steam in manufacturing but they do not necessarily abandon agriculture. Railroads did not mean the complete disuse of canals, nor do automobiles wholly replace horses. A particular social group may abandon completely an old form for a new, but other social groups may continue to use the old forms. This means that there are groups functioning in two different ways where there was only one method of functioning before. Such a process indicates that material culture becomes diversified. The complexity and heterogeneity of modern society is to be accounted for, in part, by the fact that material culture is selectively accumulative.

The material culture of a particular people or nation thus becomes diversified, resulting in heterogeneity. If we think of the material culture of the whole world, the diversification is very great indeed. Some peoples will have their culture undergo considerable change, dropping old systems and taking on new ones, while other peoples continue to use the older systems. Such differences among cultures may occur because of various factors, such as climate, resources of nature, or geographical location. Relative degrees of isolation are a most important factor in such diversification. The discussion of these factors leads to a general consideration of why culture changes and why it does not change, which is taken up in Part III.

Frequently the use of old forms of material culture is proportionately slight and of less social significance than the use of the newer forms, resulting nevertheless in complexity. There are many interesting consequences of this heterogeneity, which have effects on various social relations, such as government, customs, justice and morality. One of these consequences is specialization. A particular individual will not become acquainted with the whole of culture, but only the part which he, so to speak, specializes in. This is also true of a social group or people.

5

INVENTIONS, MENTAL ABILITY AND CULTURE

The addition of cultural forms that accumulate is the result of invention and discovery. That culture grows by means of inventions is of course universally recognized. But it is not clear just how inventions occur. It is quite customary to think of inventions as the achievement of native ability, for inventors have a high degree of mental ability. Hence it follows that an improvement in the inherent mental ability of the race would result in an increased number of inventions. This is true. But the truth of the converse statement does not follow. An increase in inventions is not always the result of an improvement in the inherent mental ability of the race, for there are other factors in the production of inventions in addition to ability. An increase in the number of inventions may flow from an increased mental ability, but the increase in mental ability may be purely cultural and not biological. A people may be more able because of training and not because of change in the germ plasm. In interpreting the phrase, mental ability, it is seen that the word does not refer exclusively to the biological element. An individual's mind at a particular moment is the result of both nature and nurture. Variations in ability may result from variations in nurture as well as from variations in nature.

In another sense it can be shown that inventions are the result of inherent natural ability. In any sample of population, the distribution of inherent mental ability, in respect to any one mental trait, conforms more or less closely to the normal probability curve; there are only a few individuals with great ability, a few with very low ability and a great many with ordinary ability. Inventors are found in an upper portion of the curve. They thus have more inherent ability than those in a lower portion of the curve. So that in this sense superior native ability is responsible for inventions. Over a long period of time the inventors will thus come from an upper portion of the distribution of native ability. While this is true, yet over this period of time the average of native ability and the distribution of native ability may remain the same. So that the superior ability of inventors is superior only with respect to the existing individuals of a particular distribution at the time, and not necessarily superior in the sense of increased native ability with respect to an earlier population. Of course over any long period of time, there may have been an increase of ability, due to mutations. And cultural achievements play an important part in selecting mutations for survival. There is no question but that mental ability plays its part in discovery, but it is desirable to see as clearly as possible just what part it plays.

The dependence of inventions on mental ability is more frequently spoken of than their dependence on the existing status of culture. A certain general dependence on the cultural antecedents is easily seen. Thus machines employing the wheel can not be constructed or invented until the existing culture has achieved the wheel. Similarly certain technical developments could hardly occur without the knowledge of smelting iron. The flaking of flints by pressure seems dependent on the knowledge of shaping stones by blows. The underlying cultural achievements necessary for the construction of a modern printing press, may conceivably run into the thousands or indeed millions. Thus, if a cultural base at any one time or in any locality be described generally, it is seen to possess certainly a limiting value in regard to the inventions possible. Where an invention depends upon a series of inventions, it seldom occurs that a single individual will make the necessary subsidiary inventions underlying the ultimate invention. The old saying that "necessity is the mother of inventions" is only a half truth. It is true that the urgency of a want spurs to greater effort. But necessity cannot create in addition to the invention the underlying cultural base. In earlier times, the necessity for quicker transportation, or a more stable food supply, or methods of preventing the deaths of babies was perhaps more urgent than now, but such wants did not produce the inventions. Primitive medicine in many diseases was powerless despite deliberate effort. It is nearer the truth to say that the existing culture is the mother of inventions.

A relevant question, is, how far a given cultural base specifically determines a particular invention, assuming a constant level of mental ability. Can it be said, for instance, that the development of the science of mathematics had reached such a stage in the latter part of the seventeenth century that the formulation of the branch of mathematics known as calculus was inevitable? The fact that Leibnitz and Newton both made this achievement is suggestive of an answer in the affirmative. Had the development of biology been of such a nature that at a certain stage the discovery of the principle of natural selection must necessarily have been made? Darwin and Wallace each made this discovery at about the same time. The difficulty in answering the question lies in describing with sufficient fullness the cultural requirements necessary for a particular invention. The inability to describe fully the conditions underlying an invention has led to the ascribing of an accidental or chance element to inventions, the unknown factors being called chance. Chance is seen when one inquires at what particular moment an invention is determined. Why was the airplane invented just when it was? Why was it not invented ten years earlier? The airplane was dependent on a light engine with great power, the steam engine of course not being satisfactory. But there were many other factors. It is difficult, however, to describe the cultural conditions fully enough to determine very closely the exact time at which the appearance of an invention is due.

However, the appearance at approximately the same time of several inventions of the same thing is very impressive evidence of the power of culture in determining particular inventions. On this point Kroeber writes:

The whole history of inventions is one endless chain of parallel instances. An examination of the patent-office records in any other than a commercial or anecdotic spirit would alone reveal the inexorable order that prevails in the advance of civilization. The right to the monopoly of the telephone was long in litigation; the ultimate decision rested on an interval of hours between the recording of concurrent descriptions by Alexander Bell and Elisha Gray. . . . The discovery of oxygen is credited to both Priestley and Scheele; its liquefaction to Cailletet as well as to Pictet, whose results were attained in the same month of 1877 and announced in one session. Kant as well as Laplace can lay claim to the promulgation of the nebular hypothesis. Neptune was predicted by Adams and by Leverrier; the computation of the one and the publication of that of the other, had precedence by a few months. For the invention of the steamboat glory is claimed by their countrymen or partisans for Fulton, Jouffroy, Rumsey, Stevens, Symmington and others; of the telegraph, for Steinheil and Morse; in photography Talbot was the rival of Daguerre and Niepce. The doubly-flanged rail devised by Stevens was reinvented by Vignolet. Aluminum was first practically reduced by the processes of Hall, Héroult, and Cowles. . . . Anaesthetics, both ether and nitrous oxide, were discovered in 1845 and 1846 by no less than four men of one nationality. . . . Even the south pole, never before trodden by the foot of human beings, was at last reached twice in one summer. . . .[6]

No doubt a striking list of inventions that have occurred only once could be made but such a record would be of little significance, for it would not imply that any invention might not have been

[6] A. L. Kroeber, "The Superorganic," *American Anthropologist*, New Series, Vol. XIX (1917), No. 2, p. 200.

invented the second time. For if an invention has been once made and has become widely known there is no occasion for a second invention. It is therefore impressive that there are these multiple instances of the same invention.[7] That some inventions are inevitable seems probable. For instance, given the boat and given the steam engine, it certainly seems highly probable that the two could be connected in the steamboat. On the other hand the inevitability of an invention does not seem so clear when one inquires, for instance, into the cultural conditions that may have made the invention of the wheel inevitable,—the wheel very probably having been invented only once. It may have been that the pulling of a load by a domesticated animal over rolling logs led to the idea of the wagon wheel. But why does it appear to have been invented in only one place in the world? Was the underlying cultural situation which was necessary for the invention of the wheel in existence in only one locality and at only one time? The answer to this question again,

[7] A longer list of inventions made by two or more persons independently has been compiled by Miss Dorothy Thomas, who has been collecting material on this subject. The list appears as an appendix at the close of this section. No doubt a much longer list could be collected from existing records, and a still longer one if the records were complete. The purpose is not so much to find a complete total but to demonstrate a great prevalence of these multiple inventions independently made.

no doubt, lies in a more complete account of the cultural conditions, which is of course difficult to make. But certainly rolling logs and domesticated animals are not an adequate account. There may also be implied certain types of cutting implements, the uses of metals, types of ground, development of technical forms, a social condition creating an urgent need, etc. Why is it, for instance, that in early times only one half of the world learned to drink the milk of domesticated animals? To give a cultural account of such a situation, a great deal must be known, of course, about the culture. And in our ignorance, we may speak of it as chance.

Although an invention is dependent on the existing culture it does not follow that the same invention demands always the same cultural history. Two different cultural situations may result in the same invention or what appears to be the same invention. Thus writing may be made on clay tablets, papyrus or on stone. Boas cites as an illustration, the fact that though pottery may have developed from basketry in Arizona, it does not follow that this is the sole origin of pottery. And, again, the social organization of primitive tribes is often characterized by a definite number of subdivisions. But this type of organization has resulted from a union of smaller divisions as in the case of the Navaho or in a subdivision of a larger group as among the Indians of the North Pacific coast of America. This phenomenon, sometimes called convergence, is of considerable theoretical significance, and has been frequently discussed. It seems to put an emphasis on the importance of a cultural need and to imply that there are various ways of meeting the need. A subdivided large group may represent a social need and may arise by union or partition.

By definition, to invent is to contrive something new. But in trying to describe the particular new thing about an invented object, it is seen that the new is sometimes quantitatively inconspicuous in comparison with the amount of old in such a newly invented object. In the telegraph, for instance, electricity, coils, batteries and circuit are all known. The sound contrivance and the code seem the newer features, but these indeed have cultural predecessors in the electric bell, the alphabet and signaling. It is rather the putting together of certain appliances that is new. In the case of the telegraph as in the case of many inventions it is the putting of an idea in use for social purposes that gives it its significance.

The social heritage of a particular people also grows through the adopting of a portion of culture in use by some other people. The culture of a particular locality is to be accounted for, therefore, either by invention or by diffusion. It is much easier to borrow culture than it is to invent it. Diffusion is known to occur even where the contacts are rare and the distances are great. The explanation of a particular culture on the basis of inventions or on the basis of diffusion, and the comparative frequency of invention and diffusion have been a central theme among anthropologists for years. The same things have been invented in different parts of the world at different times. But diffusion is relatively the much more common occurrence. Montelius [8] has discussed the early development of culture in Sweden and shown the overwhelming predominance of diffusion. Isolated communities are very good illustrations of the relative influence of invention and diffusion. The slowness of relatively isolated cultures to change has been likened to stagnation. The growth of cultures in contact with other cultures is much more rapid. The great prevalence of diffusion as a source of the cultural growth of a particular people is further indication of the importance of the cultural factor as compared to the rôle of the inventor's mental ability.

[8] O. Montelius, "Der Handel in der Vorzeit," *Praehistorische Zeitschrift*, Vol. II (1910).

A LIST OF SOME INVENTIONS AND DISCOVERIES MADE INDEPENDENTLY BY TWO OR MORE PERSONS [9]

I

1. Solution of the problem of three bodies. By Clairaut (1747), Euler (1747), and D'Alembert (1747).
2. Theory of the figure of the earth. By Huygens (1690), and Newton (1680?).
3. Variability of satellites. By Bradley (1752), and Wargentin (1746).

[9] The accompanying list of duplicate independent inventions is taken from an article, "Are Inventions Inevitable? A Note on Social Evolution," appearing in the *Political Science Quarterly*, Vol. XXXVII, No. 1. The list is collected from histories of astronomy, mathematics, chemistry, physics, electricity, physiology, biology, psychology and practical mechanical inventions. The data are thus from the period of written records, indeed the last few centuries, and largely from histories of science. The various inventions and discoveries vary greatly in their importance. The list could be extended by further research.

There are disputes concerning many of the origins in the instances listed. Disputes frequently concern priority, a matter with which the accompanying discussion is not concerned. Where the dates are doubtful a question mark has been placed after the date. Occasionally it has not been possible to get the date. The most serious difficulty in making the list is the fact that the contribution of one person is in some cases more complete than that of another. For instance, Laplace's

4. Motion of light within the earth's orbit. By Delambre (1821?), and Bradley (1728).
5. Theory of planetary perturbations. By Lagrange (1808), and Laplace (1808).
6. Discovery of the planet Neptune. By Adams (1845), and Leverrier (1845).
7. Discovery of sun spots. By Galileo (1611), Fabricus (1611), Scheiner (1611), and Harriott (1611).
8. Law of inverse squares. By Newton (1666), and Halley (1684).

account of the nebular hypothesis is in more scientific detail than Kant's. Similarly, Halley's rôle may not have been as important as Newton's in formulating the law of inverse squares. It is sometimes doubtful just where to draw the lines defining a new contribution. Our guide has been the histories of science, and where there are differences in the historical accounts we have followed the general practice. The case of the discovery of the circulation of the blood has been excluded, as there seems to be a rather wide difference in the contributions of Cesalpino (1571) and Harvey (1616). Although the rule has been to exclude such cases of doubt, in some instances where they have been included a question mark has been placed next to the name. In several cases the independence of the research of one claimant has been questioned by another claimant or by his followers. In the case of calculus the verdict on the controversy regarding Newton and Leibnitz seems to be that both justly deserve the distinction. In the case of the microscope, telescope, thermometer, steamboat and electric railways, claims are still matters of dispute. In a few cases this fact has been indicated by the words "claimed by" following the subject of the discovery or invention. Most of the cases of widely different dates have special explanations as in the case of Mendel and the discovery of the elements of phosphorus. It has also been difficult to abbreviate the description of the discovery into a short title suitable for a list.

9. Nebular hypothesis. By Laplace (1796), and Kant (1755).
10. Effect of tidal friction on motion of the earth. By Ferrel (1853), and Delaunay (1853).
11. Correlation between variations of sun spots and disturbances on the earth. By Sabine (1852), Wolfe (1852), and Gauthier (1852).
12. Method of getting spectrum at edge of sun's disk. By Jannsen (1868), and Lockyer (1868).
13. Discovery of the inner ring of Saturn. By Bond (1850), and Dawes (1850).
14. First measurement of the parallax of a star. By Bessel (1838), and Struve (1838), and Henderson (1838).
15. The effect of gravitation on movements of the ocean. By Lenz (1845?), and Carpenter (1865).
16. Certain motions of the moon. By Clairaut (1752), Euler (1752), and D'Alembert (1752).

II

17. Decimal fractions. By Stevinus (1585), and Bürgi (1592), Beyer? (1603), and Rüdolff? (1530).
18. Introduction of decimal point. By Bürgi (1592), Pitiscus (1608–12), Kepler (1616), and Napier (1616–17).
19. The equation of the cycloid. By Torricelli (1644), and Roberval (1640).
20. Logarithms. By Bürgi (1620), and Napier-Briggs (1614).

21. The tangent of the cycloid. By Viviani (1660?), Descartes (1660?), and Fermat (1660?).
22. Calculus. By Newton (1671), and Leibnitz (1676).
23. The rectification of the semi-cubical parabola. By Van Heuraet (1659), Neil (1657), and Fermat (1657–9).
24. Deduction of the theorem on the hexagon. By Pascal (1639), MacLaurin (1719–20), and Bessel (1820).
25. The principle of least squares. By Gauss (1809), and Legendre (1806).
26. The geometric law of duality. By Poncelet (1838), and Gérgone (1838).
27. The beginnings of synthetic projective geometry. By Chasles (1830), and Steiner (1830).
28. Geometry with an axiom contradictory to Euclid's parallel axiom. By Lobatchevsky (1836–40?), Boylais (1826–33), and Gauss? (1829).
29. Lobatchevsky's doctrine of the parallel angle. By Lobatchevsky (1840), and Saccheri (1733).
30. Method of algebraic elimination by use of determinants and by dialitic method. By Hesse (1842), and Sylvester (1840).
31. A treatment of vectors without the use of coördinate systems. By Hamilton (1843), Grassman (1843), and others (1843).
32. Principle of uniform convergence. By Stokes (1847-8), and Seidel (1847–8).
33. Logarithmic criteria for convergence of series. By Abel, De Morgan, Bertrand, Raabe, Duhamel, Bonnet, Paucker (all between 1832–51).

34. Radix method of making logarithms. By Briggs (1624), Flower (1771), Atwood (1786), Leonelli (1802), and Manning (1806).
35. Circular slide rule. By Delamain (1630), and Oughtred (1632).
36. Method of indivisibles. By Roberval (1640?), and Cavalieri (1635).
37. Researches on elliptic functions. By Abel (1826–29), Jacobi (1829), and Legendre (1811–28).
38. The double theta functions. By Gopel (1847), and Rosenhain (1847).
39. The law of quadratic reciprocity. By Gauss (1788–96), Euler (1737), and Legendre (1830).
40. The application of the potential function to mathematical theory of electricity and magnetism. By Green (1828), Thomson (1846), Chasles, Sturm, and Gauss.
41. Dirichlet's principle in the theory of potentials. By Dirichlet (1848?), and Thomson (1848).
42. Contraction hypothesis. By H. A. Lorentz (1895), and Fitzgerald (1895).
43. Mathematical calculation of the size of molecules. By Loschmidt, and Thomson.

III

44. Structure theory. By Butlerow (1888), Kekule (1888), and Couper (1888).
45. Law of gases. By Boyle (1662), and Marriotte (1676).

46. Discovery of oxygen. By Scheele (1774), and Priestley (1774).
47. Liquefaction of oxygen. By Cailletet (1877), and Pictet (1877).
48. Method of liquefying gases. By Cailletet, Pictet, Wroblowski and Olzewski (all between 1877–1884).
49. Estimation of proportion of oxygen in atmosphere. By Scheele (1778), and Cavendish (1781).
50. Beginnings of modern organic chemistry. By Boerhave (1732), and Hales (1732).
51. Isolation of nitrogen. By Rutherford (1772), and Scheele (1773).
52. That water is produced by combustion of hydrogen. By Lavoisier-Laplace (1783), and Cavendish (1784).
53. Law of chemical proportions. By Proust (1801–9), and Richter?
54. The Periodic Law. First arrangement of atoms in ascending series. By De Chancourtois (1864), Newlands (1864), and Lothar Meyer (1864). Law of periodicity. By Lothar Meyer (1869), and Mendeleeff (1869).
55. Hypothesis as to arrangement of atoms in space. By Van't Hoff (1874), and Le Bel (1874).
56. Molecular theory. By Ampère (1814), and Avagadro (1811).
57. Hydrogen acid theory. By Davy and Du Long.
58. Doctrine of chemical equivalents. By Wenzel (1777), and Richter (1792).

59. Discovery of elements of phosphorus. By Brand (1669), Kunckel (1678), and Boyle (1680).
60. Discovery of boron. By Davy (1808–9), and Gay-Lussac (1808).
61. Discovery of ceria. By Hisinger (1803), Berzelius (1803–4), and Klaproth (1803–4).
62. Process for reduction of aluminum. By Hall (1886), Héroult (1887), and Cowles (1885).
63. Law of mass action of chemical forces. By Jellet (1873), Guldberg-Waage (1867), Van't Hoff (1877), and others.
64. Comparison of refractivity of equimolecular quantities by multiple function. By L. V. Lorenz (1880), and H. A. Lorentz (1880).

IV

65. Resistance of vacuum. By Torricelli-Pascal (1643-6), and von Guericke (1657).
66. Air gun. By Boyle-Hooke (prior to 1659), and von Guericke (1650).
67. Telescope. Claimed by Lippershey (1608), Della Porta (1558), Digges (1571), Johannides, Metius (1608), Drebbel, Fontana, Janssen (1608), and Galileo (1609).
68. Microscope. Claimed by Johannides, Drebbel and Galileo (1610?).
69. Acromatic lens. By Hall (1729), and Dolland (1758).
70. Principle of interference. By Young (1802), and Fresnel (1815).

71. Spectrum analysis. By Draper (1860), Angstrom (1854), Kirchoff-Bunsen (1859), Miller (1843), and Stokes (1849).
72. Photography. By Daguerre-Niepce (1839), and Talbot (1839).
73. Color photography. By Cros (1869), and Du Hauron (1869).
74. Discovery of overtones in strings. By Nobb-Pigott (1677), and Sauveur (1700–03).
75. Thermometer. Claimed by Galileo (1592–7?), Drebbel? (1608), Sanctorious (1612), Paul (1617), Fludd (1617), von Guericke, Porta (1606), De Caus (1615).
76. Pendulum clock. Claimed by Bürgi (1575), Galileo (1582), and Huygens (1656).
77. Discovery of latent heat. By Black (1762), De Luc, and Wilke.
78. Ice calorimeter. By Lavoisier-Laplace (1780), and Black-Wilke.
79. Law of expansion of gases. By Charles (1783), and Gay-Lussac (1802).
80. Continuity of gaseous and liquid states of matter. By Ramsay (1880), and Jamin (1883).
81. Kinetic theory of gases. By Clausius (1850), and Rankine (1850).
82. Law of conservation of energy. By Mayer (1843), Joule (1847), Helmholz (1847), Colding (1847), and Thomson (1847).
83. Mechanical equivalent of heat. By Mayer (1842), Carnot (1830), Seguin (1839), and Joule (1840).

84. Principle of dissipation of energy. By Carnot? (1824), Clausius (1850), Thomson (1852).
85. Law of impact, earlier conclusions. By Galileo (1638), and Marci (1639).
86. Laws of mutual impact of bodies. By Huygens (1669), Wallis (1668), and Wren (1668).
87. Apparent concentration of cold by concave mirror. By Porta (1780–91?), and Pictet (1780–91?).
88. Circumstances by which effect of weight is determined. By Leonardo and Ubaldi.
89. Parallelogram of forces. By Newton (1687), and Varignon (1725?).
90. Principle of hydrostatics. By Archimedes, and Stevinus (1608).
91. Pneumatic lever. By Hamilton (1835), and Barker (1832).
92. Osmotic pressure methods. By Van't Hoff (1886), and Guldberg (1870).
93. Law of inertia. By Galileo, Huygens, and Newton (1687).
94. Machinery for verifying the law of falling bodies. By Laborde, Lippich and von Babo.
95. Centre of oscillation. By Bernouilli (1712), and Taylor (1715).

V

96. Leyden jar. By von Kleist (1745), and Cuneus (1746).
97. Discovery of animal electricity. By Sultzer (1768), Cotuguo (1786), and Galvani (1791).

98. Telegraph. Henry (1831), Morse (1837), Cooke-Wheatstone (1837), and Steinheil (1837).
99. Electric motors. Claimed by Dal Negro (1830), Henry (1831), Bourbonze and McGawley (1835).
100. Electric railroad. Claimed by Davidson, Jacobi, Lilly-Colton (1847), Davenport (1835), Page (1850), and Hall (1850–1).
101. Induction coil. By Page and Ruhmkorff.
102. Secondary battery. By Ritter and Planté (1859).
103. Electrolysis of water. By Nicholson-Carlisle (1800), and Ritter.
104. Method of converting lines engraved on copper into relief. By Jacobi (1839), Spencer (1839), and Jordan (1839).
105. Ring armature. By Pacinotti (1864), and Gramme (1860).
106. Microphone. Hughes (1878), Edison (1877–8), Berliner (1877), and Blake (1878?).
107. The phonograph. By Edison (1877), Scott?, and Cros (1877).
108. Self-exciting dynamo. Claimed by Hjorth (1866–7), Varley (1866–7), Siemens (1866–7), Wheatstone (1866–7), Ladd (1866), Wilde (1863–7).
109. Incandescent electric light. Claimed by Starr (1846), and Jobard-de Clangey (1838).
110. Telephone. By Bell (1876), and Gray (1876).
111. Arrest of electro-magnetic waves. By Branley (1890–1), Lodge (1893), and Hughes (1880).
112. Electro-magnetic clocks. By Wheatstone (1845), and Bain (1845).

113. Printing telegraphs. By Wheatstone (1845), and Bain (1845).

VI

114. Theory of infection of microörganisms. By Fracastoro (1546), and Kircher.
115. Discovery of the thoracic duct. By Rudbeck (1651), and Jolyff and Bertolinus (1653).
116. That the skull is made of modified vertebræ. By Goethe (1790), and Oken (1776).
117. Nature of the cataract. By Brisseau (1706), and Maitre-Jan (1707).
118. Operation for cure of aneurisms. By Hunter (1775), and Anil (1772).
119. Digestion as a chemical rather than a mechanical process. By Spallanzani and Hunter.
120. Function of the pancreas. By Purkinje (1836), and Pappenheim (1836).
121. Solution of the problem of respiration. By Priestley (1777), Scheele (1777), Lavoisier (1777), Spallanzani (1777), and Davy (1777).
122. Form of the liver cells. By Purkinje (1838), Heule (1838), and Dutrochet (1838).
123. Relation of microörganisms to fermentation and putrefaction. By Latour (1837), and Schwann (1837).
124. Pepsin as the active principle of gastric juice. By Latour (1835), and Schwann (1835).
125. Prevention of putrefaction of wounds by keeping

germs from surface of wound. By Lister (1867), and Guerin (1871).

126. Cellular basis of both animal and vegetable tissue. Claimed by Schwann (1839), Henle (1839?), Turpin (1839?), Dumortier (1839?), Purkinje (1839?), Muller (1839?), and Valentin (1839).
127. Invention of the laryngoscope. By Babington (1829), Liston (1837), and Garcia (1855).
128. Sulphuric ether as an anaesthetic. By Long (1842), Robinson (1846), Liston (1846), Morton (1846), and Jackson (1846).
129. That all appendages of a plant are modified leaves. By Goethe (1790), and Wolfe (1767).

VII

130. Theory of inheritance of acquired characteristics. By E. Darwin (1794), and Lamarck (1801).
131. Theory of natural selection and variation. By C. Darwin (1858), and Wallace (1858).
132. Some results of heredity. By Mendel (1865), DeVries (1900), Correns (1900), Tschermarck, (1900).
133. Theory of mutations. By Korschinsky (1899), and DeVries (1900).
134. Theory of the emotions. By James (1884), and Lange (1887).
135. Theory of color. By Young (1801), and Helmholz.

VIII

136. Sewing machine. By Thimmonier (1830), Howe (1846), and Hunt (1840).
137. Balloon. By Montgolfier (1783), Rittenhouse-Hopkins (1783).
138. Flying machine. Claimed by Wright (1895–1901), Langley (1893–7), and others.
139. Reapers. By Hussey (1833), and McCormick (1834).
140. Doubly-flanged rail. By Stephens and Vignolet.
141. Steamboat. Claimed by Fulton (1807), Jouffroy, Rumsey, Stevens, and Symmington (1802).
142. Printing. By Gutenberg (1443), and Coster (1420–23).
143. Cylinder printing press. By Koenig-Bensley (1812-13), and Napier (1830).
144. Typewriter. Claimed by Beach (1847–56), Sholes? (1875), and Wheatstone (1855–60).
145. Trolley car. By Van Doeple (1884–5), Sprague (1888), Siemans (1881), and Daft (1883).
146. Stereoscope. By Wheatstone (1839), and Elliott (1840).
147. Centrifugal pumps. By Appold (1850), Gwynne (1850), and Bessemer (1850).
148. Use of gasoline engines in automobiles. By Otto (1876), Daimler (1885), and Selden (1879?).

6

THE RATE OF CULTURAL GROWTH

The social heritage in its material aspects thus grows through inventions, and in particular areas by diffusion, and is selectively accumulative. It is desirable to consider somewhat the rapidity of change and the rate of growth of material culture. A brief perspective of the growth of culture from its beginnings shows that the change was quite slow in very early times. Based on the finds in stonework, the development of the material culture of the Chellean period to the Acheulean and the Acheulean to the Mousterian required an interval of about 25,000 years each, according to Osborn's chronology. From the beginnings of Aurignacian culture to the beginnings of the Magdalenian was a period of some 10,000 years, though it is not clear that this development took place in Europe by means of inventions. The neolithic culture appeared in Europe 5,000 years later. From neolithic times to the historic period and from the historic period on, the changes in material culture have been much more rapid. At the present time both the change and the accumulation of material culture are quite rapid and may be measured in such brief intervals as generations or even decades.

As to the causes of the changes in rate of this accumulation, it is thought a most important factor is the extent at any one time of the existing material culture. This point is important and the relation between the existing technical equipment and the number of inventions made should be examined. It would seem that the larger the equipment of material culture the greater the number of inventions. The more there is to invent with, the greater will be the number of inventions. When the existing material culture is small, embracing a stone technique and a knowledge of skins and some woodwork, the number of inventions is more limited than when the culture consists of a knowledge of a variety of metals and chemicals and the use of steam, electricity, and various mechanical principles such as the screw, the wheel, the lever, the piston, belts, pulleys, etc. The street car could not have been invented from the material culture existing at the last glacial period. The discovery of the power of steam and the mechanical technology existing at that time made possible a large number of inventions. It is certainly true that when the material culture was small inventions were few, and now when the material culture is large the inventions are many, though, of course, there are other factors than the number of elements of material culture.

In the preceding pages it has been pointed out that the material culture grows by accumulation, and the additional point is now made that the size of the material culture, that is, the number of different kinds of material-culture objects is a factor in determining the number of inventions of new material-culture objects. In general, growth occurs when more new units are added than there are disappearances of old units. And very frequently there are definite relationships between the number of existing units and the number of new ones produced. These relationships may be expressed in various mathematical formulæ, which describe various types of curves. The fact that material culture is accumulative, that is, new inventions are not lost but added to the existing stock, and the fact (if it be a fact) that the larger the stock the greater the number of new inventions, suggest at first glance the compound interest law. It is recalled that with compound interest the interest is not spent but is added to the principal and the succeeding sizes of the growing principal mean a larger amount of interest, the rate of interest remaining the same.

If any newly invented material object be taken as unit, then a curve representing its growth for the very long period of time that culture has existed would presumably have an upward trend although its slope might be small. The historical record of culture would seem to indicate that in the very early times, the slope was probably slight but in modern times probably sharper, at least there are many more inventions now than formerly. The growth of material culture may not be found to lend itself to statistical and graphical representation, but by speculating as to its possible resemblance to the compound interest curve, we may come to some better insight into the nature of the growth of material culture. We shall discuss the compound interest curve in relation to the growth of culture, but using it as a standard only for purposes of comparison not description. One difference between the compound interest curve and the possible curve of growth of culture has already been noted, namely, that the growth of material culture is not as consistently accumulative as is compound interest. For certainly there is some loss of the knowledge of making cultural objects for the world as a whole and much more loss for a particular locality or people.

Another difference is that the units of money in compound interest are the same, whereas the various invented material objects have the utmost variety. Regarding the point that the number of cultural objects is a determining factor in the number of new inventions somewhat as the size of the principal is a determining factor in the amount of interest, it is seen that some inventions are relatively insignificant while some are profoundly significant in promoting new inventions. Thus the discovery of the new source of power, steam, really meant that a whole host of inventions involving applications of this power followed, necessitating many rapid changes in material culture. Whereas, the invention of the turbine engine did not mean nearly so many changes as did the invention of the ordinary steam engine. Inventions thus differ on the basis of their effect on possible future inventions. This difference in the nature of inventions means that the curve of growth of material culture is very irregular in its upward trend and not as smooth as the exponential curve.

The facts of the growth of material culture seem to indicate a development by jumps. There will be a period of stability or of relatively slight change. Then occurs a fundamental invention of great significance which precipitates many changes, modifications and other inventions which follow with relative rapidity for a time. These rapid changes are then followed by another period of relative stability—unless another fundamental discovery be made. The adoption of the domesticated horse from the Spaniards by the Plains Indians is such an illustration, as seen from the record of changes recorded by Wissler.[10] Certainly the discovery of the power and uses of steam precipitated many rapid changes. Accounts of the changes that have followed the use of steam have for many years been published in almost all branches of social science, so great is the number of these changes. The latter part of the generalization that the period of active change is followed by a period of relative stability is not verified by the industrial revolution, perhaps because the period of time since the beginning of the use of steam as power is short. Indeed, before such a period of stability arrives, some other significant invention may be made.

This jump-like nature of social change has recently been the subject of comment by Professor

[10] Clark Wissler, "The Influence of the Horse in the Development of Plains Culture," *American Anthropologist*, New Series, Vol. XVI, No. 1, pp. 1–25.

R. A. Lehfeldt in a mathematical paper on "The Normal Law of Progress." He has there considered three sets of data, British trade statistics, the German birth rate, and the growth of British population. His data when plotted show this period of stability, then a rapid change followed by another period of stability.[11] Lehfeldt's problem is not exactly the same as that now being discussed. His data do not represent the accumulation in inventions. They rather represent the statistical measurements of a limited effect of an invention or a few inventions. Thus, the lowering of the German birth rate may be due largely to the spread of the knowledge of the newly discovered methods of birth control and the statistical formula thus measures the rate of diffusion, the quantitative spread of a single social change. Similarly the curve of the growth of foreign trade measures the rate of diffusion for a particular country of the effect of a series of inventions on manufacturing and trade. The extent of change, therefore, may mean the spread of culture and

[11] *Journal of the Royal Statistical Society,* New Series, Vol. LXXIX, (1916.) An equation to the curve describing these data he has worked out to be the following:

$$\log q = \log q_0 + kF\left(\frac{t}{T}\right), \text{ where } F(x) = \frac{1}{\sqrt{\pi}} \int_0^x e^{-x^2} dx,$$

q_0 is q at a certain moment (the period), t is the time in years before or after the epoch and T is a constant period.

amount of change measured in terms of some unit, rather than the accumulation of inventions.

It seems very probable, however, that the rate of cultural growth as measured in terms of increase in inventions is uneven, slow then rapid, then slow, and so on, because of the difference in the fundamental natures of inventions. Such a course would seem to be particularly true with respect to a restricted portion of culture, as, for instance, mechanical development of steel appliances. Combining the rates of growth for all portions of material culture, however, might smooth out the curve somewhat.

Another difference, therefore, between the compound interest law and the growth of culture lies in the fact that in cultural change the rate of growth is not constant as in the formula for compound interest. The fact that inventions vary greatly in their influence on further cultural changes makes this point clear. There are, of course, many variable factors affecting the number of inventions made other than the extent of the existing material culture, as, for instance, the hostility shown by a people towards innovations. Increased populations may mean more applied mental ability. Increased cultural contacts resulting in diffusion of elements may result in greater modifications. The larger cultural base may not only mean that there is more material culture to invent with; but it may also mean that it is easier for a given mental ability to invent than would be true where the material culture is small. This would affect the time-rate at which inventions would be made. In other words, the time of appearance of an invention when the material culture is large would be shorter than when it is small.

The number of existing cultural elements is also limited as a determining factor in the production of new inventions by the non-material culture, as for instance, the social attitude towards the new. Thus religion may discourage sculpture. Religious leaders may try to prevent discoveries in science. The social attitude will vary in different periods in its hostility towards innovations; or it may specifically encourage discovery. Western civilization to-day is less hostile to change than in the Middle Ages or than primitive cultures. We, perhaps, exaggerate this lack of hostility, and only in some respects can we be said to welcome change. It should also be noted that the increasing cultural base has also probably had an effect on determining the social attitude towards invention as truly as has the social attitude had an effect on determining the size of the cultural base.

A detailed verification of the foregoing analysis by data on inventions is desirable. For instance, a statistical record of inventions year by year would furnish material for measuring the rate of growth. But no complete record of inventions by years can be made. A partial list of such inventions by years would show the record for later years unduly large in comparison with earlier years, for the reason that records are fuller for later years.

We have the statistical records of patents granted by the United States patent office since 1838, and this record is valuable, though fragmentary, evidence. A patent is granted

> to any person who has invented or discovered any new and useful art, machine, manufacture, or composition of matter or any new and useful improvement thereof, or any new, original and ornamental design for an article of manufacture not known or used by others in this country before his invention or discovery thereof, and not patented or described in any printed publication in this or any foreign country before his invention or discovery thereof or more than two years prior to his application, and not in public use or on sale in the United States for more than two years prior to his application, unless the same is proved to have been abandoned.[12]

The number of patents by five-year periods

[12] *Rules of Practice in the United States Patent Office,* Revised July 17, 1907, Rule 24, p. 10.

since 1840 granted by the United States patent office is shown in the following table. [13]

1840	...	473	1870	... 13,321	1900	...	26,499
1845	...	503	1875	... 14,817	1905	...	30,399
1850	...	993	1880	... 13,947	1910	...	35,930
1855	...	2,013	1885	... 24,233	1915	...	44,934
1860	...	4,819	1890	... 26,292	1920	...	39,882
1865	...	6,616	1895	... 22,057			

The foregoing series shows that the number of patents is increasing rapidly but the rate of increase is declining. The growth in the number of patents granted in the United States over the eighty-year period from 1840 to 1920 is represented by a straight line with sharp upward slope more accurately than by a line curving upward. In fact it is difficult to conceive of any growth under actual conditions increasing for long according to the compound interest law. Such an increase in money for a long time is not found. Malthus said that population tended to increase in a geometric progression; but it is only a tendency for there are actual checks. Lehfeldt's curves of progress, previously referred to, curve upward for a while but later the rate diminishes markedly.

The growth of culture has been characterized by Lowie as follows:

[13] *Report of the Commissioner of Patents to Congress for Year Ended 1920*, p. 7.

We may liken the progress of mankind to that of a man a hundred years old, who dawdles through kindergarten for eighty-five years of his life, takes ten years to go through the primary grades, then rushes with lightning rapidity through grammar school, and college. Culture, it seems, is a matter of exceedingly slow growth until a certain 'threshold' is passed when it darts forward, gathering momentum at an unexpected rate.[14]

Such a vivid picture of social change makes one wonder about the future. Will the rate of inventions continue to increase? How rapidly will the accumulation of material culture continue? Many interesting thoughts are stimulated by these questions. How will life be with such rapidity of change, as indicated by the projection into the future of these processes? At the present time, parents are outdistanced in a short time by their children. We no sooner begin to get adjusted to a change, before a new one sets in. A particular cultural change not only necessitates an adjustment to it on the part of individuals but it demands sometimes rather far-reaching adjustments in other parts of culture, where cultural interrelations are widely ramified, as is often the case. Furthermore it takes a rather long period of one's life to assimilate through education the existing culture. If our social heritage accumulates still

[14] Robert H. Lowie, *Culture and Ethnology,* p. 78.

more and more, the length of time required to assimilate this increased social heritage and the difficulty in assimilating it will be even greater. Will it take forty or fifty years of a person's life to prepare one for life? Or will it mean increasing specialization and differentiation in human activity so that one becomes quite narrowly a specialist? And of this great social heritage, will one never assimilate any but that narrow portion in which one specializes? Will the specialization become narrower and narrower and take longer and longer to acquire? It is difficult, of course, to predict the future course of material culture even in very general terms. The preceding discussion has approximated, it is thought, a description of the growth of material culture, but for the past. Even though a mathematical formula were constructed to fit the facts of cultural growth, such a formula would only be descriptive within the limits of past experience. Extrapolation might prove inaccurate. But from a long-time view of the cultural record, if the past be a guide to the future, there should be expected a greatly increasing cultural growth and much more rapid social changes.

However, there are conceivable several conditions which might result in a slowing up of cultural growth. It is thinkable that the number of possible inventions might be limited, for instance, by the satisfaction of human needs and wants. The material culture existing to-day meets very satisfactorily a great many of our material wants. Our housing, clothing, foods, transportation, and much other equipment seem fairly satisfactory. May it not be argued that our wants are already well met by the abundance of the existing material culture? Such considerations seem very doubtful, however. A writer two thousand years ago might have commented that the material wants of human beings were fairly satisfactorily met then, as there were houses, clothing, methods of transportation, etc. Yet improvements proceeded at an unprecedented rate. Another point that raises doubt, is the fact that though wants may be described in psychological terms as few, their expression in cultural terms may be endlessly varied. And finally it is highly doubtful whether definite wants are important determining or limiting factors of specific cultural forms. The urgency or lack of urgency of a want is conditioned in its production of inventions by the existing culture. It is possible that cultural growth might be limited by the capacity of human society to assimilate so large an accumulation of culture. The capacity of society to assimilate culture is, however, greatly increased through specialization resulting in differentiation. If cultural forms are increasingly discarded, there would result change without so much accumulation. But such speculations are highly imaginary.

It is probable that the social development of the future will be affected by changes in the quantity and nature of natural resources such as soil, minerals, forests, etc. The natural environment has always had an effect on the development of material culture, and very broad variations in geographical factors have been a conditioning element in the production of new cultural forms. So changes, shortages, or discoveries in natural resources will have an effect on the material culture of the future.

In the preceding pages, enough has been presented to show roughly something of a picture of the growth of material culture from its beginnings to the present time, and it has been seen that certain factors inherent in culture itself may be the cause of this particular cultural growth. The writers on social evolution, it is recalled, have not kept distinct the process of cultural change from the process of biological change. Often the assumption has seemed to be that the cultural evolution was caused by biological evolution. The foregoing considerations of cultural change have been made without reference to biological evolution. We shall now discuss briefly some facts and principles concerning the evolution of biological man, particularly for the purpose of trying to get a brief picture of the biological evolution that has occurred in man since the beginnings of culture and also some idea of the rapidity of biological evolution as compared with the rapidity of cultural evolution. Such a consideration of biological evolution will make easier an appraisal of the biological factor in social evolution.

7

BIOLOGICAL CHANGE IN MAN

The remains of the animal who formed eoliths, if indeed these stones were artificially flaked, have not been found. The remains of *Pithecanthropus erectus* are of the same general period as the eoliths, but no eoliths were found with these skeletal fragments. There is some doubt as to the period in which Pithecanthropus lived, but he is either of the late Pliocene or early Pleistocene period, a half-million years or more ago. The most significant measurement of this find is his skull capacity, which is estimated at 850-900 c.c. The largest simian brain case is 600 c.c. while the skulls of men living to-day average 1450-1500 c.c. These comparative measurements indicate that Pithecanthropus was a "missing link," in the matter of skull capacity intermediate between ape and man. This find was made in Java and it is not known that man descended from this creature, or rather that the lineal ancestor of man at this period had the measurements of Pithecanthropus.

Not until the Mousterian period, 50,000 years, more or less, ago, are skeletal remains of man or man-like creatures found with a sufficient degree of completeness to give estimates of his whole bodily structure, particularly the capacity of the skull. The Mauer jaw of Heidelberg man, closely resembling neither the jaw of apes nor of men, was found dating at a period between Pithecanthropus and the Mousterians; but it cannot be told from the jaw what capacity his skull was or what were his other bodily measurements. Regarding the Piltdown man, there is such disagreement that we may pass over those fragments without consideration. But placed at the beginning and middle of the last glacial epoch, with the Mousterian culture twenty or more finds have been made, some fragmentary and some more or less complete but all resembling each other. These finds establish man without doubt, but this man differed from modern man, probably more than the yellow races differ from the blacks. The capacity of his skull was large, larger than the average of modern man judged by the small number of skulls that could be measured. This is shown from the following measurements on six skulls, cited from Osborn: Spy II, 1723 c.c. (probably); La Chapelle, 1626 c.c.; Spy I, 1562 c.c.; Neanderthal, 1408 c.c.; La Quina (female), 1367 c.c., and Gibraltar, 1296 c.c. The skulls of modern man vary between the limits of 950 c.c. and 2020 c.c. The size of the brain is considered to be correlated with mental ability. Such a correlation is true over a very broad range of life, as seen from the fact that the anthropoids have small brains and men have large brains. But there are other factors than the size of the brain determining mental ability. The structure of the brain is as truly important as the size and weight, within limits of normal variation. This Neanderthal type had skulls somewhat more flattened than modern man, with protruding brow ridges and prominent face but small chin. Just what significance these measurements, as, for instance, rounded chins, have for mental ability is not known. The literature on this race is vast and the descriptions and analyses of the various measurements are very erudite and technical. However, it is permissible to observe that at the time many of these discussions were made there was a decided expectancy for "missing links" and a search for simian characteristics. The Darwinian theories created such a situation. And if there was any bias in these accounts, it would probably be in the tendency to find simian resemblances. But no one questions that the Neanderthals were of the *genus homo*. Certainly man was living in Europe 50,000 years ago during the earlier part of the last ice age. But how direct our descent is from this race is not known. In other words, it is not possible to tell positively from the evidence of this race whether our own ancestors were more developed or less or different. Neanderthal man in his ancient form has not survived to-day.

By the time of the Aurignacian culture, there were probably several types of men living in Europe, all rather closely resembling modern man and hence differing a good deal from Neanderthal man. The type of which there are the most finds and the best descriptions is called the Cro-Magnon. The Cro-Magnons resembled modern man, especially the American Indian, quite closely, particularly in the facial formations. They were taller than modern man and their heads were larger. The skull capacity of the "old man of Cro-Magnon" was 1590 c. c. and of the woman 1550 c.c. The Cro-Magnons found at Grimaldi had skulls which are said to average 1800 c.c. The skeletons found for periods later than the Aurignacian were somewhat smaller than the Cro-Magnons and with smaller brain cases. The anatomical finds of man during the late stone age and the neolithic age, though varied, resemble quite closely the measurements of modern men. Modern Europeans seem to be somewhat taller and larger than Europeans of several hundred years ago, but this may be due to purely environmental influences such as a better food supply. Man is to be compared with the domesticated animals rather than with the wild animals. Domestication means a more continuous food supply which has an effect on bodily measurements.

From skeletal measurements, therefore, there is strong indication of evolution in man since the beginning of the Pleistocene period. And this evolution had developed man certainly by the last ice age, from 50,000 to 25,000 years ago. But the evidence of biological evolution, as seen in anatomical measurements, since the last ice age, is certainly very slight, if existing at all. It is realized, of course, that measurements of bones are only one of many possible indices of variation. The meagreness of these data as indications of evolution of mental ability is also appreciated. Other criteria, if existing for this long period, might show other and different evidences of evolution. Considering the scantiness of skeletal evidence and the absence of other data, it seems desirable to inquire briefly into what is known in general regarding the possible rate of biological change, and to make certain comparisons with the rate of cultural change.

The question, What is the rate of biological change? is so simplified that it may never be possible to answer in as simple a manner. The rate of biological change may be very rapid at one time and very slow at another. Or it may be rapid in one species and slow in another. Or again only one part of the bodily mechanism may be undergoing change and the other parts remain stable, except in so far as internal readjustments may be occasioned. And then of course it will be difficult to express rates of biological change in measurable and comparable units. All these difficulties, particularly in the light of the present data, mean that the most that can be expected from an inquiry into the rate of biological change will necessarily be quite general. But it should be remembered that the purpose for which this knowledge is wanted in the present discussion is to make comparisons of the rapidity of change in man with the rapidity of cultural changes. It is known from common observation that biological changes are slow as seen against the span of human life. This will be admitted when it is recalled that until Darwin's discoveries, a little over a half-century ago, it was not admitted generally that the species changed at all. They were supposed to have been created as they are now. It was assumed that they continued to exist as created without change. The stability of plants and animals was indeed hardly questioned and the idea of biological evolution came as a shock.

Since the records of biological change in point of time are few, it may be well to approach the subject by a brief consideration of the way in which changes occur. The evidence of changes occurs in connection with the study of heredity. This study of heredity has already developed quite an elaborate technique and terminology, and the research is too extensive to give a detailed summary. But briefly, it may be said, the process of change occurs through variations and a transmission of these variations through heredity and a selection of particular ones favorable to survival. It will be readily seen that if the bodily variations in an organism, occurring because of use or disuse, or of acquired characteristics, were transmitted to the offspring, then the rapidity of biological changes would be great, and sociology would be of the utmost importance for biology. But acquired characteristics are not inherited; and this possible source of change is eliminated from consideration. Individuals vary, of course, but there are limits to the variation. Within these limits, variations are transmitted subject to certain rules of inheritance. But if these limits remain the same there is no change of species. Changes are sought, therefore, in variations that occur without these usual limits of variation and that are inherited. These are called mutations.

At the present time it is not known how or why these mutations occur, though much is known concerning the mechanism of their transmission through heredity. A number of mutants have been observed, however. The most extensive evidence concerning their frequency comes from the laboratory of Professor T. H. Morgan, who has conducted for many years experiments on a fruit fly, *Drosophila*. Morgan's work has been chiefly concerned with the mechanisms of heredity and not primarily with the rate of mutation. He has not published an estimate of the number of mutations observed nor of the number of flies examined for mutations. To get a rate of mutations we should need to know at least the number of flies examined, the number of traits of the fly observed, and the number of mutations found.

Although the total number of flies examined in his laboratory during the years of his investigations has not been published, Morgan gave me some rough idea of the number. He said 10,-000,000 as an estimate would be conservative. He did not think there had been as many as 30,-000,000. No actual count has of course been made. Such estimates are, however, for flies that have actually been observed under the microscope. The flies are examined more or less closely for a greater or smaller number of traits, depending on the particular problem in hand. But usually the investigators look over the eyes, the wings, the body, and the legs, so that quite a number of traits are observed on each fly.

With regard to the number of mutations, Morgan has written as follows:

The most extensive evidence is from *Drosophila melanogaster*. One of the first mutants that appeared, viz., white eyes, has appeared anew in our cultures about three times, in cultures known to be free from it before and not contaminated. The eye-color vermilion has appeared at least six times; the wing character called rudimentary, five times; cut wing has been found four times; truncate wing has frequently appeared, but has not necessarily been always produced by the same change. Certain characters such as notch wings . . . have appeared quite often. . . .[15]

These cases are mentioned as recurrent instances, and there are of course a number of other mutations that have occurred only once. In another paragraph, Morgan speaks of the twelve dominant mutations that have occurred in *Drosophila*. These of course may have occurred more than

[15] Thomas Hunt Morgan, *The Physical Basis of Heredity*, pp. 248, 249.

once. Morgan cautiously concludes that mutations occur infrequently. Even if a few hundred mutations have been observed in his laboratory, we could not arrive at so exact a measure as a rate of mutations.

It is difficult to make an estimate of the number of mutations that would have a definite meaning and could be interpreted clearly. In the first place, some of the examinations of the whole fly were done fairly rapidly, the search being made for a particular mutation. It is therefore very probable that mutations have escaped notice. Some of the mutations are small, and it is not always easy to tell when a change is a mutation. Even though the rate of mutations in *Drosophila* were known, it does not follow that other species would have the same rate.

A less vague estimate of the number and frequency of mutations is found in an article published by F. N. Duncan.[16] A large number of crosses were made with mutant stock of *Drosophila* and wild stock. A uniformly careful examination of 16,637 flies of the F2 generation was made, and three mutations were found, two of these three being of the same character. Of course, three is a very small number to make a reliable ratio, as we know from the theory of

[16] "An Attempt to Produce Mutations through Hybridization," *American Naturalist,* Vol. XLIX, pp. 575–582.

probabilities. The foregoing material is much too vague and fragmentary to form an accurate numerical rate; but it does give us some information regarding the frequency of mutations, which we see is not great.

A few other remarks on mutations may be made. The new character differs from the old, sometimes very slightly and sometimes by a larger amount. It seems that the smaller differences predominate because the larger mutations entail considerable organizational adjustments, which would give the smaller mutations greater chance of surviving. Extremely large differences between the new and old characters would thus be rare. These smaller mutations mean that the development is likely to be in the direction of the selection. Professor Morgan states the idea clearly:

Starting at any stage, the degree of development of any character increases the probability of further stages in the same direction. The relation can better be illustrated by specific cases. The familiar example of tossing pennies will serve. If I have thrown heads five times in succession, the chances that at the next toss of the penny I may make a run to six heads is greater than if I tossed six pennies at once. Not of course because five separate tosses of heads will increase the likelihood that at the next toss a head rather than a tail will turn up, but only that the chances are equal for a head or a tail.

So that I have equal chances of increasing the run to six by that throw, while if I tossed six pennies at once the chances of getting six heads in one throw are only once in sixty-four. Similar illustrations in the case of animals and plants bring out the same point. If a race of men average 5 feet 10 inches, and *on the average* mutations are not more than two inches above or below the racial average, the chance of the appearance of a mutant individual that is 6 feet tall is greater than in a race of 5-foot men. If increase in height is an advantage the taller race has a better chance than the smaller one. This statement does not exclude the possibility that a short race might *happen* to beat out in height a taller race, for it might more often mutate; but chance favors the tall. In this sense evolution is more likely to take place along lines already followed, if further advantage is to be found in that direction.[17]

The example is purely hypothetical as regards the size of mutations and the conditions of survival. The illustration shows that in biological evolution the existing stage of biological development does have a determining effect on the future development, with a large element of chance. Thus there is a certain similarity with cultural growth, where it was observed that the existing stage of culture had a determining effect on the number and the nature of the inventions.

With regard to the survival of flies with mu-

[17] *Op. cit.*, p. 268.

tant characters, the opinion among the workers in Morgan's laboratory was that in general the flies in which mutations were found could not have survived in the wild state. This fact may be of possible significance in strengthening the guess that culture may provide an environment in which probable mutations might survive.

But the especial point here under consideration is the rapidity of biological change. The data on *Drosophila* are the most extensive. Other cases of change are seen in selective breeding experiments undertaken for practical purposes. Some apparently remarkable results have been obtained. But it is difficult to tell how much is due to selection and crossing and how much to mutation. Selection will of course increase the chances of a mutation in the direction of the selecting. It is questionable whether the idea of rate of biological changes can be expressed any more briefly than has been done in the preceding summarization.

8

THE CORRELATION OF CULTURAL AND
BIOLOGICAL CHANGE

The particular purpose of our inquiry is to

compare the rate of biological change with the rate of cultural change. Comparisons would be more satisfactory if time and quantity units could be found. Realizing these inadequacies in measurement and difficulties in conceptions, there does, however, seem to be meaning and truth to the statement that within the last several hundred years the number and rate of cultural changes have been much greater than the number and rate of biological changes. For instance, Japan has made remarkable changes in her culture within a few decades. It would have been impossible for her people to have changed biologically in this time. Within the span of a single lifetime a people may now-a-days change its culture greatly. Seen in this general way, in the long period of the beginnings of culture there may have been some agreement in the rate of biological change and in the rate of cultural change; but, in the latter period of the development of culture, rates of biological change could not possibly have kept pace with the rates of cultural change. The idea may be otherwise expressed by saying that at the present time inventions are more frequent than mutations. Inventions are matters of record in the patent offices. But it is questionable whether a single definite mutation in recent man can be pointed to with certainty. Egyptian biological types have persisted as shown by the measurements on skeletons from the pyramids and on modern skulls, but how greatly has culture changed since that time!

The foregoing examination of the fragmentary record of the evolution of man shows that at least as far back as 50,000 to 25,000 years ago, man had evolved and was in Europe. There may have been mutations in man since this time. The differentiation into types which may have taken place since that time would seem to indicate such mutations. Very lightly pigmented skin appearing in different parts of the world has been spoken of as a mutation. There may also have been changes in the structure of the brain or of the nervous system. It is recalled, however, that the anatomical measurements of man 25,000 years ago compare quite closely with the anatomical measurements of man to-day. There may have been evolution in man since the last ice age, but it seems to me that it has not been definitely proved. That some changes have occurred seems theoretically probable, but just what they are or how significant they are we do not know. If four generations be reckoned to the century there are then 100,000 generations for the period, which is of course to be multiplied by the population which was a good deal smaller before the development of civilization and is smaller the further back one goes. But just what these possible changes are has not been recorded. The number of characters in man that might mutate is vast. Chance probably favors the smaller mutations and selection has probably been in the direction of greater mental ability.

While the biological evolution in man within the past 25,000 years is problematical and has not been proved, there has certainly been a great development in culture, which in recent years is very remarkable. If the biological factor has not varied over recent periods of time, then how could it account for the great variations occurring in a culture which is rapidly changing? To the readers who have hitherto assumed a high correlation between biological changes and cultural changes, the possibility of civilization's growing to what it is, with native mental ability remaining constant at the level it was during the last ice age may seem surprising, and such readers may be at a loss to account for the great development of culture. But if material culture grows through selective accumulations and inventions, in which the preceding stage of cultural development plays a large part in determining the extent, nature and rapidity of the next step in cultural development, it seems to be possible theoretically, for the development of culture to have been what it has been without the occurrence of any biological evolution in man during the process. In other words, if modern Europeans could have been set back to the last ice age, but without their culture and acquired knowledge, it is open to question whether the development of culture would have been more rapid than it has been. Such a question may be asked and though present information does not warrant a conclusive answer, one should hesitate to guess that the culture would have grown any more quickly than it has grown.

If the stability of human nature over a very long period of time, say from the last ice age to the present time, could be fully demonstrated, the significance of such knowledge would be of far-reaching importance, in many fields of thought and speculation. It would be of great importance for ethics, for sociology and especially for a study of problems of adjustment between culture and human nature. The evidence surveyed in the preceding pages suggests very strongly that changes in human nature by mutations have probably been slow and very slight over a long period of time. There were very probably changes in human nature preceding the last ice age, but it has not been proven that there have been any changes since. What has visibly changed and to a great degree is the cultural expression of human nature. But this is very probably due to changes in culture and not in the biological nature of man. Commonly the term, human nature, does not mean the original nature of man but the cultural expression of original human nature. It has been said that it is the culture which makes it human nature instead of animal nature. Of course, the cultural expression of human nature has changed greatly. Man to-day may be more spiritual and has greater ability. But this spirituality or this ability may be due to learned tendencies and acquired modifications, which hold only for the experience of a lifetime. Experience in culture produces great changes, but they are not modifications in the original nature of man, nor are they inherited. The evidence indicates a lack of correlation between cultural changes and biological changes, if not before the last ice age certainly afterward.

There is another subject, closely related to social evolution, in which a great deal of work has been done, bearing on the question of the correlation between biological variation and cultural variation. This is the subject of comparative ethnology. So extensive has been the research in this field that a brief summary would require as lengthy a presentation as has been made of social evolution. The general nature of some of the evidence relating to race and culture can be seen, however, from a few illustrations. Consider, for instance, the data from the American continent. The American Indian is generally admitted to be homogeneous from the racial standpoint. Some are tall and some are short and there is variation in head form, but as a whole they are a racial type with a fairly close resemblance. Yet the culture of the American Indian at the time of the coming of the white men showed very great variation. The culture, for instance, of the Northern Athabascans or of some of the California tribes shows a very crude material culture, only a slight development of social organization and a low development of art. These are small wandering bands living on roots, herbs and game. In contrast, there is a high development of culture along the North Pacific coast, a culture distinguished with prominence in social classes, ceremonials, decorative and dramatic art, boats and houses. In Central America and Southern Mexico were highly organized social systems, elaborate stone temples, agriculture, pottery, a numeral system, astronomical knowledge, and beginnings of writing. Certainly the variations in culture are great for a people of a rather homogeneous racial type. But it may be argued that even within a people of the same racial type a slight biological variation in mental ability may account for vast cultural differences. But this remains unproved, for the American Indian and the variation in inherent mental ability is unmeasured. There seems to be no particular correlation between the bodily measurements on stature, head form, color, or facial angle with these varying degrees of cultural development.

It may then be asked, How is this great cultural variation to be explained? This is a question the answer to which, for even a single cultural trait, can only be made after a definite historical account. The cultural history should certainly first be known before jumping to the rather obscure biological explanation. There are, however, certain general explanations that have been found to be of quite wide significance in accounting for cultural developments and hence cultural variations. Briefly, some of these are the following. The culture of a particular group grows by borrowings, which occur through cultural contacts of varying degrees. Geographical isolation acts thus as a hindrance to the spread of culture. Contacts of peoples facilitate the spread of culture. The contact in one group of two different cultures may result in new formations. The existing cultural base of a group not only has an effect on the future inventions, but it has a selective effect on diffusion. A nomadic group is not so likely to borrow pottery-making as an agricultural community. Some things spread rather easily, as, for instance, the use of tobacco. The adoption of other cultural features is more difficult. The adoption of the gun might reduce the food supply and cause extensive changes. There is in the culture of a group usually a fairly close integration or interrelation of the various parts as in a complicated machine; and a single change in one of the parts necessitates considerable reorganization, thus making barriers to diffusion. Food is always an important feature of the culture and a change in food, as, for instance, the introduction of maize, usually means many readjustments and many borrowings. If two cultures are widely different the integration of each may be such as to make adoptions difficult. Other features of cultural change and diffusion might be cited. The excellent ethnological work of the American school of anthropologists among the American Indians, has resulted in their pointing out many purely cultural accounts of cultural variations, and has led to a considerable development of theory of cultural diffusion.

Before leaving the subject of cultural explanations of cultural differences, one other point of interest may be mentioned. Some cultural differences between groups are so great as to be astounding. This is particularly true where comparisons of primitive cultures are made with the highly developed modern culture. Certainly one cause of this great discrepancy is the differences in the rates of cultural growth. The survey of the rise of culture in Europe showed it to have been very slow indeed at first, gradually getting faster and in the latter phase growing with great rapidity. The growth of a culture that has reached the point of extremely rapid change will, within a definite period of time, say, five hundred years, be immensely greater than the growth, within the same time, of a culture that has not reached the stage of such rapid change. If such a comparison be thought of as a race between two cultures, the one will in the same period of time greatly outdistance the other, which will seem to be left hopelessly behind. The original disparity between two such cultures may have been due to relative degrees of isolation or other cultural factors. Theoretically, once such a great difference is established between two such cultures, it seems difficult for the difference to be lessened, for the reason that diffusion of culture is more difficult where the differences are very great. It is true the Japanese took over in large part western culture, and China may do so, but if the Japanese culture had been in the neolithic stage it would certainly have been most difficult for it to have been brought up quickly to the stage attained in modern Europe.

SUMMARY

The presentation of the analysis of some aspects of social evolution has been quite long to read and somewhat involved. It therefore seems desirable to summarize the argument. In Part I was shown the necessity of segregating the biological factor and the cultural factor. This differentiation was thought to be desirable for the study of social evolution. Students of social evolution do not generally make such a segregation of factors; in fact, many students think social evolution is caused by biological evolution. Good methodology warrants an account of social evolution in terms of cultural records before recourse is had to the more obscure biological causes.

Accordingly the growth of material culture since its beginnings in the early ice ages was subjected to analysis. Material culture appears to grow by means of inventions which are seldom lost but which accumulate. Thus the material culture grows larger and larger. As the material culture grows larger more inventions are, on the average, made. The extent of the material culture base is a factor in the frequency of inventions. Thus material culture tends to accumulate more rapidly. The result is more rapid social change, increased specialization and differentiation. In very early times, material culture was small in amount and changed slowly. Such was the condition for a long time. Recently the material culture has grown to a vast amount and is changing very rapidly.

Considering now the biological factor, the records of ancient man indicate a significant evolution from the early Pleistocene period to the last glacial period. But since the last ice age, external measurements make it seem probable that there has been no significant evolution in these characters in man, and certainly do not prove it conclusively. Studies of heredity show that mutations occur only infrequently. Probabilities are that some change has taken place in some of the many characters of man since the last ice age; but the incomplete record does not show them and nothing is known as to what characters may have changed nor their significance. Biological change over the last two thousand years must be exceedingly slight, if it has occurred at all.

But the cultural change over the past two thousand years has been extraordinarily great. Therefore there appears to be for this period no correlation beween cultural changes and biological changes. Cultural evolution is thus not to be accounted for by biological evolution. Indeed, since the last ice age it may be that the vast cultural growth has taken place without any significant biological evolution in man. Once given a level of biological equipment, culture may go on increasing at a rapid rate without any biological change. The significance of the biological factor for the study of social evolution is thus somewhat more limited than is usually thought.

PART III

CULTURAL INERTIA AND CONSERVATISM

In the previous discussion we have been concerned with how culture changes. We wish now to inquire into why culture does not change. It has been observed that culture does not die as human beings do but goes on. The persistence of culture at times appears so strong that it seems as though culture actually resists change. There certainly is a resistance to change as any modern social reformer will testify. Why is it so difficult to change culture for those who wish to make progress? Is it due to any resisting quality in culture? Or is it due to traits in human beings that resist social change? Is the slowness of culture to change a hindrance to the improvement of social conditions or a measure of social order and stability? In the pages which follow, it is proposed to consider some of the more prominent and more frequently cited types of resistance to change, as, for instance, the so-called survivals, the more common explanations of cultural inertia, and some instances of modern conservatism. The examination will concern both cultural and psychological factors. It is hoped that such an inquiry will throw more light on the nature of the social heritage and social change.

I

VARIOUS CONCEPTIONS OF THE PERSISTENCE OF CULTURE

The study of the slowness of culture to change has been approached by the various writers from several different points of view. One of the earlier conceptions is that of survivals. Tylor in his *Primitive Culture* studied at length cultural forms that had apparently persisted beyond their usefulness and these he called survivals. Examples of these survivals are folklore, proverbs, customs, superstitions, and magical practices. Thus, the presence among European peoples of superstitions regarding sneezing is found to date back to a time when spirits, which were thought to reside in the body, passed in and out through the breath and sneezing was thus a peculiar manifestation of some spiritual activity. Hence certain bodily motions were performed after sneezing in deference to the spirit. The development of science has shown the absurdity of such beliefs yet the practices continue to survive. Tylor's main purpose, however, was not so much to note or explain a resistance to change as to find in these survivals evidence of the evolution of culture, and to show that culture passed through certain stages in the course of evolution.

The idea of survivals had previously been formed in biology in the study of embryology. According to the so-called "recapitulation theory" the life of the individual is supposed to repeat the history of the species. So signs of gills were observed at certain stages of human fœtal development and were taken as an indication that the embryo in its development passed through the fish stage in the course of evolution. Thus the signs of gills of fishes in the fœtus are a survival in man of an earlier evolutionary stage. In a somewhat similar way evidence of an earlier primitive culture survived into the modern phase of culture. Although the evolution theory seems to have been the occasion of these observations, yet it did appear that certain types of culture, especially certain customs, seemed to resist change.

Students of another field of ethnology and with a somewhat different purpose, have also called attention to the peculiar persisting quality of culture. These are the students who use etymology, and particularly kinship terms, to gain an insight into the unwritten history of an earlier period. The early Aryan culture of Europe was studied by means of the persistence of certain words in our language. For instance, the word, pecuniary, goes back through the Latin, *pecunium,* to the Sanskrit, *paçu,* meaning cattle. The etymology of certain words in the various languages shows they go back to an earlier language possessed by the Aryans; and in this way the earlier Aryan culture can be described. Similarly, existing kinship terms of a particular people give evidence of a prior family or marital condition. Thus, language as a special form of culture has a certain persistence, as the simplified spelling reformers also have had occasion to observe.

Recently, the modern ethnologists have given the name, cultural inertia, to the apparent slowness of culture to change. Their observations cover a very great variety of phenomena, from folklore to material culture. Such observations are particularly noticeable in the study of culture areas, and the influence of the diffusion of culture. Sometimes culture does not spread very quickly, when it would be expected to if judged on the basis of contact through geographical location. For instance, the cultures of the Hopi and of the Navaho though in daily contact show little tendency to merge. A people will migrate from the seacoast inland and will continue to carry certain figures of the sea in their mythologies. Boas cites from Bogoras the case of the Chuckchee who became nomadic and instead of developing the light tent, continued to use quite clumsily a complicated structure resembling their former permanent dwellings.[1] Ethnology affords many examples of what appears to be a sort of resistance of culture to change, and such a tendency is seen in many features of culture.

Still another source of interest in the slowness of culture to change is the modern social reform movement. Modern society is divided into more or less loosely defined groups, called conservative and radical. The latter group are much impressed with the slowness of social change. For instance, political reformers in the United States worked for many years to get the national government to adopt a budget system to replace the old haphazard, uneconomical, logrolling method. The old United States National Banking system lasted for many years after it was known that a centralized system of credit and an elastic bank-note system were needed. Industry paid the cost of several severe panics before the Federal Reserve Banking system was adopted. The separation of the executive and legislative functions of our government continues to exist, despite the fact that the government practically ceases to function on important and urgent issues

[1] Franz Boas, *The Mind of Primitive Man*, p. 162.

when the President and Congress are of a different political complexion. The inadequacies and wastes of private industry which is run for profit rather than service are shown in various reports, yet the system continues year after year fundamentally unchanged. Such claims of radicals and liberals to-day show the great importance of cultural inertia and furnish abundant evidence of it.

From several different sources, then, there appears to be very strong persistence of culture. Such conditions call for explanation. Such an explanation is of especial importance for theories of progress and of particular interest to those who are attempting to control and direct social changes towards social progress.

2

SURVIVALS

Our first consideration of cultural inertia will be of the survivals emphasized particularly by Tylor, and which have since been quite widely discussed. These survivals, it is recalled, are frequently old customs such as the use of mistletoe at Christmas time, the riderless horse at a funeral, the use of the ring in the marriage ceremony, children's games with the bow and arrow, and various superstitions, magical practices, and proverbs. A mere recounting of some of these old customs suggests immediately why they are thought of as survivals. Mistletoe, because of the peculiarity of its green growth in a leafless tree in the winter, presumably possessed certain magical properties which were of religious significance according to the religious ideas of early times. It was used in ceremonies of the Druids and was later fused into Christmas customs. With better knowledge concerning the growth of plants and with changed religious concepts, there is no longer any mystical religious significance to this peculiar plant. Nevertheless its use continues in our Christmas festival. The custom is therefore said to survive beyond the period of culture in which its relative significance was great. Marett has spoken of this process which results in survivals as a transvaluation of culture, and the particular type of transvaluation just discussed, he calls metataxis. He likens this process to "casting out of the parlor the unfashionable bit of furniture and placing it downstairs in a corner of the kitchen or of the children's play room," or again, "these fables, proverbs or the leechcraft prescriptions in vogue to-day among the folk are but the debased product of yesterday's official wisdom."[2]

As Marett has pointed out and as Tylor realized, these old customs do not last on as does a fossil. They are not dead in the sense of being functionless or not being put to use. Rather their valuation has been changed. Their use is no longer in the parlor or living room but is now in the kitchen or the children's play room. They survive in the sense of living on as a thing of utility rather than as lasting on as skeletal remains.

Thus, it is easily seen that though bows and arrows were useful as instruments of adult warfare, and are no longer of use in modern society for such a purpose, nevertheless they may be useful as playthings for children. Similarly, proverbs may have at one time been the highest expression of wisdom, yet they may be very useful forms of expression for ideas to-day, even though they be expressed in similes of the chase, or in phrases of a nomadic life. The vitality of Christmas as a festival may be less in our modern city life with our changed ideas of religion, but still it may serve certain purposes of social life.

The usefulness of some of those survivals called superstitions is not so apparent. Of what use or purpose, it may be asked, are certain

[2] R. R. Marett, *Psychology and Folklore*, p. 109.

taboos or beliefs in luck, or certain signs and divinations? Whether these survivals be socially useful or not they are certainly not fossils, for they do function in the life of the folk. Indeed, they may not only not serve any good social end, they may be socially harmful. The use of certain herbs, roots and quack medicines is harmful. The planting of crops according to signs of the stars may be bad agricultural practice. Funeral customs may be injurious to health. Although these features of culture are of no good social use and indeed may be socially harmful, it can be maintained, it is thought, that they possess a certain utility, that is, they attempt to supply a want or to meet a psychological need. A person is sick and wants to do something to get well. If he hasn't learned of the achievements of science in medicine he will follow the existing cultural practices of his group. There are many occasions in life when the craving to know the future is very strong. Lacking a conception of scientific standards of prediction or an ability to apply them, one may very easily use mysterious signs, particularly if this cultural practice is existing and easy of access. Similarly, though some funeral customs may be harmful, they may be a means of meeting individual desire for expressing sorrow or of meeting the group standards in this regard. As seen from the above considerations, it is maintained that, though objects of material culture, such as ruins, may survive as fossils, forms of culture such as customs, beliefs, religions, survive because of a utility they possess in meeting psychological needs.

3

THE UTILITY OF CULTURE

The idea of utility of culture can be assumed, it would seem, in nearly all cases of survival or where culture exists. Sometimes the material objects of culture may exist without being used; but nearly all cultural forms are put to some use. Utility is simply another word for usefulness with the conception of good and bad omitted. The word, wantability, has been suggested by Professor Irving Fisher as equivalent in meaning to utility.[3] The utility of the cultural forms means that they satisfy some individual or social want. Any features of culture other than material objects, such as customs, beliefs, religious practices, folk ways, superstitions, social habits, and

[3] Irving Fisher, "Is Utility the Most Suitable Term?" *American Economic Review*, Vol. VIII (1918), No. 2, p. 335.

philosophies that exist may be said to have utility to satisfy some psychological need.

It does not follow of course that the psychological need creates the cultural form; nor indeed that only one cultural form will satisfy a particular desire. One cannot start from the side of desire, assume a certain set of desires, and predict the culture. In fact, very little is known about the etiology of desires. They are very complex; they shift and change; and fuse or pull at cross-purposes, resulting in conflict. Past cultural experiences play a part in directing the motivation. A single cultural form may answer several widely differing desires. So that while a knowledge of the psychology of desires does not enable one to account for a particular type of culture, nevertheless a knowledge of desires, once a cultural form is attained, does yield a fuller understanding of its use. Thus a definite instance of a burial custom or of a taboo, or such a custom as *couvade* may be accounted for historically, yet it may be so strange as to be hardly understandable.

In such a case a knowledge of the behavior of desires, say, in the cases of mental conflict may render this cultural usage more intelligible. Thus to see individuals eat a piece of food or build a shelter or dance does not seem strange; the desires back of such activities are understood. But the fascination of a people for a myth of a man marrying his mother or an exogamous taboo or the feigning of sickness by a man at the birth of his child is not so easily understood and a greater knowledge of psychology would certainly help to understand such a cultural form. To say, therefore, that a survival is not a fossil but really meets a psychological need is a very generalized explanation of survivals. It cannot be predicted what cultural form will survive and what cultural form will not survive because the psychological need is not the only factor and because we do not know enough about psychological needs. There are also cultural or historical reasons why a particular piece of culture survives. The particular psychological desires which a survival tends to meet must be analyzed in each particular case.

From the foregoing analysis of survivals it would seem that there is no particular property of culture as such that shows a peculiar resistance to change. Culture once in existence tends to exist for the reason that it has utility, very much as a physical mass at rest tends to remain at rest. In each case the phenomenon is referred to as inertia. In case of an invention of a cultural form superior in utility, there is a displacement. Thus metal weapons replace bows and arrows and archery survives only as a children's game. Literature and science replace folklore and witchcraft in the well-to-do classes, but the replacement is slower among the more ignorant folk. It seems that the peculiarity called survival consists not so much in any new principle of resistance to change but rather in the extremely interesting way in which it furnishes clews to previously existing stages of culture. The surviving culture occupied a place of importance in an earlier culture compared to its unimportant place in modern culture, and hence helps to tell the story of an earlier culture.

Another illustration of what seems to be an impressive instance of cultural resistance to change is the case where a cultural form or activity is employed for one purpose at one time and later the same form or activity serves another and different purpose. The same piece of culture persists through several different usages. Such is the case to a certain degree in survivals. The religious significance of mistletoe has disappeared but its festival use remains. Tylor's account of the origin of drinking to one's health shows that at one time it was a ceremony performed with a mystical fluid in connection with the ceremony of the dead. Its use is now quite festive. It seems that in some of these cases of persistence, the culture persisting possessed two or more utilities, or what J. B. Clark calls a bundle of utilities; at one time the one utility being more prominent than another. In the course of time the first utility diminishes in significance while another increases. Thus, a certain rite may promote both religious and social activity. But the once dominant religious appeal may give way to the rise of the expression of sociability. Cultural forms frequently involve many different psychological responses at the same time. The church may satisfy certain religious, ethical and social needs, religion itself, of course, being a complex of psychological motives. It is thus thinkable though not necessarily probable that in the future the church may become a social or ethical institution with a diminishing religious significance. Similarly, the family as an institution answers a number of needs: economic, affectional, protective, recreative, etc. In some cultures the affectional element has been slight, affection finding an outlet elsewhere, and the economic element has been strong; in other cultures the economic element has been slight and the affectional bond strong. Furthermore, the same activity may occur from different motives. Thus one may steal to establish a reputation for cleverness or bravery as is true in some cultures, or one may steal for bodily needs as sometimes occurs among slaves. Therefore the same cultural form or activity may serve different psychological needs at different times.

4

DIFFICULTIES OF INVENTION AND OF DIFFUSION

Cultural forms may persist apparently because it is easier to use an existing form than it is to create a new one. The new idea is expressed in the old form. The Monroe Doctrine, as an expression of the foreign policy of America, was at the time of its origin a doctrine designed to protect the United States from the indirect aggression of foreign powers. It may very probably change its meaning, if the imperialistic sentiment in the United States should grow, and become an instrument for economic aggrandizement on the part of the United States. This old and revered doctrine of foreign policy might more easily be expressive of the new ideas of imperialism than some new document. Thus the difficulty of inventing and of getting the invention adopted and the ease of revaluing an old cultural form account for very striking persistences of culture. Lowie cites from Boas [4] the use of

[4] Franz Boas, "The Eskimo of Baffin Land and Hudson Bay," *Bulletin, American Museum of Natural History*, Vol. XVII (1907), pp. 75, 357.

a stone lamp by the Eskimo of Southhampton Island as such a case of cultural inertia.

Thus the Central Eskimo generally make lamps and pots out of soapstone. In Southhampton Island, where this material is lacking, they have not devised a new form but have at the expense of much ingenuity and labor cemented together slabs of limestone so as to produce the traditional shape.[5]

The difficulty of inventing and spreading an invention may mean that new demands or valuations are met by the use of old forms, it being easier to transvalue an existing form than to invent a new one.

It should be observed that the difficulty of inventing, as a cause of cultural inertia, only appears as a factor when one looks backward into the past after the invention has been made. At a particular time when an invention has not been made or conceived, the continued existence of culture does not appear as anything unusual. It is rather the ordinary thing, as was previously expressed by saying that culture once in existence and having utility continues to exist until replaced by an invention or until lost through some cause. But where there is a change in the use of an old cultural form, the trait called cultural inertia is prominent and the explana-

[5] Robert H. Lowie, *Culture and Ethnology*, p. 59.

tion may be that an old form is put to new uses more easily than a new form is invented.

The slowness of culture to change also seems notable when one observes that the culture of one people, as in the case of China in the nineteenth century, seems to resist outside influences, that is, new forms existing in other cultures are not adopted or utilized. This failure is sometimes credited to the inability of a people to take over a higher culture. Such a characterization is, it seems to me, an unsatisfactory way of expressing it because the implication is that the cause of the phenomena lies in the ability of the people, or lack of it, whereas the difficulties may be largely cultural. Thus the Mexicans seem slow to borrow the culture of the United States. The culture in the southern Appalachian mountains in Tennessee, Kentucky and North Carolina seems to be a survival of an older culture; the mountaineers have never utilized the advantages of modern industrial culture about them. Where diffusion of culture is difficult, there seems to be an inertia of culture. This apparent cultural inertia is partly a matter of perspective. From the vantage point of an outsider, it seems that the Hopi are slow to change their culture, but the Hopi probably are not so impressed with this point of view. And from the point of view of one having the higher material culture the slowness of the Mexican or mountaineer culture to change may seem a good indication of cultural inertia. Slowness of culture to change not only varies according to perspective but slowness is a relative term and implies a standard of comparison. But even granting that some cases of cultural inertia may be somewhat illusory because of the perspective, still it is quite true that a vast amount of cultural inertia is as a matter of fact due to difficulties of cultural diffusion.

What cultural difficulties are there to the spread of culture? Some of these have already been indicated in another connection in the previous section. A record of these difficulties leads to an understanding of cultural inertia or why culture does not change more rapidly. It is very easy to see how geographical isolation may act as a barrier to the introduction of new cultural ideas, and thus the isolated culture will continue to exist with relatively little change. A culture completely isolated would depend for change on inventions within itself; where it is not isolated there is the opportunity to borrow inventions made in many different areas. The culture of the isolated regions certainly appears inert by comparison with a rapidly changing culture. The culture continues because of its utilities and is relatively unchanging because cut off from new forms and ideas from the outside.

It is also easily seen that barriers to cultural dissemination may lie in climate or in absence of natural resources. The absence of coal and iron greatly hinders the introduction of the modern machine industry and the various correlated features. Trade and exchange greatly lessen these barriers.

Cultural forms or ideas vary greatly in their correlation to other parts of culture. Coffee-drinking is not closely dependent on other features of culture nor are other features of culture dependent on coffee. Presumably coffee-drinking could spread very rapidly over large areas, provided coffee could be secured. Other parts of culture that are more strongly interdependent, such as methods of transportation, or manufacture or changes in food production, entail a great many fundamental changes in the culture into which they are being adopted. Such correlated changes are obstacles to diffusion. Some object of material culture, say A, is dependent on a number of other objects or inventions, say B, C, D, E, F. It would be difficult for such an object A to be adopted into another culture which did not possess B, C, D, E, F.

Some such difficulties of diffusion exist between

two cultures where there is considerable disparity between the cultures, one being much more advanced in technology than another. The greater the difference between two cultures the greater the difficulty of cultural diffusion. There are so many fundamental parts of material culture with their many dependent subsidiary inventions, that the task of assimilating them is immense. To the person who has the advantage of the use of the higher material technology, the lower material culture seems very slow indeed in changing.

Another difficulty of diffusion lies in the fact that cultures appear to have a certain equilibrium or balance, like that of an elaborate machine, and in such a case the introduction of a new cultural feature of a fundamental sort will necessitate considerable readjustment and modification of the culture as a whole. This statement, of course, is very general. Culture also, it is admitted, has the appearance somewhat of segmentation, that is, a portion can be changed with only slight effect on the whole. Although this independence of cultural features exists, nevertheless there is considerable interdependence also. Consider, for instance, in our own culture how many cultural objects are dependent on rubber. Imagine the rubber supply cut off and think what rearrangement and readjustments would have to be made. Or, imagine the exhaustion of the supply of lubricating oils. The introduction of a new source of machine power would produce profound effects. Although the adoption of some new cultural features does involve the task of considerable social rearrangement, it is questionable how much such entailment and difficulty act as a barrier to the importation of culture. The American Indians of Washington Territory argued against any adoption of culture from the whites because of the destructive effect such contacts had had on the Indians in Oregon. But the consequences of the borrowing of culture are not always seen nor thought out beforehand.

The foregoing illustrations suffice to point out certain obstacles to the diffusion of culture. It can be readily seen from these considerations that difficulties of diffusion tend to bring into relief the phenomenon called cultural inertia. In all these cases the existing culture continues but is not changed because of obstacles to the importation of new cultural elements. In some cases, such as instances of isolation, the inertia seems most prominent, but the prominence of the inertia lies in the contrast of comparison rather than in any special quality of resistance to change inherent in culture.

5

VESTED INTERESTS

Modern social problems are an especially good field for the study of factors affecting cultural changes. For, in the first place, there is a wealth of material, because at the present time many social problems are occasioned by the frequent cultural changes. Furthermore, the student of modern social changes has a certain advantage over the student of changes in earlier cultures because of the greater detail and fuller record. Of course the factors in modern social changes are not instantly clear, but they are certainly not as obscure as the forces of the remote past. Very probably, therefore, an examination of some present-day changes may reveal additional factors affecting cultural change. It is not necessarily true, though, that the same forces operating today to effect or resist cultural change have operated at all times or operated in earlier cultures.

One factor affecting change in modern society that is quite easily observed is the power of a particular economic class. Modern society is differentiated into economic classes. Wealth and income are quite unequally distributed, so that one class or group has a very large proportion of the total amount. And there is plenty of evidence to show that the group or class that has the major portion of "the good things of life" is not so eager for change as those whose incomes and material possessions are scant. Those who derive exceptional benefit from rent, interest and profits resist changes that endanger or affect adversely these sources of income. The interests of these groups have been referred to as "vested interests." Groups not benefiting so much but suffering from the existing disposition of property are more likely to institute and support changes. Two other points should be noted in this description. One is that the possession of money and property in modern society is closely correlated with power. The other point is that economic conditions are closely interrelated with many other cultural features, so that many suggested changes to-day affect the economic situation and the effect of the economic situation in modern society reaches far into other fields of culture. The result is that an economic class is in powerful opposition to a great many forces of social change.

It is also true, however, that the power of this economic class has been very influential in promoting change. As employers they are in large part responsible for business enterprise, which has materially transformed the American continent in a very short while. Of course this material progress is not to be accounted for wholly as a result of the ability of the class of entrepreneurs. Much of this material change, through inventions, was inherent in culture; that is, such material changes as the development of steam and electrical power would probably have occurred under various systems of property distribution. Still, in the past, the opposition to business enterprise on the part of the wealthier class has not been conspicuous save in exceptional cases. In a society differentiated into social groups, some group will be identified with the forces of change while another group with interests more highly vested in the existing culture will resist the forces of change.

Opposition by the vested interests to change has not been so frequently observed among the simpler cultures. However, a somewhat similar opposition to change among peoples with more primitive cultures seems indicated by Dr. Parsons in her study of custom.[6] She points out that there is a "will-to-power" element in custom, which resists a change in the custom. This will-to-power is, however, rationalized, so that the true motive is not apparent. Thus certain rules

[6] E. C. Parsons, *Social Rule*.

of obedience for children seem designed for the comfort or power of the adult. The perpetuation of such rules may have utility for the more powerful class, here the parents and adults. So that in primitive society power is unequally distributed. The elders, males, warriors, religious leaders, may have much power, while slaves, women, or children have little. Such distribution of power may or may not be of value for survival or social welfare. The "vested interests" of these individuals thus favored by custom do not actually appear as inimical to change, possibly because the processes of change among primitive peoples are rare. The resistance of the "vested interests" to change is more evident in modern society.

Those who have "vested interests" derive a differential advantage under existing conditions and if they are likely to lose this advantage to others because of changes in the situation, then the "vested interests" will offer a resistance to change. There are of course "vested interests" in various social conditions, other than the purely economic. There are "vested interests" in schools, in churches, in political organizations, and all resist changes that shake their interests.

6

THE POWER OF TRADITION

Another reason for the slowness of culture to change is said to be a traditional hostility, inherent in the mores, towards the new among some peoples, particularly those with the simpler cultures. Numerous visitors from the Occident to the Orient have written of interesting illustrations of reverence for the past, or the old, and of marked hostility to innovations. In the west, on the other hand, there is boasting of a desire for improvement, of a willingness to experiment. Peoples living under primitive social conditions are said to have a reverence for the past, and a strong preference for doing a thing the way it has always been done. It appears possible, therefore, for the mores in a particular culture to embody a specific attitude towards change, either hostility towards change or a willingness to change.

To the traveler from modern Europe or America, the definite hostility to change on the part of the Orientals or tribes with primitive social conditions is a strange phenomenon. But the strangeness is due to his own ignorance for the usual rule is slowness of change, the exceptional is the rapidity of change as found in modern western cultures. Furthermore, this difference between the reverence for the traditional and openmindedness towards the experimental is usually exaggerated. The willingness in modern civilization to experiment is only partial; there are many suggestions that we are not willing to try. Furthermore, the difficulties of trying out new ideas by peoples of lower material cultures is not appreciated by the glib visitor. No doubt some changes that are occurring escape the eye of the casual traveler.

There are various reasons why the mores of modern peoples reveal a willingness to change. In the first place, the rate of making material inventions is much greater now than before and thus the peoples have become accustomed to changes through the appearance of these inventions, the number and frequency of which are in part determined by the existing cultural accumulation. Furthermore, experimenting is made more sure by knowledge. In the absence of science, experimenting becomes a matter of haphazard trial and error, the error sometimes being quite probable and costly. The fact that the fear of failure may have been greater in more ignorant societies and the chances of success more probable under the advancement of knowledge of the present time is a factor in the greater readiness to experiment in modern times.

Illustrating the possibility of a variety of factors that may account for a readiness to accept change, one explanation of the progressivism of the western part of the United States may be cited. It has been claimed that the natural resources were so abundant and the assurance of the growth of population so great, that the chances of failure in business were much less than in other parts of the country. Hence there was a sort of willingness, indeed a premium on trying something new, an experience which was extended to other fields than business. This account may or may not be true but it is clear that there are a number of reasons why in modern civilization there is a welcome for improvements.

A very common explanation of why the so-called primitive peoples—not primitive peoples necessarily but peoples with primitive cultures—revere the past and resist change places the cause as fear and ignorance. The customary ways of doing things seem safe because they have been tried. Trial to the best of limited observation has proven success. Perhaps the opinion in primitive cultures is not so rationalistic nor so explicit as the foregoing, but is summed up in some such remark as "it has always been done." On the other hand, the new is the unknown, and doubly so if scientific development is slight. And if, in conjunction with the trial of the new, there occurs a death, disaster, disease or an unfortunate accident, they are linked as cause and effect, as has been frequently noted. A fear reaction follows which indicates a fear of the new, the unknown.

So the mores in a culture may embody a definite attitude for or against change. The frequency of change, however, is not only a result of such an attitude but also a cause. If inventions, which are in part determined by the existing material culture, are frequent, a people becomes accustomed to change and the hostility to change tends to be broken down. On the other hand, if material culture inventions are infrequent, change may be rare and feared.

7

HABIT

Slowness to change in modern terminology is called conservatism. Conservatism is considered an attribute of a people of a particular age and locality or as a trait of a special class of individuals. Although conservatism certainly has important cultural factors, it is often thought of as a psychological trait. Existing accounts of conservatism therefore tend to be psychological explanations. A consideration of some of these more or less psychological explanations of why culture is slow to change will be undertaken.

Before discussing certain psychological explanations of the slowness of culture to change, it is desirable to call attention to certain points of methodology involved in explaining social phenomena psychologically. The subject was discussed somewhat in preceding sections, but there are so many aspects of the relation of sociology and psychology that the treatment never seems completed. The point has been taken that in analyzing social phenomena the explanation should first be historical or cultural. Very often when this is done, there seems no psychological problem left. But it is true that every cultural form or manifestation of behavior has its psychological side since it could not exist except through the agency of human beings. But because prior psychological analyses have frequently led theorists astray, we are hardly justified in becoming doctrinaire in our devotion to the historical method. On the other hand there are cases where a special knowledge of the psychology of behavior makes our understanding of social forms and social behavior more complete than would be the case if the cultural factor only were considered. For instance, incest taboos and marriage regulations may be quite fully described historically and culturally, yet there is something decidedly strange about incest and about marriage prohibitions. One's curiosity is not satisfied by the cultural facts. Psychology may be able to make the custom much clearer by its researches into mental conflict and repression of desire centring around the relation of a child to its parent. Even when the psychology of incest is known, it does not necessarily follow that regulations of incest will among all peoples be of the same form and of the same degree. The cultural situation may be a factor in determining the particular form. But the psychology of incest may also be necessary for understanding a particular form of regulation of incest. Another illustration of the value of psychology is in the prosecution of crime. Crimes, no matter what their cultural forms may be, are not understood without a knowledge of motives. A historical description of the crime helps to reveal the motive, but a knowledge of the motive also helps to determine the facts, as every detective knows.

Having pointed out certain relations between psychological and cultural causes, we shall now examine some of the psychological causes of conservatism. Perhaps the most commonly noted psychological trait that resists change is habit. Habit is popularly thought of as the doing of a thing over again in the same way, that is, not in a new way; and the determining force of this repetition, of the use of the old or previously used method, is supposed to come from within, from psychological or physiological sources. It therefore follows that a part of our nature predisposes us to behaving conservatively, that is, doing things in the same old way. How shall we evaluate this factor, habit, in cultural inertia? A number of points may be noted.

In the first place our actions are not wholly governed by desires to do things in the same way. We love adventure, we are restless, we like to try new things in new ways. It may therefore be part of our nature to love the new as well as to love the old. And, if the problem could be thus simplified, what we should want would be some sort of quantitative estimate of these two tendencies.

It should also be observed that in so far as habit as a purely psychological factor is an influence in slowing up cultural changes, it operated in ancient times as truly as now, for the psychological mechanisms of habit were present as truly in ancient man as in modern man. Of course one type of culture may call forth habitual behavior more than another type, but such changes in habit reactions will be due to a cultural factor and not a psychological factor, since the variation is in the culture and not in the original nature of man.

Furthermore, a good deal of what is called habit is attributed to forces inherent in the original nature of man when it should be attributed to culture. The doing of certain activities over and over again, frequently called habits, is required by culture and not by inward cravings. For instance, the daily routine of life is imposed in large part by the processes of social and industrial life; yet this is the type of activity that causes the remark that man is a creature of habit.

A culture with orderliness and routine engenders repetition, which is called habit. If culture were extremely chaotic and continuously so, would the force of habit be so impressive? A part of the phenomenon called habit instead of being a cause of cultural inertia is a result.

Perhaps, also, slowness to change is accredited to habit when it is caused by ignorance. If an American goes to Europe it will take him some time to get rid of his peculiarly American ways, and to adopt European manners. The difficulty and time required in learning these new customs is due in part to their strangeness or his ignorance, as well as to habit. The response to stimuli along new lines in a new culture often has to be learned through knowledge, and in ignorance the response is along the old familiar channels. A youth leaving home and the high school for college makes a fairly sharp change in cultural environment. It is usually estimated that it requires the whole freshman year to break the old habits and form the new. There seems to be a "hanging over" of old customs, resembling the previously discussed survivals. And no doubt the old habits have a certain utility, meet a psychological need, despite the fact that new customs are superior.

Nevertheless, even after all the foregoing qualifications and misinterpretations are admitted, there still remains the psychological phenomenon of habit. Certain responses to stimuli tend to follow a previously used channel somewhat more readily than to find a new one. That habit acts to make changes in social conditions slow seems to be a fact. That habits operate during a lifetime will be admitted; but at death these habits are broken and at birth new habits form. But the forces that made habits in the adult make habits in the young, particularly through the powerful influence of parents. In a culture that is rapidly changing, social forces will make habits in the young which will be somewhat different from the habits of adults because culture has changed within a generation. If the deaths in a society occurred all at one time and the births all at once, the change in culture would be more easily seen and such an abstraction illustrates the idea of the influence of habits in conserving culture. But deaths and births in a society are a more continual process. Nevertheless, the dying of influential elders speeds up somewhat cultural changes.

Education is a force which conserves culture from one generation to another, that is, education in a very broad sense as the learning that takes place outside the schoolroom as well as inside. Education is thus in very large measure the making acquainted of the young with the existing culture, and tends to strengthen the force of habit. Education of course can be made in part a training in experimentation and invention or even in spreading the newest culture instead of the old and thus assist cultural changes, but such a process will be a small part of education thus broadly conceived. A knowledge of habit does then throw some light on why culture changes slowly. It is well to remember, however, that habits are the result of cultural inertia as well as its cause, and that the purely psychological mechanisms of habit were the same ten thousand years ago as they are to-day. If culture continues to grow with an increasing number of changes, we shall become habituated to change.

8

SOCIAL PRESSURE

Another type of resistance to change, frequently discussed by social psychologists, is socially enforced conformity to group standards. Individuals are forced to abide by existing folk ways and rules by some sort of social pressure and fear of ostracism or punishment. Such forced conformity is usually to the existing standards and hence appears to hinder change in the existing culture. Social pressure is also exerted in times of social change to force conformity to the new as in war time or as in fashion and styles of dress. But such group control seems to be much more prevalent in maintaining the present order by cutting off deviations from existing conditions and by restraining those who want to make radical changes.

There are many reasons why one abides by custom. Habit is one such factor. But in addition to habit, conformity to custom seems to be insisted upon, consciously or unconsciously by a group of others. One hesitates to deviate from a code of manners. A pressure to conform is felt if the prescribed regulation is broken. Conformity is found not only in connection with folk ways and customs, but social rules are quite consciously made, as in legislative enactments, and departure from them is prevented by the force of police, courts and penal institutions. These social phenomena have been described and analyzed as a form of social control by Ross and Giddings. Giddings, in describing the forces of social control, makes use of statistical terms, pointing out that, in society, there are modes which most behavior closely resembles and that extreme deviations from those modes are not allowed to occur.[7] Social pressure is like natural selection in biology. Distributions of biological specimens of a class cluster around a type or a mode. The reason for such a distribution is thought to be that there is a type adaptation and that extreme variations from type are eliminated by environmental forces. Natural selection tends to mold a type. In a somewhat similar way, in social phenomena, deviations from type are prevented by distinctly social forces. There is a social pressure which makes conformity to type. Thus there are certain rules and practices, in re-

[7] F. H. Giddings, *Studies in the Theory of Human Society*, Chap. XII, p. 197.

gard to the employment of children in factories, which approach a standard or type, and there is a group force tending to make manufacturers and parents conform to this type as determined by law.

Such control and conformity may be observed daily but the question is, How are such phenomena to be explained? No doubt under the term social control many diverse phenomena of various origins have been classified. But some of the more conspicuous factors will be considered, with particular references to their psychological and cultural nature. There is a distinct group aspect to such control. It is as though the opinion or will of the group is imposed on the individual. Individuals are particularly sensitive to the opinions of others and much of one's action is shaped with regard to the possible opinion of others. The drive to such behavior of individuals may be quite fundamental and have its roots in gregariousness, sociability or self-submission. The imposition of such rules of behavior implies a purely psychological basis of collective behavior. Also, collective effort towards the doing of anything, other than the simplest like response to stimuli, involves teamwork and coöperation. The individual who interferes with such collective effort will tend to experience in some form of expression the resentment of the group.

The cultural expression of such behavior will vary according to the particular type of culture. The cultural situation may be so ordered that for a time a minority or a single individual may thwart the unorganized or only partly realized desires of the majority.

Collective activity is expedited through orderliness and definiteness, and one wonders if the fact that changes may disturb the orderliness of social organization tends to make changes less welcome. Civilization is orderly; its order is commented upon with pride. But is the order in society necessary because of the nature of culture or because of the original social nature of man? It has been said that habit is a law of our being because habit by reducing actions to the automatic makes it possible for attention and consciousness to be fixed on choices and problems of importance. But such a statement unfortunately implies that the supposed purpose is the cause. However, social order does in a somewhat similar way expedite social activities. Traffic along a crowded highway is aided by regulations. Living together in various social activities is made easier by the knowledge that comes from the definiteness and repetition of organization.

Such organization aids prediction and facilitates the making of correct judgment, all quite desired in the business of living. A man who transacts business, constructs a plan, or undertakes a venture, makes his judgments on a great many of the details by certain surface indications without conducting a thoroughgoing piece of research into the details. Consider the employment of a new employee. A very few data are often all that is necessary for such a purpose. Honesty, ability, loyalty, and certain other qualities are judged from the few data as indications, without knowing the full history and heredity of the individual employed. We can "size up" a person by his manners or his dress or his language, which could not be so easily done if customs were changing rapidly. It is a very important function of manners that they do facilitate opinions and judgments. The desire for certainty, definiteness, facility and knowledge may be partly responsible for the orderliness of organization and resistance to changes that introduce confusion.

Of course, the variations in the degree of organization or orderliness are due more to variations in the cultural situation than to variations in human beings. One cultural situation may mean a high degree of order, while another may mean considerable confusion, with no fundamental change in human nature of the people. Still there seem to be certain psychological forces that tend to produce orderliness. There is therefore probably a social pressure towards orderliness, a tendency to prevent deviations in the direction of social confusion. It was previously pointed out that the slowness of culture to change was particularly noticeable in language, especially in written language. It is not wholly clear why language is so slow to change, but it would seem that no purely cultural explanation would be entirely satisfying. The psychological utility of orderliness would appear to be in large part the explanation of the stability of language.

Another psychological aspect of social control lies in the social necessity of curbing egotism and selfishness. The functioning of one's desires is usually quite immediately and directly in the interests of one's self and not particularly in the interest of others. One usually feels one's own desires more urgently than the desires of others. In fact the appeal of one's own desires often overshadows and obscures the interests of others. It sometimes is necessary, therefore, for others to impose restrictions on the selfish desires of the individual. The individual must therefore conform; and the danger of deviating from the accepted standard lies in the egotism of the particular individual's desires. It has been said, with some truth, that in all eccentricity there is a grain of egotism. Particularly in the breaking of customs is an outlet found for egotism, and in the requirements of custom is likely to be seen the resentment against the egotism of others. The desirability of controlling the selfishness of the individual for the sake of the welfare of others does appear as a factor in social pressure. That social pressure is a force which frequently prevents deviations in the direction of the new, the stories of martyrs indicate.

9

FORGETTING THE UNPLEASANT

Another psychological process that strengthens conservatism is the tendency to forget the things that are unpleasant to remember, a tendency frequently observed by psychoanalysts. If memory is thus selective, the past appears really brighter than it is and we are loath to change from the conditions of the past.

The reader may be skeptical regarding the accuracy of the statement that there is a tendency to forget things that are unpleasant to remember, especially since one readily recalls a number of unpleasant events of the past. We learn from the unpleasant experiences of life certain guidances for the future. The child who burns his finger on the stove remembers the fact, and this remembrance controls his actions in the future. The use of the whip is of value to the animal trainer as truly as are the rewards of praise. But the statement is not that we tend to forget certain events that were unpleasant at the time, but rather that we tend to forget certain events that are unpleasant to remember. It may indeed yield a good deal of satisfaction and pleasure to recall certain events that were painful at the time. It is only to the extent that unpleasant events are unpleasant to remember that we tend to forget them.

This tendency has been studied somewhat by the use of experiments but the observations have been most abundant where psychoanalysis has been used. With psychoanalysts such forgetting is so common as hardly to be doubted. The great body of phenomena of conflict and repression so widely observed in neurotic characters results in the forgetting of the unpleasant. We put the distasteful, the disagreeable out of our mind. We seek forgetfulness by will power, by seeking pleasure or diversion, and by various other devices. There are, of course, cases of morbidness and compulsive fears where one dwells on the unpleasant, but these have been explained on the basis of repression and by no means run counter to the tendency to forget the unpleasant.

Many of the facts of life and of history are in harmony with the theories of the repression from consciousness of the unpleasant. For instance, it is generally agreed that childhood appears in retrospect happier than it really was. The home, its surroundings, playtime, food, all tend to be idealized in remembrance. College alumni remember the good old days at college. The glorification of the past is seen in the phrase "the good old days." We love to remember the glorious events of war and not the errors. We remember less and less the defects in our national heroes, recalling their noble qualities. George Washington is mythical and Lincoln is rapidly becoming so. All these illustrations have other psychological factors and are not to be explained solely by a tendency to forget the unpleasant. However, these and many other instances do conform to what psychoanalysis shows to be true in individual lives. If the past is glorified by such selective forgetting, it is to be expected that we would not want to change from these conditions of the past. And in so far as our wants and wills and purposes in regard to changing conditions operate and are effective, culture will be slow to change because of this purposeful amnesia.

It is interesting to inquire to what extent cultural conditions may modify this tendency to forget the unpleasant things and to overestimate the good things of the past. Under the hand of the psychoanalyst the patient is made to recall these experiences that are unpleasant to remember and after working out a more wholesome attitude towards them, the past is no longer unpleasant to remember, the result supposedly being a wholesome one for the personality. A person may find it distinctly satisfying to recall some painful event, if by recalling it he can prevent a repetition in the future. In other words, when there is a way out, an appreciated knowledge gained by experience or a prospect of improvement, the unpleasant events of the past are not so unpleasant to remember. And so it would seem that if there is a prospect of improvement in social conditions, something to be gained by avoiding a repetition of these objectionable situations, the past may be less glorified and past conditions may be seen more nearly as they were. In a rapidly changing culture, individuals identify themselves with these changes, work with hope for improvement and the concept of "better times" may tend to replace the notion of "the good old days."

PSYCHOLOGICAL TRAITS AND CONSERVATISM

The element of fear is another psychological factor in human beings that tends to cause them to resist changes. Fear may appear too strong a word; perhaps anxiety is more accurate, or the degree of fear found generally in uncertainty and in ignorance. The fear in uncertainty may be the reason for the use of the phrase, "let well enough alone." There is, for instance, some such uncertainty in the minds of voters who reject the proposal to adopt "proportional representation." Although the reasons given for not adopting the new may often be rationalized expressions for some other reaction, still, the element of uncertainty is manifested noticeably with regard to many proposed changes. There is more human risk in social experimentation than in a scientific laboratory. The uncertainty may be particularly prominent because of the high degree of interdependence and orderliness necessary in social organization.

Since human beings are always active agents in all cultural change, these changes could be reviewed against the background of each and all human traits, if we could count and define them all, and each trait appraised in regard to its relation to cultural change. But such a procedure would be more an exercise than of practical significance. So only some of the human traits more conspicuously affecting the stability of culture have been presented.

There are also psychological factors that tend to hasten cultural changes. Curiosity is probably such a factor, and is an element in inventiveness. The repression of desires may lead to a restlessness that furnishes a drive for change. Pain in many instances furnishes an impetus to change. We not only love regularity and orderliness and act according to habit, but we also love adventure, we love to travel, we have an ambition to improve. So there are unquestionably psychological bases of change as well as resistance to change. The inquiry of this chapter has been rather to inquire into the nature of the more apparent resistances to cultural change. However, one might conceivably raise the question, a very general one indeed, as to whether human nature predominantly resists change or is essentially change-loving. Presumably a brief general answer would be practically meaningless. In some situations human beings want to change and in others they do not. Running over a long list of psychological traits and examining which motives facilitated change and which impeded change and then totaling the results would probably give, if it could be done, an uncertain picture due to the variety of changes and the variety of those traits.

It is also remembered that in any large sample of the population, there will be great variation in the psychological equipment of the different individuals. Some individuals are by original equipment or very early experiences more conservative in the general situations of life while others are more radical. This will be true within virtually the same general environment. For instance, some individuals are to-day understandably radical for the reason that "they have nothing to lose but their chains." There are occasionally others, however, who are very well blessed with the world's goods but yet are generally radical. An explanation of such radicalism may very well be largely psychological, as the following analysis indicates. The world is, with difficulty, bearable to such radicals not because of any material situation, but because of an internal conflict of whose true nature they are more or less unconscious. Radicalism is often found with certain neurotic tendencies. The nervous instability which predisposes one to radicalism is probably found in a minority of modern population. So that in any large sample of population there will be both radicals and conservatives, made so both by psychological equipment and by the cultural situation, the latter being more variable over time.

SUMMARY

We have now examined some of the more conspicuous aspects of the slowness of culture to change. And out of this analysis comes the hypothesis that culture once in existence persists because it has utility. Forces that produce changes are the discovery of new cultural elements that have superior utility, in which case the old utilities tend to be replaced by the new. The slowness of culture to change lies in the difficulties of creating and adopting new ideas. These difficulties are quite numerous and usually not appreciated by observers. An examination of some of the more frequently cited types of survival and cultural inertia does not indicate any other new principle of cultural stability, such as a peculiar resisting quality in culture to change. The understanding of cultural inertia lies largely in appreciating the various difficulties of change. Some difficulties are predominantly cultural; and others are psychological.

The strangeness of cultural survivals does not lie in any mystical principle of evolution. These survivals persist not as fossils but because they have utility and there are usually in such instances of survivals difficulties and utilities making understandable why there has not been a replacement by new forms and new ideas. Cultural inertia is sometimes exaggerated due to faulty observation. There are certain instances of seemingly extraordinary inertia, where the same cultural form is used at one time for one purpose and later for a quite different purpose, that is, a cultural form has persisted so long that its meaning or value has quite radically changed. Such instances arise because a particular form has or may have a number of quite different utilities and apparently it is easier to use an old form than to acquire or invent a new one. Perhaps the most numerously observed cases of cultural inertia are due to difficulties of diffusion of culture. A comprehensive and far-reaching study would reveal a great variety of difficulties of a purely cultural sort, which might or might not be classified into a few general types, applicable to all cultural conditions. Detailed studies of the difficulties of diffusion make in particular instances the strangeness of cultural inertia appear less strange. Particularly in modern times can the processes of change be seen frequently and in great detail. In modern society, divided into classes, those classes deriving differential benefits from existing conditions tend to resist any change that will lessen those benefits. Difficulties of changing the social conditions are also found to have a prominent psychological aspect as well as a cultural side. Some of the more conspicuous psychological resistances to change are seen in the phenomena of habit, the social pressure for conformity, and the process of forgetting the unpleasant which results in a distorted view and admiration of the past. Of the great number of human traits, some tend to make us conservative and some to make us radical. We cannot take a census of these traits and classify them with regard to change. Therefore only a few have been discussed.

The preceding analyses are not comprehensive but are in the nature of an inquiry into some of the more frequently mentioned aspects of the slowness of culture to change. In this age of great change, those who are working for changes in the direction of progress are much concerned with the obstacles to change. It is hoped that the foregoing discussion throws some light on the subject. There remains, however, another very important nature of social change yet to be discussed. This will be done in Part IV. The thesis is there advanced that the source of most modern social changes to-day is the material culture. These material-culture changes force changes in other parts of culture such as social organization and customs, but these latter parts of culture do not change as quickly. They lag behind the material-culture changes, hence we are living in a period of maladjustment.

PART IV

SOCIAL MALADJUSTMENTS

That this is an age of change is an expression frequently heard to-day. Never before in the history of mankind have so many and so frequent changes occurred. These changes, it should be observed, are in the cultural conditions. The climate is changing no more rapidly, and the geological processes affecting land and water distribution and altitude are going on with their usual slowness. Nor apparently is the biological nature of man undergoing more rapid changes than formerly. We know that biological man changes through mutations which occur very rarely indeed and we have no biological evidence to show and little reason to think that mutations in mental or physical man are occurring more frequently now than in the past. These changes that we see taking place all about us are in that great cultural accumulation which is man's social heritage. It has already been shown that these cultural changes were in early times rather infrequent, but that in modern times they have been occurring faster and faster until to-day mankind is almost bewildered in his effort to keep adjusted to these ever-increasing social changes. This rapidity of social change may be due to the increase in inventions which in turn is made possible by the accumulative nature of material culture. These conclusions follow from the preceding analyses.

I

THE HYPOTHESIS OF CULTURAL LAG

This rapidity of change in modern times raises the very important question of social adjustment. Problems of social adjustment are of two sorts. One concerns the adaptation of man to culture or perhaps preferably the adapting of culture to man. This subject is considered in Part V. The other problem is the question of adjustments, occasioned as a result of these rapid social changes, between the different parts of culture, which no doubt means ultimately the adaptation of culture to man. This second problem of adjustment between the different parts of culture is the immediate subject of our inquiry.

The thesis is that the various parts of modern culture are not changing at the same rate, some parts are changing much more rapidly than others; and that since there is a correlation and interdependence of parts, a rapid change in one part of our culture requires readjustments through other changes in the various correlated parts of culture. For instance, industry and education are correlated, hence a change in industry makes adjustments necessary through changes in the educational system. Industry and education are two variables, and if the change in industry occurs first and the adjustment through education follows, industry may be referred to as the independent variable and education as the dependent variable. Where one part of culture changes first, through some discovery or invention, and occasions changes in some part of culture dependent upon it, there frequently is a delay in the changes occasioned in the dependent part of culture. The extent of this lag will vary according to the nature of the cultural material, but may exist for a considerable number of years, during which time there may be said to be a maladjustment. It is desirable to reduce the period of maladjustment, to make the cultural adjustments as quickly as possible.

The foregoing account sets forth a problem that occurs when there is a rapid change in a culture of interdependent parts and when the rates of change in the parts are unequal. The discussion will be presented according to the following outlines. First the hypothesis will be presented, then examined and tested by a rather full consideration of the facts of a single instance, to be followed by several illustrations. Next the nature and cause of the phenomenon of cultural maladjustment in general will be analyzed. The extent of such cultural lags will be estimated, and finally the significance for society will be set forth.

A first simple statement of the hypothesis we wish to investigate now follows. A large part of our environment consists of the material conditions of life and a large part of our social heritage is our material culture. These material things consist of houses, factories, machines, raw materials, manufactured products, foodstuffs and other material objects. In using these material things we employ certain methods. Some of these methods are as simple as the technique of handling a tool. But a good many of the ways of using the material objects of culture involve rather larger usages and adjustments, such as customs, beliefs, philosophies, laws, governments. One important function of government, for instance, is the adjustment of the population to the material conditions of life, although there are other governmental functions. Sumner has called many of these processes of adjustments, mores. The cultural adjustments to material conditions; however, include a larger body of processes than the mores; certainly they include the folk ways and social institutions. These ways of adjustment may be called, for purposes of this particular analysis, the adaptive culture. The adaptive culture is therefore that portion of the non-material culture which is adjusted or adapted to the material conditions. Some parts of the non-material culture are thoroughly adaptive culture such as certain rules involved in handling technical appliances, and some parts are only indirectly or partially so, as for instance, religion. The family makes some adjustments to fit changed material conditions, while some of its functions remain constant. The family, therefore, under the terminology used here is a part of the non-material culture that is only partly adaptive. When the material conditions change, changes are occasioned in the adaptive culture. But these changes in the adaptive culture do not synchronize exactly with the change in the material culture. There is a lag which may last for varying lengths of time, sometimes indeed, for many years.

An illustration will serve to make the hypothesis more clearly understood. One class of material objects to which we adjust ourselves is the forests. The material conditions of forestry have changed a good deal in the United States during the past century. At one time the forests were quite plentiful for the needs of the small population. There was plenty of wood easily accessible for fuel, building and manufacture. The forests were sufficiently extensive to prevent in many large areas the washing of the soil, and the streams were clear. In fact, at one time the forests seemed to be too plentiful, from the point of view of the needs of the people. Food and agricultural products were at one time the first need of the people and the clearing of land of trees and stumps was a common undertaking of the community in the days of the early settlers. In some places, the quickest procedure was to kill and burn the trees and plant between the stumps. When the material conditions were like these, the method of adjustment to the forests was characterized by a policy which has been called exploitation. Exploitation in regard to the forests was indeed a part of the mores of the time, and describes a part of the adaptive culture in relation to forests.

As time went on, however, the population grew, manufacturing became highly developed, and the need for forests increased. But the forests were being destroyed. This was particularly true in the Appalachian, Great Lakes and Gulf regions. The policy of exploitation continued. Then rather suddenly it began to be realized in certain centres of thought that if the policy of cutting timber continued at the same rate and in the same manner the forests would in a short time be gone and very soon indeed they would be inadequate to supply the needs of the population. It was realized that the custom in regard to using the forests must be changed and a policy of conservation was advocated. The new policy of conservation means not only a restriction in the amount of cutting down of trees, but it means a more scientific method of cutting, and also reforestation. Forests may be cut in such a way, by selecting trees according to their size, age and location, as to yield a large quantity of timber and yet not diminish the forest area. Also by the proper distribution of cutting plots in a particular area, the cutting can be so timed that by the time the last plot is cut the young trees on the plot first cut will be grown. Some areas when cut leave a land which is well adapted to farming, whereas such sections as mountainous regions when denuded of forests are poorly suited to agriculture. There of course are many other methods of conservation of forests. The science of forestry is, indeed, fairly highly developed in principle, though not in practice in the United States. A new adaptive culture, one of conservation, is therefore suited to the changed material conditions.

That the conservation of forests in the United

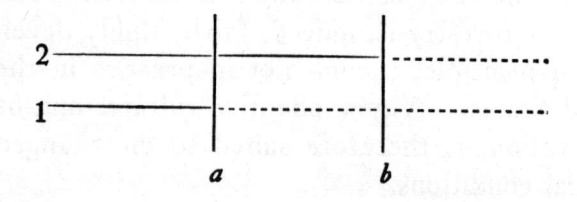

States should have been begun earlier is quite generally admitted. We may say, therefore, that the old policy of exploitation has hung over longer than it should before the institution of the new policy. In other words, the material conditions in regard to our forests have changed but the old customs of the use of forests which once fitted the material conditions very well have hung over into a period of changed conditions. These old customs are not only not satisfactorily adapted, but are really socially harmful. These customs of course have a utility, since they meet certain human needs; but methods of greater utility are needed. There seems to be a lag in the mores in regard to forestry after the material conditions have changed. Or translated into the general terms of the previous analysis, the material conditions have changed first; and there has been a lag in the adaptive culture, that is, that culture which is adapted to forests. The material conditions changed before the adaptive culture was changed to fit the new material conditions. This situation may be illustrated by the figure. Line 1 represents the material conditions, in regard to forests in the United States. Line 2 represents the adaptive culture, the policy of using the forests. The continuous lines represent the plentiful forests, with the sparse population and the mores of exploitation, the dotted lines, the new conditions of forests which are small in relation to the population and the new policy of conservation. The space between *a* and *b* represents the period when the old adaptive culture or mores exists with the changed material conditions, and is a period of maladjustment.

It is difficult to locate exactly the points *a* and *b*. Consider first the location of point *b*, or the time of the change from the policy of exploitation to the policy of conservation. The policy of conservation of forests certainly did not begin prior to 1904, when the first National Conservation Congress met. It was during Roosevelt's administration that many active steps in the direction of conservation were taken. Large areas of national forest lands were withdrawn from public entry. Gifford Pinchot was very active in spreading the gospel of conservation, and the House of Governors called by President Roosevelt was in large measure concerned with programmes of conservation. About this time many books and articles in magazines and periodicals were written on the subject. The conservation movement can hardly be said to have started in any extensive manner before this time. It is true that, earlier, papers had been read on the subject before scientific societies and there had been some teaching of scientific forestry, but prior to this time the idea of forest conservation was little known and the movement was certainly not extensive. Nor had the government taken any significant steps in a genuine policy of conservation. Indeed it might be argued with some success that we have not yet adopted fully a policy of conservation. For a great many of the private holdings are still exploited in very much the same old way. Reforestation is still largely a matter of theory in the United States. It is true that the government has taken a number of steps to preserve the forests but the conservationists are far from being satisfied with the progress of the movement to date. Certainly we have not attained the high mark maintained in western Europe.

It is also difficult to locate point *a*, that is, to determine when we should have started the conservation movement. Some features of conservation probably should have been instituted perhaps early in the last century. Thus the allotment of permanent forest areas might very well have been done coincidently with the extension of our domain; and the destruction of forests on land little suited to agriculture might have been prevented as the population spread to these new regions. At the time of the Civil War the population had become quite large, and shortly afterward the era of railroad-building set in followed by a great development of industry, insuring large population and concentration. It was at this time that the wonderful forests of the Great Lakes region were cut down, and the cuttings in the Appalachian regions increased greatly. Some close observers saw at that time what development of population and industry would take place, but the relation of the forests to such a condition was not appreciated. If scientific forestry had been applied then, many of the unnecessarily wasted forests would still exist and now be furnishing lumber. There would not have been such a washing of soil and the danger of floods would have been less. While some methods of forest conservation might have been applied to advantage shortly after colonial days, the proper time for more extensive developments of conservation was probably in the era following the Civil War. The population was becoming large; the west was being settled; the Pacific coast had been reached; the territorial boundaries had been fixed; industries, railroads, factories, corporations, trusts were all growing with rapidity. The east was in greater need of conservation of forests than the Pacific Northwest or Alaska; nevertheless very probably for the whole country, though its stages of development were unequal, an extensive conservation movement should have been instituted about the middle of the last half of the nineteenth century. It would seem, therefore, that there has been a lag of at least a quarter of a century in changing our forestry policy.

The foregoing discussion of forestry illustrates the hypothesis which it is proposed to discuss. It is desirable to state more clearly and fully the points involved in the analysis. The first point concerns the degree of adjustment or correlation between the material conditions and the adaptive non-material culture. The degree of this adjustment may be only more or less perfect or satisfactory; but we do adjust ourselves to the material conditions through some form of culture; that is, we live, we get along, through this adjustment. The particular culture which is adjusted to the material conditions may be very complex, and, indeed, quite a number of widely different parts of culture may be adjusted to a fairly homogeneous material condition. Of a particular cultural form, such as the family or government, relationship to a particular material culture is only one of its purposes or functions. Not all functions of family organization, as, for instance, the affectional function, are primarily adaptive to material conditions.

Another point to observe is that the changes in the material culture precede changes in the adaptive culture. This statement is not in the form of a universal dictum. Conceivably, forms of adaptation might be worked out prior to a change in the material situation and the adaptation might be applied practically at the same time as the change in the material conditions. But such a situation presumes a very high degree of planning, prediction and control. The collection of data, it is thought, will show that at the present time there are a very large number of cases where the material conditions change and the changes in the adaptive culture follow later. There are certain general theoretical reasons why this is so; but it is not desirable to discuss these until later. For the present, the analysis will only concern those cases where changes in the adaptive culture do not precede changes in the material culture. Furthermore, it is not implied that changes may not occur in non-material culture while the material culture remains the same. Art or education, for instance, may undergo many changes with a constant material culture.

Still another point in the analysis is that the old, unchanged, adaptive culture is not adjusted to the new, changed, material conditions. It may be true that the old adaptive culture is never wholly unadjusted to the new conditions. There may be some degree of adjustment. But the thesis is that the unchanged adaptive culture was more harmoniously related to the old than to the new material conditions and that a new adaptive culture will be better suited to the new material conditions than was the old adaptive culture. Adjustment is therefore a relative term, and perhaps only in a few cases would there be a situation which might be called perfect adjustment or perfect lack of adjustment.

It is desirable, however, not to make the analysis too general until there has been a more careful consideration of particular instances. We now propose, therefore, to test the hypothesis by the facts in a definite case of social change. In attempting to verify the hypothesis in a particular case by measurement, the following series of steps will be followed. The old material conditions will be described, that part of the adaptive culture under consideration will be described, and the degree of adjustment between these two parts of culture shown. Then the changed material conditions and the changed adaptive culture will be defined and the degree of adaptation shown. It is necessary also to show that the unchanged adaptive culture is not as harmoniously adjusted to the new conditions as to the old and not as harmoniously adjusted to the new conditions as is a changed adaptive culture. Having made such a series of descriptions, the next step will be to measure the lag, which should be done by locating the point of change in the material culture and the point of change in the particular adaptive culture.

2

VERIFICATION BY THE FACTS OF WORKMEN'S COMPENSATION FOR ACCIDENTS

Sufficient data are available to test this hypothesis by a study of workmen's compensation as a means of dealing with industrial accidents. In studying the possible delay in developing workmen's compensation in the United States, the various steps outlined in the preceding paragraph will be followed but, for purposes of presentation, not in the exact order there listed.

There are to-day a great many accidents occurring in industry. Hoffman estimated that in 1913 there were in the United States around 25,000 fatal industrial accidents and 700,000 industrial accidents causing disabilities lasting four weeks or longer.[1] A recent estimate by Hookstadt of United States Bureau of Labor Statistics places the fatal industrial accidents at 28,000 in 1917 and the disabilities, partial and total, lasting four weeks and longer, around 875,000. He estimates that for this same year there were 3,000,000 temporary total disabilities lasting less than four weeks. The year 1917 was a year of unusual industrial activity, however. These accidents are so numerous now, not solely because our population has grown large, but because so many workmen to-day work with or near machines which are dangerous to life and limb. The accidents fall with severity upon the workmen and their families, for the annual earnings of workmen are low in comparison with the cost of an adequate standard of living and there is little saved for a crippled life or for a period of temporary disability. Furthermore, since these injuries are due in large part to the nature of modern industry, it is not just to make the workmen bear all the financial burden. It seems fair that industry itself should bear a part of it. If industry doesn't bear the burden, much of the cost eventually falls upon the State in the form of support to the aged, cripples, widows and young children.

[1] Frederick G. Hoffman, "Industrial Accident Statistics," *Bulletin, No. 157, U. S. Department of Labor*, p. 6.

So the States of the United States have passed workmen's compensation laws which provide for payment to injured workmen according to the nature of the injury. These compensation laws make a fair adaptation to the industrial accident situation for the reasons just cited, particularly as the financial cost of these injuries falls in part upon industry rather than upon the workmen. It is therefore a better adjustment than when the cost is borne by the workman. It is also a better adjustment than is provided for by the most advanced employers' liability laws, for various reasons. Under these laws the workman to recover must sue the employer unless, as in some cases, settlement is made outside the courts. Resort to courts means always delay and frequently very long delays. The Illinois Employers' Liability Commission found in a survey that only fifty-three per cent of the injured receiving compensation were paid inside of two years. The Ohio Employers' Liability Commission found an average delay of one year and one-half month.[2] The costs of the judicial and legal machinery are high and of amounts awarded in the verdicts rendered, a large part, from ten to fifty per cent, goes to defray legal expenses. Under workmen's com-

---

[2] Carl Hookstadt, "Comparison of Experiences under Workmen's Compensation and Employers' Liability Systems," *Monthly Labor Review,* Vol. VIII, March, 1919, No. 3, pp. 846–864.

pensation acts the remuneration is almost automatic. Workmen's compensation reaches the unskilled workers better than the employers' liability laws, as the unskilled worker was less apt to use the courts than the skilled worker. Workmen's compensation funds provide, also, of course for a much larger number of workmen than the very few who were helped by fraternal or benevolent insurance societies.

Another piece of evidence of the suitability of workmen's compensation laws is the fact that they tend to reduce the number of accidents. Presumably, this is so for if the costs of accidents are made part of the immediate costs of production such costs tend to reduce profits. Accidents being expensive, the management of industry tries to reduce this source of expense. Certainly it is a fact that the "safety-first" movement in the United States started almost from the beginning of the workmen's compensation period. Accident prevention campaigns have been almost contemporaneous with the period of enforcement of workmen's compensation. It is not true that workmen's compensation laws are the sole causes of accident prevention. The loss of good workmen to industry through accidents, for instance, without any enforced compensation to the injured, nevertheless makes it good business policy to limit the number of accidents. Although accident prevention work has been well under way in many industries for the past ten years, the record of accidents is not sufficiently complete for the whole country to say positively that there is a diminishing frequency of accidents. But certain special investigations indicate that this is a fact. For instance in a report published by the United States Bureau of Labor Statistics [3] it is shown that for a group of iron and steel plants, about 25 per cent of the industry, both the frequency and severity accident rates fell from 1907 to 1917 and have fallen continuously since 1912. The frequency rate fell from 1912 about 50 per cent and the severity rate about 25 per cent.

The present workmen's compensation laws in the United States are not of course a case of perfect adaption. These laws are not perfect. Many of them are optional to employers, and many of them do not provide State funds. The compensations for the various injuries are too low. There are many more details that could be improved, as, for instance, the medical service and the waiting period. A better classification of hazardous occupations could be made.

Not all employees are reached by the laws as

---

[3] Chaney and Hanna, "The Safety Movement in the Iron and Steel Industry, 1907 to 1917," *Bulletin, No. 234,* June, 1918, p. 16.

now drawn, in most cases perhaps not over 75 per cent.[4] The list of industries in some cases might well be extended. Indeed, adequate compensation laws should probably cover all industries and all employees, and it is probably desirable to eliminate the so-called hazardous industries from the terminology. Furthermore it is possible that even some better method than the present compensation laws may yet be found.

Workmen's compensation laws are of course not the sole method of adjustment to the accident problem of modern industry; nor are employers' liability laws. Factory inspection, machinery safeguards, rest periods, rates of speed of production, and perhaps prohibition of the sale of intoxicating beverages, are all adaptations to the accident situation. But in so far as workmen's compensation laws alone are considered as the adaptive culture, it is true that they are not a perfect adaptation but are better than the adaptive measures that immediately preceded them.

We have now described the new material conditions of industry making the accident situation and have described the method of adjustment to the situation as shown in workmen's compensation laws. The degree of satisfactory adaptation

---

[4] Carl Hookstadt, "Comparison of Experiences under Workmen's Compensation and Employers' Liability Systems," *Monthly Labor Review*, Vol. VIII, No. 3, pp. 846–864.

between the material culture and the adaptive culture has been shown.

In earlier times before the rise of modern industry with complex machines driven by artificial power, the economic activities were largely agricultural. Such manufacturing as was done was done by hand. During this period of handicraft production only a very small per cent of the population lived in towns and cities. In these times the accidents of industry were few. The tools of industry were simple and not particularly hazardous, either on the farms or in the towns. The relationship between master and servant was a personal one, the contact being quite close.

Since under such material conditions the accidents were few, individual liability seems not a bad adjustment to such accidents as did occur. The law regarding accidents was the law of negligence and was a branch of the common law. In a case arising under the law of negligence, attempt was made to find the individual who was at fault in the neglect of duty in causing the accident, and damages were assessed upon the guilty party. For instance, if a vicious bull was loose and gored a man, damages in such a case might be recovered under the law of negligence.

The adjustment to accidents in these early times was shown by the development of the common law of negligence. Suits for damages for injuries sustained because of the employer's negligence had occurred for many hundreds of years. But with the development of industry in the nineteenth century, certain defenses, particularly that of "common employment" and of "contributory negligence" were developed, which employers sought for protection against suits for damages. The first cases developing these defenses were, in the United States, in 1841, *Murry v. South Carolina Railroad Co.*, and in England *Priestly v. Fowler*, in 1837.[5]

One of these defenses is called the "assumption of risk" and under this doctrine the master is not liable to his servant for injuries occurring in the ordinary risks of the employment as the servant assumes these risks on entering his employ. Another defense is called "contributory negligence," and under this doctrine the master is not liable if the servant has by his own negligence contributed in any way to the occurrence of the injury. And finally the third defense is known as that of "common employment" or "the fellow-servant rule." Under this principle the employer was not liable if he could show that the accident was the result of negligence on the part of any fellow-servant of the injured em-

[5] Lindley D. Clark, "The Legal Liability of Employers for Injuries to their Employees in the United States," *Bulletin, No. 74, U. S. Bureau of Labor Statistics.*

ployee. Therefore if the employer could show to the court that the employee assumed the risk on entering his employ, or that the accident occurred because of his own negligence or that of any fellow-servant, he would not be liable for the accident. This legal protection to the employer was thus very formidable.

The common law therefore proved inadequate to meet the situation caused by the accidents arising from the development of industry. There was truly a maladjustment because of the increasing accidents and the inadequacy of the law. But as more accidents occurred, the common law was later modified to a considerable extent by statutory enactments and by judicial interpretation, as will be pointed out in following paragraphs. The particular purpose here is to show that in earlier times before the increase of accidents due to the complexity of machine industry, there was no serious lack of adjustment between the accident situation and the common law. The adaptive culture was fairly well suited to the material conditions. This is seen from the descriptions just given of the common law and the earlier economic conditions, when the tools were simple and the accidents were few.

It is now necessary to measure the period of maladjustment between the adaptive culture and the material conditions, that period which may be temporarily described as the time when the industrial accidents were numerous and there were no workmen's compensation laws. It will also be necessary to show that the adjustment during this period was less satisfactory than in the preceding period and in the period which followed. It is not very difficult to locate the upper limit of this period. Prior to 1910 there were no State workmen's compensation laws in force in the United States. The national government had passed a law applying to its own employees, however, in 1908. Certain State benefit and compensation laws quite limited in scope and application had been passed earlier: Maryland in 1902, United States Philippine Commission in 1905 and Montana in 1909. The Maryland and the Montana laws were declared unconstitutional, however, as was also the general workmen's compensation act of New York of 1910. By the beginning of 1912, however, five State workmen's compensation acts were in force; by 1913 there were 13 States with acts in force; by 1914, 18 States; by 1915, 22 States; by 1916, 29 States; by 1917, 32 States; by 1918, 35 States; by 1919, 37 States; by 1920, 40 States; and by 1921 two more States had put into force workmen's compensation acts.[6]

[6] Carl Hookstadt, "Comparison of Workmen's Compensation Laws of the United States and Canada up to January 1, 1920," *Bulletin, No. 275, U. S. Bureau of Labor Statistics.*

Only six of the 48 States in January 1922 have no workmen's compensation acts in force, viz., Arkansas, Florida, Mississippi, Missouri,[7] North Carolina and South Carolina, States not very largely industrial. Thus in less than a decade compensation laws had spread through nearly all of the States of the Union. Indeed, by the close of 1915, within five years after the first State law was put in force, all of the highly industrialized States except Pennsylvania and Delaware had these laws. It can be said, therefore, that within two or three years of 1915 this particular adaptive culture changed to fit the changed material conditions. Thus point b of the illustrative figure is located with some precision.

To locate point a of the figure, the time at which the material conditions changed, is somewhat more difficult for the reason that the change in the material culture was more gradual than the change in the adaptive culture. At what time can it be said that industrial accidents became sufficiently numerous that workmen's compensation laws should have been adopted? Unfortunately there are no statistics of the number of early industrial accidents. Since industrial accidents are to a certain extent correlated with the

[7] Missouri adopted a law in 1919 but it was repealed by referendum vote. A new law has been passed in 1921 but it had not been put into force during 1921.

growth of modern industry, some sort of estimate as to time can be made by observing the statistics of the growth of industry. Good criteria of the growth of industry are the production of iron and coal, the miles of railroads in operation and the percentage of the population that is urban. Such records are seen in the following table.

Years	Population (ooo's omitted)[8]	Percentage of the population living in urban places of 8,000 persons and over [9]	Miles of railroads in operation [8]	Pig iron produced, in long tons (ooo's omitted)[8]	Coal produced, in long tons (ooo's omitted)[8]
1790		3.3			
1800	5,308	4.0			
1810	7,240	4.9		54	
1820	9,638	4.9		20	3
1830	12,866	6.7	23	165	286
1840	17,069	8.5	2,818	287	1,848
1850	23,192	12.5	9,021	564	6,266
1860	31,443	16.1	30,626	821	13,045
1870	38,558	20.9	52,922	1,665	29,496
1880	50,156	22.8	93,267	3,835	63,823
1890	62,948	29.1	167,191	9,203	140,867
1900	75,995	33.1	198,964	13,789	240,789
1910	92,175	38.8	249,992	27,304	447,854

From this table the development of industry is seen to be gradual; there is no sharp break in the curve of industrial progress. However, in the two decades from 1850 to 1870, there was a very

[8] *Statistical Abstract of the United States, 1920*, pp. 764, 801, 802, 811.
[9] Reports of the Bureau of Census, Department of Commerce.

appreciable beginning of industrial development. In 1870, one-fifth of the population lived in cities and towns over 8,000 in population. A million and a half tons of pig iron and about 30 million tons of coal were produced.

Another index of the development of industry and one that bears a closer relation to the estimation of the number of accidents, is the number employed in gainful industrial occupations. The census classification of occupations is for the following groups: agriculture, manufacturing and mechanical pursuits (including mining), transportation and trade, professional service, domestic and personal service, and clerical occupations. Of these classes, those engaged in manufacturing and mechanical pursuits, transportation and trade, roughly correspond to those workers to whom workmen's compensation funds are potentially applicable. Perhaps some of those engaged in trade are not peculiarly liable to accidents and are not covered by compensation acts, but such a number probably roughly balances with others omitted when only these classes are counted. There are census figures showing the number engaged in these classes of industrial occupations as far back as 1870. Thus in 1910 the number of males 10 years old and over, engaged in manufacturing and mechanical pursuits and in transportation and trade, was 15½ million; in 1900,

10 million; in 1890, 7¾ million; in 1880 about 5 million; and in 1870, 3½ million. In 1860 and in 1850 there were no doubt smaller numbers. The census classifications prior to 1870 are not comparable with those in later decades. The records, however, show that in 1860 there were 1⅓ million employees in manufacturing industries and in 1850 very nearly a million. The figures since 1860 quoted above are for males only, as estimates for accidents can be made somewhat better for males than for females; and since the number of accidents among females in industrial pursuits is relatively small, perhaps no great error is involved in using only the figures for males.

There were in 1870, then, 3½ million males engaged in these industrial occupations in the United States. If the accident rate per thousand engaged in these industrial pursuits was known, this rate could be applied to the 3½ million so employed and some sort of estimate of the number of accidents could be made. It is possible to find such an accident rate for the present time, but it is not known that there was the same accident rate in 1870 that there is now. Still such an approximation would give information better than none at all. Hoffman estimated a rate of fatal accidents in 1913 for all industrially occupied males of 0.73 per thousand occupied.[10] But in getting this rate, those employed in agriculture, the army, the navy, and a group of "all other occupied males" were included. If these groups are excluded from the calculations and a new rate is computed it will correspond somewhat more closely to the workers who would be affected by workmen's compensation and to those males engaged in manufacturing and mechanical pursuits and in trade and transportation. A new rate calculated after such exclusions are made is found to be approximately 1.0 per thousand employed. If this same rate of fatal accidents held in 1870, there were 3500 fatal accidents in that year. Hookstadt's figures for 1917 show that disabilities lasting four weeks or longer are 30 times as numerous as the fatal accidents and the disabilities lasting less than four weeks are 100 times as numerous as the fatal accidents. These relative proportions approximate closely those found in standard accident tables.

If these ratios held in 1870, then there were about 100,000 accidents causing disabilities lasting four weeks or longer, 350,000 accidents causing disabilities lasting less than four weeks. It would seem therefore that the year 1870

[10] Frederick G. Hoffman, "Industrial Accident Statistics," *Bulletin, No. 157, U. S. Bureau of Labor Statistics.*

was hardly too soon to have developed workmen's compensation acts, even if the accident rates were a good deal lower than the estimates for 1913. Even if they were half as low, there were in 1870 a fairly large number of accidents. Had workmen's compensation acts been in force in the United States from 1870 on, a very great many accidents would have been cared for with much less burden to the worker. If the accident rates for the intervening years between 1870 and 1910 were the same as those quoted above, then during this forty-year period there were 300,000 fatal accidents among males engaged in industrial occupations, 9,000,000 disabilities lasting four weeks or longer and 30,000,000 disabilities lasting less than four weeks. The total number of industrial accidents over this period must have been very large, even if the accident rate in the earlier years was lower than present-day rates. The earlier accident rates may indeed have been higher.

Of the vast number of accidents, some few recovered damages through the courts no doubt. A very few may have carried insurance. Relatives living in rural districts may have helped some to bear this burden; and for a very large number probably the varied economic opportunities of an expanding country helped to lighten the burden. If workmen's compensation acts had been in force from 1870 on, many accidents that did occur would never have occurred, for accident prevention campaigns would probably have started earlier. From a table published by the Prudential Insurance Company, the fatal accidents per million of population in the years 1906-1910 were greater for the United States than for any other of twenty-three countries for which there were data, and was very nearly twice the number recorded in Germany and in England and Wales. The United States was the last of the larger western nations to adopt workmen's compensation laws. In the '80's acts were enacted in Germany and in Austria; in the '90's in Norway, Finland, Great Britain, Denmark, Italy, and France; and from 1900 to 1910 in New Zealand, South Australia, Netherlands, Greece, Sweden, Western Australia, Luxemburg, British Columbia, Russia, Belgium, Cape of Good Hope, Queensland, Hungary, Transvaal, Newfoundland, Alberta, Bulgaria and Quebec; and since 1910 compensation acts have been enacted in a number of other countries.[11] The fact that the United States was one of the very last nations to enact compensation laws certainly does not alone explain why her accident rate is so markedly un-

---

[11] Lindley D. Clark, "Workmen's Compensation Laws of the United States and Foreign Countries," *U. S. Bureau of Labor Statistics Bulletins, Nos. 203 and 243,* p. 298, and p. 96, respectively.

favorable in comparison with other countries; but it is very probably an important factor. It seems probable that if compensation laws had been enacted here, say, in 1870, or earlier, probably a large number of accidents that did occur would never have occurred.

The year 1870 is the earliest date for which the census gives occupation statistics that are comparable with occupation figures for late years. It is possible indeed that earlier than 1870 industrial accidents may have been sufficiently numerous to warrant compensation laws. But prior to 1870, industry was not very far developed as seen from the statistics in the previous table. The fact that the first suit in which the employer sought protection under the defense of "common employment" occurred in 1841, suggests that prior to 1840 there was not much pressure for compensation. In 1840 there were not 3000 miles of railroads in operation and not 2 million tons of coal were produced. Industry when young is said to need protection but financially there is little reason to think that the industry or the public could not have borne the burden imposed by compensating for accidents from the very beginning in this country; certainly industry could have borne the burden as well as the workmen. It would appear, therefore, that the material conditions changed so that workmen's compensation systems were needed at least between the years 1850 and 1870. The material conditions changed therefore in the period 1850–70, while the adaptive culture did not change for a satisfactory adjustment until about 1915.

Since during this interval from the period 1850–70, until 1915, there were changes in the adaptive culture as well as in the material culture, it remains to show that, during this period, there was maladjustment, namely, a less satisfactory adjustment than in the years which preceded and in the years which followed. This has already been partly done in describing the degree of adaptation during the earlier and late periods. When industrial accidents began to occur with some frequency, the injured person at times entered suit against the employer under the common law of negligence. But the employer became extraordinarily well protected because of the development of the defenses of "assumption of risk," "contributory negligence," and the "fellow-servant rule." It was realized that under these doctrines it was very difficult for the injured employee to get justice. So these defenses were modified or abrogated by statutory enactments and by judicial interpretation. Now, if these old defenses had been completely abrogated, it might be argued that a fairly satisfactory adjustment would have been made to the accident situation, without workmen's compensation laws, and solely through improved or changed employers' liability laws. It is therefore of importance in the analysis to ascertain to what extent these old employers' liability laws were modified by statutory enactments.

The first statutory modification of the common law of employers' liability was made in Alabama in 1885,[12] following closely the British model of 1880. This act was not an abrogation of these old defenses of the employers, but was only a modification of the defense, the fellow-servant rule, and enabled the representatives of the deceased employee to recover damages for death caused by negligence. Although this British act made only a partial change for the better in the common law, acts following this model have been adopted in only seven States of the United States. These enactments were made at the following dates, 1885, 1887, 1893, 1893, 1902, 1902 and 1907. Twenty States have either abrogated or modified the fellow-servant rule for railroads; in a majority of these States it has been abrogated. Nearly all of these acts applying to railroads were passed after 1900. Three States have special laws for mines. A

[12] Lindley D. Clark, "The Legal Liability of Employers for Injuries to their Employees in the United States," *Bulletin, No. 74, U. S. Bureau of Labor Statistics.*

few States, notably Oregon and Ohio, have made extensive and significant changes by statutes in the common law of employers' liability. However, seven States have made no change whatsoever. It is thus seen that the common law which was hanging over into a period of changed material culture, to which it was not fitted, was undergoing change by the State legislatures. But in only a few States were sweeping changes made in the common law that applied to industry in general. The significant changes in the common law came in for the most part around the beginning and early part of the twentieth century.

As to the extent that the common law defenses were modified by judicial interpretation, it is difficult to determine quantitatively. But there are some ways of estimating the effectiveness of the modification of the changes in the common law of employers' liability both by statute and judicial interpretation. Figures which show the proportions of the total number injured who received compensation under modified employers' liability laws would be such an indication. Samples of statistics taken in New York and in Pennsylvania show that of married men killed in industry the families from one-quarter to one-third received no compensation at all.[13] Similar proportions

---

[13] Crystal Eastman, *Work Accidents and the Law*, pp. 121 and 271.

are quoted for Wisconsin by the Wisconsin Bureau of Labor and Industrial Statistics.[14] In a study made of accidents by the Labor Department of New York, out of 902 accidents investigated, 44 per cent received no compensation at all, not even medical expenses.[15] More comprehensive statistics are found in the records of the insurance companies, doing employers' liability insurance. In New York, such companies reported a payment to one case out of every eight reporting injuries, during the first decade of the twentieth century after New York had passed an employers' liability law. These statistics, which were collected just prior to the passage of workmen's compensation acts, are not truly representative, because many accidents were no doubt never recorded and for this the injured were probably not compensated. It is questionable whether at that time, in States other than Pennsylvania, New York, and Wisconsin as large a proportion of injured received settlement.

The awards under the employers' liability laws were often very inadequate. In a study of 902 cases of temporary disability in New York, 397 injured employees received no compensation whatever, and 304 cases recovered from the employers less than 50 per cent of the money loss

[14] Vol. XIII, p. 54.
[15] Crystal Eastman, *Work Accidents and the Law,* p. 274.

of wages and expenses.[16] Miss Eastman in her study of employers' liability in New York concludes that only a small proportion of injured workmen get substantial damages under the employers' liability law. The foregoing figures indicate that in those States where the common law of employers' liability was considerably modified, the accident situation was far from being satisfactorily met by employers' liability law both in the amount recovered and in the number of injuries reached. Material assembled by Hookstadt proves quite definitely this conclusion.[17] Such results might have been surmised from the fact that the States swung so rapidly from employers' liability to workmen's compensation laws. But even if a very large number of injured employees had been reached by the operation of employers' liability laws and even if the awards had been large, this system would have been less satisfactory than that of workmen's compensation, because of the delays of the court and legal expense, and of the antagonisms occasioned.

It is therefore quite clear that between the time when the number of industrial accidents became significantly large due to the growth of ma-

---

[16] Crystal Eastman, *Work Accidents and the Law*, p. 274.
[17] Carl Hookstadt, "Comparison of Experience under Workmen's Compensation and Employers' Liability Systems *Monthly Labor Review*, Vol. VIII, No. 3, pp. 846—864.

chine industry and the time of the adoption of workmen's compensation, there was a very unsatisfactory adjustment to the accident situation. During the period of maladjustment, the old adaptive culture, the common law of employers' liability, hung over after the material conditions had changed. But this common law was not wholly unchanging. It was being modified some as time went on, but never sufficiently to meet the new conditions even approximately. In conclusion, therefore, of the investigation of this particular test of our hypothesis, the delay in the adoption of workmen's compensation or the lag in common law of employers' liability after the material culture had changed was about a half-century, from 1850–70 to 1915. The investigation might have included other arguments and more data. Such additional data would have made the treatment too long for general consideration, and without such additional investigation, it is thought that the hypothesis is sufficiently substantiated. The lag might have been measured somewhat more precisely for a single State than for the United States as a whole.

3

ILLUSTRATIONS: TAXATION, FAMILY, INTERNATIONAL RELATIONS, TRADE UNIONS, REPRESENTATIVE GOVERNMENT, PUEBLO DWELLERS

An attempt to prove the hypothesis with data from other cases of supposed maladjustment would involve in each case a somewhat lengthy presentation which would interest only the reader who is especially concerned with the particular maladjustment. A number of cases of what seem to be lags in the adaptive culture, however, may be listed quickly, without an attempt at proof. In all these cases, however, it is thought that a lag could be measured and a maladjustment proven if the necessary research were undertaken.

The general property tax. One such case of lag, is the general property tax in the United States. Since the formation of the various States of the union, State revenues have been raised largely by assessing the amount of general property and levying a tax on the assessed value of the general property, at a rate established at such a point as will yield the necessary revenue to meet estimated State expenditures for the ensuing year. Although such a system of taxation has been praised highly in the past, it is now quite generally admitted by taxation authorities to be unsatisfactory, for several reasons. Perhaps the most important reason is the fact that personal property now tends to escape taxation under the general property tax. According to the theory of the general property tax, it is a just tax because all property is taxed. But in practice only realty, i. e., land and the fixtures thereto, is reached. Personal property, particularly the intangible personalty, such as stocks, bonds and the various other securities largely escape taxation. This is definitely shown by Seligman in his *Essays on Taxation,* from which the following facts and quotations are taken.

The proportion paid [in New York State] by personal property has decreased steadily almost every year until according to the last figures [1911] it pays but five per cent of the State taxation, as against ninety-five falling on real estate. In forty years the valuation of real estate has increased eight billions while that of personalty has increased only thirty millions. . . . In California, personal property was assessed in 1872 at 220 millions of dollars, in 1880 at 174 millions and in 1887 at 164 millions—a net decrease in fifteen years of 56 millions. Real estate increased during the same period from 417 to 791 millions. Personal property paid 17.31 per cent, real estate 82.69 per cent of the taxes. . . . In Cincinnati the valuation in 1866 was: realty, $66,454,602; personalty, $67,218,101. In 1892 the realty had increased to $144,208,810; the personalty had decreased to $44,735,670. . . . These figures become ridiculous when it is remembered that in our modern civilization the value of personal property far exceeds that of real estate, as understood by the taxing power.

Under the general property tax, personal property thus tends to escape taxation. This condition was, however, not always so. Under early agricultural conditions, when the amount of personal property was small and easily visible to the tax assessor, personalty was taxed in fair proportion to realty. But with the growth of industry, corporations and modern finance, it has not been possible to reach all personalty for taxation. Personalty has also grown in the western States which are still agricultural and the "auditor of Washington tells us that, if a true valuation could be reached, it is 'clear and incontestable that the wealth of the territory in personal property, for the purposes of taxation would largely predominate over that of real estate.'" Yet practically none of our States has discarded the general property tax, although a few have remedied the situation somewhat by a more or less satisfactory development of special corporation taxes, inheritance taxes and income taxes. Seligman, writing in 1919, says:

> It [the general property tax] is the cause of such crying injustice that its alteration or its abolition must become the battle-cry of every statesman and reformer.

The analysis of the general property tax seems to show that when the material culture was in its economic aspects simple agriculture, this tax was suitable to those conditions; but with the changing of the material culture from simple agriculture to modern industry, the general property tax was a maladjustment for the reason that personal property escaped taxation. It is necessary, therefore, to abandon the general property tax or to alter it in order to reach property that escapes taxation under the general property tax. This can be done through the separation of State and local revenues, by the development of corporation taxes, inheritance taxes, income taxes, and various special taxes. But as yet only a very few States have done this. The lag in this adaptive culture has certainly been a number of years.

The family. Another case that seems to show a good many lags in the adaptive culture is the delay in adjustment of the family to modern machine industry. Under earlier agricultural conditions, the family, it is generally admitted, had worked out a fairly satisfactory adjustment to these conditions. The family was an economic institution as well as an affectional and biological one. In fact, under agricultural conditions, it was a most significant unit in society possessing in addition to biological and economic functions, many other functions such as recreational, educational, protective and religious. Woman's economic function was most important, and a woman of ability was of great economic value to the farm. Marriage was, in part, the taking of a business partner, and early marriage was of economic advantage because it was entering business early. The wife's duties, spinning, weaving, sewing, preparing foods, the manufacture of different articles, and various other tasks around the farm, were quite comparable, in economic return, with the husband's work. The education that was necessary for life and business success was acquired in large part in the home, with the exception of such elementary book education as the three r's. It was an excellent institution for supervising the activities of children because the child's future life as an adult was to be spent on the farm. Divorce was a particularly serious event because it meant a rupture to so many economic and social activities. The agricultural family was also in a fortunate position to render protection to the dependent kin. The functioning of the family under these conditions indicates an excellent adjustment between the family as a social organization and the material culture, though no doubt there were tyrannies, repressions of instincts and resistances to new ideas.

The immediate effect of the growth of large-scale production meant taking from the home an increasing number of economic functions and placing them in factories. This was particularly true of the work which was formerly woman's share. The services performed by the family living in a modern city apartment illustrate what a great change has taken place in the functions of the family. Such profound changes in the economic functions of the family and the creation of new forms of economic activity meant that new adjustments would have to be made by the family, since it was hardly possible to stop or change significantly the march of material progress.

The educational function, for instance, can not now be performed as satisfactorily by the family as was once possible. The diversification and the specialized technique of industry and the transfer of occupations from the home to the factory have meant the necessity of special vocational and trade education outside the home. Manual training which was formerly quite readily learned at home must now be taught in city schools. The technical efficiency demanded by modern industrial life has necessitated changes in the curricula of the schools. These are all special adjustments of education to the changed material conditions. The juvenile court has arisen as an adjustment agency to the changed material conditions through the failure of the family to make the proper adaptation. With the industrial revolution came the great growth of cities, little adapted to child life. The congestion of cities was accompanied almost nowhere with adequate development of play space for children. Coupled with these conditions was the breaking up of homes and the drawing of mothers into industry.

The factory immediately brought children to work within its walls, with unsatisfactory results, and a better adjustment was made through child labor laws and compulsory school laws, with inspectors and attendance officers. Such special laws were unnecessary under the old material conditions. Special forms of State insurance and various types of pensions seem a desirable form of adjustment to the new conditions which face the family. The agricultural family with a relatively more stable abode was very well suited for caring for widows, the aged, and dependent kin. There were rooms and food, and light tasks to be done. But with the scattered and more migratory family living in congested centres, such care of dependents can be effected in fewer families and with more difficulty. Women have not become satisfactorily adjusted to these new material conditions of the factory system. Their work as producers has largely been taken away, so that many are idle, or do work which is only slightly productive of substantial economic values; or else they go into industry under such chance conditions as they may find. The introduction of women into industry may call for special adaptations in regard to such matters as sanitary conditions, hours of labor, and maternity insurance. A somewhat wider life for woman outside the home seems desirable, since so many of the home occupations are now found outside the family. The extension of the franchise to women is only a minor step in that direction. Finally, the reduction of the economic function of the family together with other functions has rendered the marriage union of man and woman less stable.

It is thus seen that the change from agriculture to the modern factory system has necessitated changes in the family organization. There is abundant evidence to show that the old agricultural family organization is no longer adapted to industrial life as seen in modern cities. Many functions which were performed reasonably satisfactorily by the family in farm life have been or are being taken over by the State, by industry, by special organizations. Special organizations have been developed to perform functions affecting women, children, education, dependency, recreation, etc. In these cases, it is no doubt difficult to measure the delay in each case in developing the new forms for performing these functions. But it seems quite clear that there has been a delay. Few would maintain that child labor laws, compulsory education, vocational and industrial education, playgrounds, and social insurance, for instance, have been developed as promptly as they should. The material culture has gone forward, while the adaptive culture has lagged behind.

International relations. Many writers have argued that changes in international relations have not kept pace with the industrial changes affecting the United States. The theory, which, however, is not wholly accepted, runs somewhat as follows. In early times the United States was more or less physically isolated from many of the other nations, particularly the nations of Europe. Problems of international relationships were not in general pressing with the United States, except on certain critical issues. The policy of no entangling alliances, though a somewhat brief and inaccurate descriptive phrase, indicated a fairly satisfactory form of relationship, it would seem.

A high organizational development of activity and efficiency was not particularly urgent in the State Department of our government, nor especially in the consular and diplomatic service. In time material changes occurred which have, in part, destroyed this isolation. With the steam engine, boats now cross the Atlantic Ocean in a few days, whereas formerly the period of crossing was measured in weeks. Cables have been laid and the wireless telegraph developed. Newspapers carry immediately records of events in other countries. Most important is the growth of foreign trade as measured by the volume of imports and exports. Foreign investments are growing, as is also foreign travel. The natural resources of the world are being appropriated in one way or another. Because of these material changes other nations are brought closer as neighbors and their activities are of increasing concern to the United States. The changed material conditions are apparent, while, it is claimed, our international policies and organizations of foreign relations have not been developed sufficiently to meet these changed conditions satisfactorily. This is a debatable point; but there is some evidence to indicate that the efficiency of the diplomatic and consular service and of the State Department has not in the past been adequate to meet properly the problems arising from the changed material conditions. Until the recent great war the mass of the population of the United States was ignorant of and indifferent to foreign relations. And even after the war there is a strong feeling that we should concern ourselves less with foreign relations. Aside from the merits of a particular League of Nations, there is much indifference to such a project even though it has been introduced under exceptionally dramatic conditions. There is certainly some evidence that the older mores hang over into the new conditions, and that a proper adaptive culture has not been developed.

Trade unions. The theory of industrial unions for wage-earners is another illustration. Employees in modern industry have found it to their advantage, it is usually admitted, to organize into labor unions. Hitherto these organizations have been, with few exceptions, along trade or craft lines. The organization of workers in a trade has meant greater bargaining strength than the individual laborer has, and the workers have used such collective bargaining power to their advantage in matters of hours of labor, wages and working conditions. There are of course some who are opposed to any labor organizations in the interests of industry or of society. But granting the general point of view in favor of labor organization, it seems questionable whether organization along craft lines is the type of organization which gives the desired strength to compete with the recently developed powerful organizations on the side of capital. Very large corporations and trusts began to grow up in the last quarter of the nineteenth century. The influence of financial organizations became quite powerful. This consolidation developed through various interlocking devices between the different corporations and other industrial and financial organizations. The strength of capital became very great through these powerful organizations which have grown greatly during the past quarter- or half-century. The strength of craft unions seems less, relative to the power of capital, now than at the time when capital was less highly organized. It would seem that the strength of labor would be greater and more able to cope with these large industrial organizations if labor were organized along industrial lines rather than trade lines. From this labor point of view, therefore, the trade unions are not as satisfactorily adapted to the large industrial combinations as would be industrial unions. It is true that the affiliations of unions in city, State and national organizations have remedied somewhat such deficiencies. But it seems probable that labor unions would have become more powerful if the organization had developed a number of years ago directly along industrial lines. In this illustration the adaptive culture considered is the organizations of labor, and the culture to which adjustment is being made is, in part, the development of industry.

Representative legislative government. It is also argued that the present forms of representative legislative assemblies are not as satisfactorily adjusted to modern social conditions as they were in earlier times. Representation in the United States is now on the basis of localities. The principle of locality-representation was highly important before the development of rapid transportation. Localities that are relatively isolated have local differences and interests peculiar to the local group. Hence the interests of a people living in various localities relatively isolated need to be presented by representatives chosen on the basis of locality. The railroad, the postal service, telephone, telegraph, newspapers, travel, trade and the spread of business development have all tended to reduce the barriers that accentuated locality interests. Mere physical distance, of course, still is a barrier. The wards of a city have not so many distinct local interests as for instance do the various States of so large an area as the United States. Localities within States are midway between these two extremes. Locality-representation in so large a country as the United States was even more important in early times than other forms of representation because wealth was fairly equally distributed and there was a good deal of homogeneity in occupations. In modern society the interests of the people are differentiated on the basis of economic classes and of occupations as well as on the basis of locality. There are of course many of these classes. And it would seem that a sampling for purposes of representation should take into consideration such a differentiation of interests. Theoretically it is possible for random sampling by locality to yield representation of classes; but practically the representation of special interests is not proportional in the United States. Proportional representation is a device to meet this situation. It is difficult to say whether it is a satisfactory device as it has not been adequately tested in modern legislative assemblies. Other changes in the nature of representation have also been suggested.

It is true that in the United States at the present time legislative bodies are not the most highly admired of the governmental organs, particularly in our States and cities. This is certainly not due wholly to the principle of locality-representation. One reason, for instance, for the rise of the executive in comparison to the legislature and of his power over legislation is probably the fact that, upon the executive attention is more readily focused and responsibility more easily fixed than on a large group of representatives, in this age when there are so many demands on a voter's time. Furthermore, the newspaper has to a certain extent usurped some of the functions of legislative representatives. The executive can frequently determine the various opinions from newspapers as well as from elected representatives. Important government policies are announced at times in notices to the press or in speeches delivered elsewhere than in legislative halls. There are, of course, many other criticisms of our legislatures. The functioning of modern legislatures has been frequently criticised by students of political science, and the causes traced to various special factors. Although there may be particular causes, a fundamental trouble may be due to the great changes that have occurred in the material conditions of life. It is argued that representation by localities was adjusted in a fairly satisfactory manner to the pioneer conditions of the first part of the last century; but since that time our material culture has greatly changed while the nature of our representation and the organization of the assemblies have remained substantially the same. Just what changes in the representative assemblies should be made, we do not know. The material culture has changed, and there is evidence that the adaptive culture is not adjusted satisfactorily. Political scientists do not appear to be certain just what changes in the adaptive culture should be made. The conditions of modern legislation do suggest the need of change, however, and further research might substantiate the hypothesis, mentioned here all too briefly.

Pueblo dwellers. Another possible illustration from a different culture may be observed among the Hopi Indians of Arizona. These Indians are pueblo dwellers and live on the tip end of three long mesas—flat table-lands that run down into the desert from the north like three great fingers. The inducements to live at the mesas are the permanent springs of water found at the foot of these mesas. The few springs and streams that are found elsewhere in this semi-desert region are not permanent; the region shows the beds of many streams now dry. It is not clear why the Hopi live on top of the mesas rather than at the foot, but there is some reason to think that such a location provides good defenses in time of warfare. It appears to be a sort of natural fortress, rather difficult to attack and a good place to store the limited and precious supplies of grain. It is known that in earlier times, the Hopi, an agricultural people, were greatly harassed by the various nomadic bands of other Indian tribes of this region. Their folklore and history furnish evidence of this. It certainly appears that such a location of dwellings is a very good adaptation to a condition of warfare initiated by powerful nomadic tribes. But the question arises, Why do they live on top of these mesas now that there is a condition of peace enforced by the United States government? The Hopi have not been subject to attack since the Navaho last went on the warpath and were effectively dispersed by Kit Carson, who, in the 'sixties, scattered them and deported large numbers. Such a location of dwellings does not appear now in times of peace to be the best adaptation. The mesas are several hundred feet high. Women must toil daily up this ascent with their heavy jugs of water and the men with their corn and firewood. It is a long climb for the children who go to the government schools which are built at the foot of the mesas. However, these pueblo dwellers are now beginning to move their habitations to the foot of the mesas. But why didn't they move down before this? Probably a strong incentive to move down is the trading stores and the government schools which have been built below. But it would seem that if they had moved down a half-century earlier, they would have been saved much labor and inconvenience. The danger of attack, if this was the cause of living on top of the mesas, has not existed for fifty years. A custom, whatever may once have been its justification, seems to have lagged after the conditions had changed.

The foregoing illustrations have been cited as cases that upon investigation would probably show lags in the adaptive culture and degrees of maladjustment. A great many more such cases from modern social problems could be listed. If one should attempt to verify the hypothesis from data in each of these illustrative cases and to measure in years the time of the lag, the following difficulties would be encountered.

It is difficult to show that the adaptive culture is at one time adapted and at another time not adapted, and particularly to measure the degree of adaptation. Thus to show that legislative assemblies chosen on the basis of locality-representation are satisfactorily adapted at one time and not at another is not easy to do. And it is hard to prove that the United States has at the present time a less satisfactory organization for handling relationships with other nations than in the past. It frequently seems to be, in these cases, a matter of argument and opinion rather than a matter of fact. Adaptation is a condition of degree, complete lack of adaptation or perfect adaptation being rare. The lagging adaptive culture will of course have some utility of the nature discussed in Part III.

Furthermore, thinking in terms of an ideal, the adaptive culture is never wholly harmoniously adapted to the material conditions, for the reason that there is no ideal limit to this harmonious relationship. For instance, workmen's compensations, or feminism, or conservation of forests, may be more satisfactory than former mores, but who shall say that these adjustments are ideal? When we can think of better adjustments, that is, when we make inventions in the adaptive culture, the old adaptive culture will appear to lag, since it will take, in a purely physical way, some time for an invention to spread or be adapted, even after it has been thought out or applied once.

It should not be assumed, of course, that every suggested improvement in the adaptive culture is a real improvement. There are many social reforms in the air to-day, but certainly not every such suggested reform is desirable or will prove satisfactory. Thus there are various plans for dealing with unemployment and some are quite impracticable. Every suggested improvement does not prove that there is a lag.

Another difficulty encountered in measuring lag is that changes are sometimes quite gradual. Where a change in the material culture or in the adaptive culture is abrupt, it is easy to locate the point of change. But this is not always the case. When, for instance, did machine industry reach such a point in its development in the United States that it could be called an industrial nation? At what point had industry developed so that workmen's compensation was desirable because of industrial accidents? In such cases the development of adaptation or maladjustment is gradual and the ends of a period of maladjustment will be somewhat indeterminate. But of course such an indeterminate nature of a lag does not mean that the lag is any less real.

Another possible difficulty, in determining a lag in adaptive culture, lies in the task of defining the two variables, particularly in defining the adaptive culture. In any particular form of culture which is adjusted to material conditions, not all of this particular form is adaptive to the material conditions. Thus, it is hard to describe just how much of the family organization is subject to variation because of a change in the economic system.

4

REASONS FOR CULTURAL LAG

Up to this point in the consideration of the hypothesis, there has been little attempt to generalize. A number of particular cultural situations have been partially described, and it is clear that there are many cases where material conditions have changed and where the culture that was adjusted to the old material conditions has lagged appreciably behind. More and more such cases might be collected but at the cost of considerable time for the reader. Rather than an enumeration of more cases, it is desirable to consider the causes of such lags to see if the causes are sufficiently general to give an indication of how widespread these cultural lags are. Such a consideration of causes may give as good an idea of how extensive the phenomenon may be as does the more tedious method of considering individual cases.

A general inquiry into causes can best be approached by citing a number of specific causes. It would be possible here to make a thoroughgoing analysis of causes in a single instance, but that would hardly give us the scope of causes that is desired. These causes cited will be listed without any particular significance as to sequence.

Scarcity of invention in the adaptive culture. Sometimes, the adaptation of a culture to changed material conditions necessitates what might be called an invention in the adaptive culture. Lack of change in governmental forms, for instance, may be due to lack of inventions. It has been previously pointed out by others that in the field of government there is a marked lack of inventiveness. Our city governments followed, for instance, certain earlier town models and made certain borrowings from State governments. The rise of cities following the industrial revolution has created new conditions to which our city governments have not been well adapted. So acute an observer as the distinguished author of *The American Commonwealth* has said that the most conspicuous failure in government in the United States was in the government of cities. Of recent years there has been a good deal of experimenting with forms of city government; but for a long while, during an era of unprecedented corruption and bad government, there was a dearth of new ideas. The commission form of government itself was an invention almost by accident. Quite conceivably some new form or method of representation in legislative bodies would bring an improvement. The growth of industrial accidents because of the use of modern machines necessitated an invention in the adaptive culture, which is called workmen's compensation. However, the lack of knowledge of the invention was not the cause of the delay in developing workmen's compensation in the United States, for Germany had the plan in 1884, as has already been pointed out. Some adjustments to material culture may be made without any special invention. Thus the family makes certain adjustments to industry without involving a special invention; although such adaptations as playgrounds, juvenile courts and pension systems may be called inventions.

Mechanical obstacles to adaptive changes. What, is perhaps more frequently true is that the invention in adaptive culture is known but there is difficulty in getting the invention adopted. Some one in comparing invention and diffusion has made the remark that it is easier to spread butter than it is to make it. It is not, however, as easy to spread culture as it is to spread butter. A good deal that was said in Part III regarding resistance of culture to change is applicable here to the special case of lag, as, for instance, habit, love of the past, and various utilities of the old culture. There does seem to be, however, at times a purely physical or mechanical obstacle to the spread of some forms of culture. For instance, in the United States most State legislatures meet only every two years and frequently for short and limited periods. For this reason alone it takes some time for statutory enactments to spread throughout the States. The management of a subway once attempted to get the passengers to enter the end doors of the cars and go out the centre doors, for the purpose of expediting traffic. The plan was given up, and one of the difficulties seemed to be the vast number whose habits had to be changed, particularly during rush hours. In a democracy such as we have in the United States, the people have to become familiar with proposed reforms before they are sanctioned. This takes time, as every practical reformer knows. It involves setting up extensive machinery of education and propaganda. Indeed the obstacles to the spread of any invention in the non-material culture are many.

The heterogeneity of society. A good many of these special obstacles to changes arise because society is heterogeneous, consisting of many classes and groups. The need of the change in the adaptive culture is felt by only one class or group, whereas the change must be made by the society as a whole. For instance, workmen's compensation laws are passed by representatives of the whole group, whereas they apply to only a special class in the whole group. Very probably if the whole group were made up exclusively of workers liable to injury in industry, there would not have been so long a delay in the adoption of such laws. Changes in the adaptive culture work at times for the interests of one group but against the interests of another group. A great many proposed reforms to-day are for the purpose of providing better adjustments for classes who are not the rich and powerful classes. Many of these proposed reforms, such as remedies for unemployment, cost money which must be raised by taxation or fall as a burden on the wealthier classes, who do not appear to derive a special benefit from them. It is this raising of money which is an obstacle. The class situation in modern society is therefore a source of resistance to some changes in the adaptive culture. It is not clear, however, that the heterogeneity of society is a source of resistance to changes in the material culture. Perhaps to a certain extent it is so. In so far as social classes are causes of lags in the adaptive culture, such causes would presumably be more frequent in modern society than in primitive society.

The closeness of contact with material culture. Another general reason why the adaptive portions of the non-material culture lag behind the changes in the material culture is the fact that the relationship between the adaptive culture and the material culture is not very close, but several steps removed. Thus the form of a city government is not so close to industry as the corporate organization of industry itself. And a general philosophy like the *laissez faire* doctrine is a little further removed from the machinery of industry than are labor policies. Governmental organizations would be expected to adjust themselves somewhat more slowly to industrial changes than organizations of labor and capital. Trusts would be expected to develop rather quickly with changes in industry. In so far as the absence of closeness of contact is responsible for a delay in the changes of the adaptive culture, this cause would operate in any state of society, whether it be changes from hunting to domestication of animals or from agricultural to industrial conditions.

The connection of the adaptive culture with other parts of culture. Another cause of delay in the adjustments is the fact that the particular adaptive culture is sometimes correlated with some other part of the non-material culture, as perhaps the non-adaptive non-material culture. The mores of exploitation may be related to business in general as well as to a particular situation like forestry. If exploitation continues a good policy in business though not in forestry, presumably exploitation in regard to forestry would be more difficult to change because the exploitation is a general policy which continues satisfactorily applicable to other parts of culture such as business. If the adaptive culture, x, is correlated with another part of culture, z, as well as with the material culture, y; then, if y changes and z does not change, x will be more slow to change than would be true if it were not correlated with the third factor, z. Thus the position of women, x, is adapted to the industrial situation, y; but it is also related to the family-husband-children situation, z. The industrial situation, y, changes, but the family-husband-children situation, z, remains; therefore it would seem that changes in the position of women, x, would be slowed up some in its adjustment to industry, y, because of the correlation between x and z and the fact that z is stable. Another illustration is the fact that the desirability of individualism as a general policy in education, the family, or in business, may make it difficult to give it up in government or social reform.

Group valuations. Still another reason why some forms of non-material culture are slow to change appears to be the strong position they occupy in the valuations of the group. This is particularly true of morals, mores and some customs. Customs become mores because of the strong approval of them as a policy by the group. The group decides that certain ways of doing things are right and there is group pressure to enforce conformity. Certain emotional values of approval become attached to these ways of doing things. These emotional values of group approval appear to be forces resisting change, perhaps partly because of habit, conditioned reflexes, social pressure, love of the past through forgetting the unpleasant, and perhaps the recognition that these ways of doing things have worked in the past. It is possible the group approval may attach itself somewhat more strongly to these ways of doing things as seen in morals, customs and institutions than to material objects. It is of course true that individuals love the soil or a ship, or hate a drug, but group valuations of institutions and mores are very strong. Thus the family, the Constitution of the United States, a political party, individualism, monogamy, all seem to be protected by a group pressure or approval which constitutes a distinct force operating at least for a time against modification. This is what is meant by the saying that institutionalism resists change.

There seem to be various special reasons why adaptive non-material culture is slow to adjust to changed material conditions. The purpose of this essay, however, is not so much to ascertain causes, as to establish the fact of maladjustments between material culture and the adaptive non-material culture due to lags in the adaptive culture. The consideration of causes was primarily for the purpose of seeing whether they were of such a general nature as to make the phenomena widespread. Of course, the phenomenon of lag would be found only in a situation of cultural change. Since it is in recent times that cultural changes are so frequent, the lags in adaptive culture are expected to be a problem of only modern times. In very early times changes were not sufficiently numerous and frequent to give rise often to any very significant problem of this nature, though the Hebrews after migrating to the "promised land" had difficulty, as recorded in the Old Testament, in giving up mores of the old nomadic life and adjusting to the new agricultural conditions.

5

THE CORRELATION BETWEEN PARTS OF CULTURE

The problem of a harmonious adjustment between the material culture and the adaptive culture appears to be a part of a larger problem, namely, the harmonious adjustment of all parts of a culture in a period of change. This problem may be stated in the form of certain questions. How closely correlated are the various parts of culture? How nice an adjustment is necessary or desirable between the different parts of culture? And to what extent is this adjustment maintained in periods of cultural change? These questions are altogether too large to be considered in any detail. And it is questionable whether any sort of quick general answer can be given upon which reliance can be placed. Hobhouse attacked this problem in part in the volume, *The Material Culture and Social Institutions of the Simpler Peoples*. He attempted to correlate social institutions with material cultures. The correlation did not appear to be very great. The data of ethnology show a great many possible combinations between different parts of culture. For instance, there are hunting peoples with polygamy and monogamy, and pastoral cultures with polygamy and polyandry. The position of women may be high or low in hunting cultures and equally high or equally low in agricultural conditions. Tracing descent through the father's side only is found in a great variety of cultural conditions, so also is descent traced through the mother's side. Finer analyses will no doubt show closer interrelations between some parts of culture. Thus while polygamy or monogamy is found in a variety of cultural situations it may be true that the functions performed by the family are closely related to the economic conditions, as is claimed by Grosse.[18] Lowie has shown some significant changes that oc-

[18] Ernest Grosse, *Die Formen der Familie und die Formen der Wirtschaft*.

curred when the Chukchee changed from seal-hunting and fishing to reindeer-breeding.[19] Wissler has described certain changes that occurred among the Plains Indians after the introduction of the horse.[20] Private ownership of large-scale industry is correlated with some form of labor union. Some parts of culture appear to be quite closely interdependent, whereas other parts appear more or less independent. Various parts of the non-material culture are correlated with each other as well as with the material culture. No satisfactory presentation of this larger general problem can be made here; we shall do well indeed to present, in so short a space, the smaller problem of the maladjustment between material culture and certain adaptive cultures.

It does seem to be true, however, that people can live, society can exist, under very varied combinations of different parts of culture. Thus there are possible many different degrees of adjustment. But varied conditions under which people live furnish evidence as to what are the most harmonious combinations. Society can exist without unemployment insurance, but unemployment insurance may be a much better social condition. People can live in periods of consider-

[19] Robert H. Lowie, *Primitive Society*, pp. 198-201.
[20] Clark Wissler, "The Influence of the Horse in the Development of Plains Culture," *American Anthropologist*, New Series, Vol. XVI, No. 1, pp. 1–25.

able social maladjustments, but it does not follow that such a life is the most satisfactory or that effort should not be made to make better adjustments in the social heritage.

6

MATERIAL CULTURE AS A SOURCE OF MODERN SOCIAL CHANGES

There remain, however, a few other considerations to be made in inquiring how generally the hypothesis of lag may justifiably be applied. It has been shown that when the material culture changes there are frequently lags in the old adaptive culture before changes providing satisfactory adjustment have been made. It is not to be implied, of course, that changes may not be made in the non-material culture and that part which is adaptive to material conditions while the material culture remains constant. Indeed, it is conceivable that a change may first occur in non-material culture and later the material culture be adjusted to such a change. Thus religion may change and an adaptation affecting material conditions may be made to the religious ideas, as in the development of taboos against the use of certain animals as foods or the development of architecture in houses of worship. There may be progress in science, to be followed by changes in the material culture, which may be thought of as adaptations of material culture to science. Moralists may argue that the material culture is adjusted to moral principles, rather than a moral adjustment to the material conditions. There are, therefore, some changes in the non-material culture that precede and to which the material culture is later adjusted, and we wish to know whether in our modern culture most of the initial changes are in the material culture or in the non-material culture.

Concerning the question of whether in modern times the initiation of the vast cultural changes that are taking place so rapidly lies more largely with the material culture or with the non-material culture, it should be recalled that there are a great many changes occurring in the material culture because of inventions. As an illustration, there are thousands and thousands of different types of machines for production, all recently invented. Many changes are being made in the material factors in transportation, by means of steam, electricity and gasoline, by land, sea and air. There are new types of dwellings; and the variety of new types of consumption goods is bewildering. Why are there these multitudinous changes in material culture to-day? And more particularly, are these changes in material culture consequent to changes in the non-material culture and adaptive to the various forms of non-material culture?

It certainly does not appear that the uses of steam, or electricity, or gasoline are undertaken for the purpose of making adjustments to a changed form of social organization, or a particular concept of morals, or to a religious doctrine or to any other form of non-material culture. These material inventions appear to be made and adopted with the idea of satisfying individual wants, because they bring comfort, rest, speed, enlightenment, or wealth. The power of steam saves human energy and steam is used instead of the human arm to turn machines. But the introduction of steam makes changes in home production, the growth of cities, changes in the position of women, new causes of war. It has its effect upon the birth rate, the functions of the church, and the nature of education. If, for illustration, there had not been discovered these sources of power for turning wheels, that is, if we were still producing by the energy or power of human beings and domesticated animals only, cities would have been few, concentration of production in factories would not have taken place, production would be largely on the farms and in the home, the position of women would have been much as of old. Some changes would have occurred in education, in religion and in morals. But there seems to be no doubt that the influences on non-material culture flowing from the use of steam have been profound. There is no reason to think that steam was adopted in order to make an adjustment to some part of the non-material culture.

Certainly a large part of the non-material culture appears to be by nature a method of adjustment either to material culture or to natural environment or to both. The phrase, ways of doing things, is a generalized characterization of a large part of non-material culture. Social organization, customs and morals are the means of a collective way of doing things, in large part to and with the natural environment and material culture, either simply, directly and individually, or somewhat indirectly, remotely and collectively. Such methods of behavior would therefore presumably change if the natural environment or the material culture changed. While initial changes may occur through invention in social institutions, religions, laws, etc., one would hardly expect the material culture to change frequently for the purpose of making adaptations to these ways of doing things.

But some forms of non-material culture are ways of doing things valuable for their own ends and not particularly concerned with material conditions. Thus art serves aesthetic desires, relatively free from considerations of material culture. The sex instinct functions with little relation to material culture. Religion as a form of culture meets certain needs, irrespective of material culture. And social organization may not only be a way of adjustment to material conditions but it may serve independently certain other human desires such as the desire for sociability. So, much of non-material culture has purposes quite its own, which may be attained with very little use of material culture in almost any environment. This difference in the nature of the parts of non-material culture led us in the analysis to the segregation of the part which is more closely adapted to material culture; and this was called adaptive culture. While it is true that much of non-material culture is not highly adapted to material conditions, it is also true that the material culture is not adapted to such types of non-adaptive non-material culture. In other words, we should not expect frequent changes in material culture to be made for purposes of adjustment to types of non-material culture, such as religion, art, ceremonies and literature.

It would be interesting to know whether there is anything in the nature of material culture or of non-material culture which would make a greater frequency of inventions in one or the other. The accumulative nature of material culture resulting in increasing cultural base was thought to be in part responsible for the great number of material changes to-day. Is the non-material culture similarly accumulative resulting in increased cultural base? The non-material culture is so diverse that it is difficult even to make a general guess. But religion does not appear to be particularly accumulative, neither is the family organization. Art, literature, government seem to be somewhat accumulative but probably not so much so as material culture. Science seems to be rather highly accumulative. The cumulative aspect of customs, mores, and "ways of doing things" would appear to rest in part on the cumulative nature of material culture. It may therefore be that the increasing cultural base as an immediate factor in producing inventions or change may be more characteristic of material culture than of non-material culture. There are of course other factors affecting inventions and change, and in earlier times the non-material culture may have been quite heterogeneous and complex while the material culture may have been simple.

Evidence as to the susceptibility to change of the different parts of culture may be drawn from studies in the diffusion of culture. Which is the more easily adopted by a people, the material culture or the non-material culture? Wissler, whose studies of the culture areas of the American Indian furnish excellent perspectives of the borrowing of cultures by one tribe from another, remarks:[21]

The term culture as used by anthropologists generally includes such groups of traits as social organization, ceremonial activities, art and material culture. Of these it appears that social organization is less readily changed in contrast to the last. It is food, shelter and transportation complexes of material culture that the intruding group will take over bodily. Then the chances are that one by one the associated ceremonies always found intimately connected with food production will be taken over to displace those now made useless, and ultimately drag in their social counterparts. Even a superficial view of the data so far accumulated by anthropologists will show how well this hypothetical picture fits the facts for several culture centres.

While Wissler's generalization may be true for the data he has dealt with, a statement that material culture spreads more easily from one group to another than other features of culture, such as social organization and ceremonies, is probably only true in general, or on the average. There are many exceptions and qualifications. Some ceremonies and religious movements have

[21] Clark Wissler, "Aboriginal Maize Culture as a Typical Culture Complex," *American Journal of Sociology*, Vol. XXI, March, 1916, p. 661.

swept over areas with great rapidity. But the statement that material culture is borrowed first and non-material culture later suggests that the adoption of inventions in material culture will be somewhat earlier than changes in the non-material culture, and that obstacles to change are found in connection with non-material culture that are not found with the material culture.

The foregoing analysis has been undertaken for the purpose of inquiring whether there is anything in the nature of culture which would indicate whether the vast number of cultural changes taking place to-day were initiated largely in the field of material culture or in the field of non-material culture. If the foregoing analysis is sound, it would seem that a preponderant number of changes are begun in the material culture causing changes in the non-material culture. And while there may be some changes occurring in the non-material culture, not initiated or caused by changes in the material culture, these changes do not in themselves very frequently precipitate changes in the material culture. It therefore follows that if to-day a great number of the cultural changes occurring are started by changes in the material culture, thereby causing changes in the non-material culture, particularly adaptive culture, the hypothesis of lags is widely applicable. Whether this lag is appreciable in length of time or in severity of effect can only be told in each instance by analysis and measurement.

These considerations give prominence to material culture as a factor in the changing society of to-day. This prominence is due to three facts. First is the great accumulation of material culture. Second, the material culture is changing so frequently and so rapidly. And third, the material culture causes so many changes in other features of society. The magnitude of material culture to-day is very striking. Greece had developed a non-material culture to a high degree, comparing well with our own. But the material culture of Greece was much less advanced. The material culture of modern society is also much more elaborate than the material culture of so-called primitive peoples. Among these peoples the environment and natural resources were of very great significance to them, determining within limits their food supply, their shelter, their clothing. Climate, geographical conditions, and natural resources made, for instance, many differences between the pueblo dwellers of Mexico and the Eskimo of the north or the Indians of the plains. Material culture to-day, particularly since the development of trade, is conquering limitations imposed by climate. And on account of its size and increased significance, adjustments not only have to be made to geographical conditions as was true in primitive culture, but we must also make adjustments to material culture. From the point of view of adjustments, then, material culture is replacing in significance to a certain extent the geographical environment of old. But there is this distinction, the material culture to-day changes frequently whereas the changes in geographical conditions are slow. This makes problems of adjustment ever-recurring.

The very fact that material culture is to-day undergoing such rapid changes means that it is significant as a cause of social phenomena. In the analysis of causes of any phenomenon, it is the factors that are variable that are said to be causes. The variability of modern material culture is one of the reasons for the prominence of the modern doctrine of the economic interpretation of history. Ethnologists are as a rule not so much impressed with the theory of the economic interpretation of history as are students of modern culture, and perhaps for the reason that the material culture was neither so large nor so variable in primitive society as in the modern era.

A recognition of the significance of material culture in modern society need not identify one with what is sometimes called materialism. Contrasts are made usually between the material and the ideal, spiritual or religious in reference to life's values rather than in reference to sociological factors. One can recognize the influence of material culture, without of course denying the influence of other cultural factors. And one may work, of course, towards shaping material culture to ends and purposes that may be in accord with the ideals and the spirit. It is only by a recognition of the significance of material culture that social reformers can hope in a practical way to modify or direct it.

SUMMARY

The development of the hypothesis considered in this chapter may be summarized as follows: Material culture in changing causes other social changes in what was defined as adaptive culture. But frequently there is a delay in the changes thus caused, so that the old adaptive culture hangs over into the new material conditions. This lag in the adaptive culture produces a period of maladjustment, which is less harmonious as an adaptation than the period which precedes or follows. This hypothesis was considered carefully in the case of workmen's compensation for industrial accidents. The lag in the old adaptive culture was measured in years and the hypothesis was verified by the facts. It was thought that similar proof could be given in many such instances, and a number of such probable cases were cited. The further application of the hypothesis by data and statistics was abandoned on account of the limitations of space, and some considerations as to nature and causes were undertaken to inquire how widespread was the situation described in the case of workmen's compensation.

It was thought probable from the nature of material culture and its changes, and the nature of non-material culture and its changes, that at the present time a great many initial changes were occurring in the material culture which were causing changes in other parts of culture. Special forces and causes were thought to exist which caused changes in certain parts of non-material culture to spread less rapidly than changes in the material culture. There are, therefore, a great many instances where the material culture changes first and the other social changes which it causes follow later. In some cases these lags may be so brief as to be insignificant, but in a great many cases the lags causing maladjustments may be so long as to be socially very significant. The extent of the lag and the severity of the maladjustment should be measured in each instance. The great size of material culture to-day, its rapidity of change, and its significance as a source of other changes in society make the material culture in modern society play a most important part.

Since lags in social movements causing social maladjustments follow changes in material culture, and since there are many rapid changes in material culture, it follows that there will be an accumulation of these lags and maladjustments.

According to the analysis made in Part II, the growth of material culture was shown to become faster and faster. If the material culture should continue to accumulate and change with increasing rapidity, it would seem that the cultural lags will pile up even more than at the present time. Such a development creates quite a task for those who would direct the course of social progress, the task of eliminating these maladjustments by making the adjustments to material changes more rapid. It is thinkable that the piling up of these cultural lags may reach such a point that they may be changed in a somewhat wholesale fashion. In such a case, the word revolution probably describes what happens. There may be other limiting factors to such a course of development; and our analysis is not sufficiently comprehensive and accurate to make definite prediction. But certain trends at the present time seem unmistakable.

PART V

ADJUSTMENT BETWEEN HUMAN NATURE AND CULTURE

In the preceding chapter, the discussion concerned the harmonious adjustment of the different parts of the social heritage, particularly during a process of rapid social change. It was there shown that a number of social problems arise because the different parts of culture change at unequal rates. In the present chapter we wish to consider some of the problems that arise, not from the lack of adjustment of the various parts of culture, but from the lack of adjustment between human nature and culture. Since the publication of the *Origin of Species,* there has been a great deal of discussion of the adaptation of man to environment. Our problem, though, deals not with the whole of environment but with that part which is called culture: and the concern is not with man as a whole, but with man's inherited psychological equipment. Furthermore, the emphasis in the problem is not wholly on the adaptation of human nature to culture, but on the adjustment between human nature and culture, which includes the possibility of an adaptation of culture to human nature. Naturally, the question is raised as to how satisfactory an adjustment between human nature and culture exists, particularly when we consider the possibilities of making better adjustments. The question is such a broad one, that its many phases ramify into a large number of special hypotheses, which may in time be verified by detailed data. No detailed study is to be made here, however. Our purpose is rather to chart the problem and draw such conclusions as the general analysis and present status seem to warrant.

I

THE THEORY OF THE CAVE MAN IN THE MODERN CITY

Evolution in man. The problem can best be outlined by approaching it from the point of view of social evolution, developed in Part II. The consideration of social evolution there made concerned the possible changes, in the course of time, in human nature and in culture. Man has been on the earth for 50,000 years or possibly for several hundred thousand. Skeletal remains indicate that his evolution has been slow. The evidence we have of the way biological evolution takes place confirms the view as to the slowness of evolution. Mutations are infrequent. It was claimed in the second chapter that no proof had been made that there had been any significant biological evolution of man since the last glacial period. It is of course possible that there may have been significant changes in man's biological nature since that time, although we do not have conclusive proof; and it would seem probable that there may have been some mutations, but of just what significance it is not known. The whole question of the significance of biological evolution in man for sociology has been confused by the vast cultural changes that have taken place. But it seems possible for the tremendous cultural evolution since the last ice age to have occurred without any significant biological change. Human nature as thought of in terms of hereditary equipment may very probably be fundamentally the same now as in the last glacial period. Indeed in many respects man's psychological nature is quite similar to that of the anthropoids. It certainly is true that man's nature is much more like that of the cave men than the appearance of cultural differences would lead one to think. The apparent differences may be cultural, acquired since birth in the course of a lifetime. The fact that this is difficult to conceive lies in our ignorance of the cultural process and our failure to understand the power of culture.

Cultural evolution. On the other hand, cultural change is not so slow as biological change, especially in modern times. In early times, to be sure, the rate of cultural change was very slow. Man for a very long time was in the rough stone age, probably for hundreds of thousands of years. Then culture developed quickly through the neolithic age and through the use of metals up to the high mechanical achievements of to-day. That the latter stages of this cultural development occurred without any significant biological changes is practically certain.

The primitive nature of man and the artificial nature of civilization. The course of cultural evolution and of biological change in man as set forth in the foregoing paragraphs throws some light on the problems of adjustment between human nature and modern culture. Man is the same biologically as he was in the late ice age, while his culture has suddenly become vastly different. The problem may be popularly expressed as that of cave men trying to live in a modern city. Suppose we could place a group of Cro-Magnon men in a modern city. What would be some of the difficulties of adjustment for them? It is fairer to imagine a group of their children being brought up in a modern city. Can we, being biologically the same as Cro-Magnon men, adjust ourselves to the sedentary life demanded of office workers? If we suffer from indigestion, can it be due to the fact that we do not eat the food that the cave men ate; or that we do not take the muscular exercise which the life of the primitive hunter demanded? Do we have difficulties in adjusting ourselves to our institution of marriage and a rigid sex code? May these difficulties be due to our primitive nature which may have been adjusted in the age of the cave dwellers and anthropoids to a more promiscuous expression? May our wanderlust tendencies be traced to the fact that primitive men were wandering hunters? Is the monotonous and specialized work on a machine for many hours a day for every week in the year and for many consecutive years the type of life to which our equipment is naturally adapted? These questions suggest the nature of the problem of adjustment as it is popularly conceived and suggest the idea that modern civilization is essentially artificial, that is, not like the culture of the hunting peoples which is assumed to be more natural.

It is claimed that a great many social problems such as war, crime, sexual phenomena and disease arise because of the inability or difficulty of the original nature of man to adapt itself to modern conditions and cultural standards. So also it is claimed that much of our unhappiness, nervousness and insanity is traceable to the same general causes. Certainly human nature is at the bottom of many of our social and individual ills in the sense that if human nature were only different these problems would not exist. If we were less selfish, less passionate, less pugnacious, more reasonable, more kindly, and more tolerant, our social problems would not be so numerous nor so difficult, and it is quite possible that certain standards of civilization are set rather high for our primitive nature to conform to.

Evidently to understand the problem of adaptation we must know what human nature is like and we must understand the nature of modern culture and the extent of its artificiality. Can it be that we are really cave people trying to adjust ourselves to factory life? This strange but plausible theory may be taken as a point of departure for a critical estimate of the problems of adaptation between human nature and culture. As previously indicated, two assumptions may be taken as strongly probable; one is that modern man is biologically very much the same as the men of the old stone age, and the other is that modern civilization is recent, of short history, and very different from the hunting culture. While this much of the theory is sound, as appears from the analysis of Part II, the remaining parts of the theory we have not examined. This will be done in the following paragraphs.

The adaptation of cave man. It is true that

man, or some creature much like man, lived for many hundreds of thousands of years hunting wild animals, gathering herbs, nuts or fruits, and inhabited trees or caves. There must have been some measure of adaptation to this environment and type of life, but it should not be too readily assumed that the adaptation was perfect. It may have been only a partially satisfactory adaptation, however; we do not know very much about what this life was like. On the physical side, for instance, it was an outdoor life as contrasted with life in our modern houses. The cave men lived a much more physically active life than modern office workers. Certain surmises can be made regarding the type of food eaten and the type of physical activities engaged in. But guesses as to the instinctive life, as to how much they fought, loved, hated, feared, or were gregarious, are probably wide of the mark. At least speculation by theorists as to how peoples with primitive cultures function psychologically has often been far from the facts as observed by field workers. So we have very little basis to go on for forming an estimate of the psychological adaptation of primitive man of very early cultures.

Objection should also be made to the use of the phrase, "cave man," as biologically or psychologically descriptive of man. A description in terms of instincts, capacities and mechanisms is preferable. The term, "cave man," suggests a type of cultural life rather than a biological equipment. Any description of human nature in terms of cultural activities is misleading, for it is conceivable that the psychological equipment may function equally well in a thousand different cultures. Satisfactory adaptation is not necessarily confined to any one type of cultural life, even though that may have been the type of life existing for hundreds of thousands of years. Thus one may take exercise in a gymnasium as well as in the hunt. And many different stimuli may arouse fear as satisfactorily as a wild beast. As a descriptive term "the cave man" is bad because of the misleading associations that inevitably come to mind, as a result of childhood tales or novel-reading or Sunday supplements to the newspapers, or what not. These associations are just as misleading as popular notions about savagery and barbarism are false. Though we may be cave people trying to live in a modern city, we are little the wiser for this knowledge because we know little of what the cave man is biologically and psychologically.

The slowness of the biological process of adaptation. Another point in the theory of the cave man in the modern city is that our biological nature is not adapted to civilization because of the comparatively short time that we have been living in civilization. If the adapting is all to be done from the biological side then certainly the two or three thousand years of civilization and the one hundred and fifty years of industrialism are not long enough times to make biological adaptations, acquired characteristics not being inherited and mutations occurring rarely. But it does not follow that there is not adaptation. Such an assumption is wholly from the biological side. Adaptations may be made on the side of culture. And the two thousand years of civilization in Europe are conceivably not too short a time for culture to be adjusted to man.

The artificiality of modern civilization. Furthermore, the argument stresses the fact that modern civilization is very different from the culture of the ice ages and that the amount of this difference is an indication of the lack of adaptation. This great difference may simply appear to be different in physical outlines. From the point of view of the functioning of instincts, the difference may not be so great as the objective measurements of the material culture would indicate. Thus one's appetite may be satisfied by any one of a very great number of foods. The type of material culture does not necessarily cause variations in the extent to which we are pugnacious or become angry. We love irrespective of the particular fashion of courtship. We may find adventure in modern life as truly as it was found in the hunter's life. Monotony is by no means confined to the modern factory; unquestionably routine existed in the primitive life of man. It may be that the instinctive life of modern men is greatly different from that of cave men, but the theory based merely on the objective differences between modern and early culture does not of itself prove such a great difference.

Instinctive activities of modern and ancient man. Perhaps the method of testing the theory under consideration that most readily comes to mind is that of comparing the emotional and instinctive life of man in ancient society with that of man living in modern society. Such a method implies a listing of the different instincts and a consideration of the functioning of each one both in the hunting cultures and in modern industrial society. If such a comparison could be made it would yield the information we want. But think of the difficulties of making such a comparison. Lists of instincts and emotions have been made, but such a list tells us little about their nature, interrelations, or relative significance. It is even difficult to describe adequately the emotions and instincts involved in a single act; how much more difficult is it then to characterize even roughly the instincts and emotions involved in the many different acts of a people. We have no statistical record of the behavior of the instincts of man from the hunting cultures, or of man in modern civilization. Perhaps the best that could be done in comparing the life in modern and ancient cultures is to point out, roughly, certain obvious differences in cultural activities, leaving to surmise the instincts involved. But in such a comparison, which of the early cultures shall we choose and which type of the very heterogeneous modern society? These comparisons will at best be fragments and guesses, as the following illustrations indicate.

For instance, with some individuals in modern life there is probably greater intellectual activity involving concentration, thought, sustained attention and concern with abstractions, than would be found among primitive hunters; though primitive hunters probably functioned much more frequently along these lines than is commonly supposed. Laborers who work twelve hours a day seven days a week doing the same tasks in the steel mills may have a smaller variety of emotional and instinctive reactions expressed in daily behavior throughout a year than did the men of the simpler hunting cultures. The emotion of fear may not find as frequent expression in modern times as formerly, but it may be that the great prevalence of anxiety in modern life is another form of fear expression. In some classes of modern society fighting is less frequent, though irritation and temper may be other forms of expression of pugnacious tendencies. Tendencies towards gregariousness may, on the other hand, find more frequent expression in modern cities than among the small hunting bands of former times. As for example, the sex instinct functions in ways not natural to the hunting peoples where large numbers are unmarried, as among the male groups working as migratory, casual laborers in some sections of the United States. Similarly the instincts of soldiers in prolonged trench warfare probably do not function as among primitive hunters. It is thus possible to make some random observations, but they are far from being a complete picture and are subject to error.

Civilization may afford a better adaptation. A conclusion in the theory we are considering is that we are less satisfactorily adapted on the psychological side to civilization, because we are after all cave men and because civilization is new and different. Although our natures may be much the same fundamentally as that of the cave people, and although modern culture is recent and different, it does not follow from such theoretical considerations that we are less satisfactorily adapted. If the adaptation were wholly a biological adaptation, this would be more probable; but the culture that has grown may have become a more rather than a less satisfactory adjustment for human nature. Indeed this would seem to be true if culture were simply the result of human needs. If culture were solely the result of desires, then the longer the history of culture, presumably the more satisfactorily desires would be met. And if adaptation be the satisfaction of desires, then we should expect modern civilization to afford a better adaptation to human nature than the hunting cultures of the stone ages. The easy gratification of wishes, however, may not be the best adaptation for our organisms. Growth and development within a life-time, for instance, may proceed best with some effort, some denial or struggle. The collective whole of our desires may find a better adaptation than by a ready yielding to the immediate individual impulses.

It is also somewhat questionable to what extent culture as a whole may in its growth come to satisfy more and more adequately our desires. There is some relationship between culture and human needs, but it is not easy to state what this relationship is. Many single material inventions are adopted because they answer a particular desire or render a specific comfort. But the adjustments they occasion may be many more than the particular immediate adjustment at their first adoption. Thus steam was used because it saved a certain amount of human effort; but the cultural changes precipitated by the widespread use of steam concerned many other needs than that of labor-saving. The effects of a material invention are not only far-reaching; but it seems impossible to foresee the full social consequences, and these unforeseeable consequences may be much greater than the immediate desire gratified by its adoption. Inventions and discoveries may create unpredictable situations that may indeed be even dangerous. Thus a hunting people may by the adoption of the gun kill off its food supply; just as we may create inventions that may exhaust our natural resources.

In a previous analysis of cultural growth, it was pointed out that the nature of its future growth depended a great deal upon the past. What was called the cultural base plays a very large part in determining what the future trend will be. This fact, therefore, limits the effort of human will and desire in creating new forms. It is not as though human desire were unlimited in creating as it wills. These considerations make one less assured that the growth of culture is towards the greater satisfaction of desire or towards a better adaptation. From such general considerations it is difficult to say whether we should expect modern civilization to afford a better adaptation to the original nature of man than the simple cultures of food-gatherers and hunters. It may or it may not. Perhaps some parts of our heterogeneous culture may afford a better adaptation and some parts may not. The question can probably be better answered by considering specific instances and problems rather than by such general consideration.

What is meant by adaptation or adjustment between culture and human nature is a question which must have occurred to the reader in following the preceding analysis. The idea is taken over from biology. We say that a polar bear is adapted to the environment of the Arctic circle, but not to life at the equator. It means a harmony in the functioning of all parts of an animal's equipment in a certain environment. The question here arises as to what is such a proper functioning of human nature in a given environment. Probably any definition which covers all such situations would be so general as to be of little value. More light will be thrown on the conception of adjustment, when the repression of the instincts is discussed later on. It should be observed that one's notion of adaptation in some cases depends somewhat on one's attitude towards life, one's idea of progress, or one's religious beliefs.

Human nature changes within a lifetime. Another point in the foregoing theory of human nature about which there may be confusion is the idea of its slowness to change over a long period of time. When it is said that man has probably not changed much in thousands of years, what is meant is that the part that is passed on by heredity has probably not changed much. Mankind may not change over a long period of years, yet there may be very great changes occurring in an individual during a lifetime. But such changes are acquired characteristics and are not transmitted by heredity. The apparently extremely great variations of human nature within different generations are in part deceptive, because what is thus seen to be varied is not alone human nature, but the cultural expression of human nature. In our modern culture an individual may utilize opportunities in higher education and develop to a considerable extent the personality of the student or the scholar. On the other hand, if born into a situation where the opportunities to read and to write were denied, a personality different in some respects would be developed. To say that we are cave people trying to live in a modern city means that we bring to modern culture a human equipment that is relatively fixed over centuries, but not wholly fixed within a generation. This indicates how it is possible for the same human nature to appear so different in two very different cultures.

Partial use of the instinctive equipment. Another source of difficulty in getting a clear meaning out of the theory that we are cave people living in a modern city lies in differences in the understanding of the requirements of human nature. Must our instinctive equipment be fully employed? The point at issue may be set forth in the following manner. Men of the old stone age had a muscular system that fitted them excellently for running, climbing, hitting and for performing the various acts involved in hunting and getting food. We have this same muscular equipment. But many of us no longer run, climb or hit. We are carried about in vehicles and spend a great deal of time sitting at a desk. We probably do not make use of this muscular equipment as fully as did the primitive hunter. It was a very necessary mechanism in adapting him to his environment. In the adaptation of the modern office worker to his environment the varied assortment of muscles is less actively employed. Failure to exercise adequately our muscles is said to involve serious consequences affecting kidneys, blood pressure and digestion. Using the muscles is found to have distinctly beneficial effects upon our health. If we take the proper amount of exercise we feel better and stronger and the different bodily organs function more satisfactorily. So it has become necessary to devise some artificial means of exercising. This physical equipment of muscles cannot with safety be allowed to fall into disuse.

There comes down to us from our remote ancestors not only a set of muscles, but also, it is said, a group of instincts, such as the sex instinct, the pugnacious instinct and the gregarious instinct. These instincts were of adaptive and survival value for the early primitive hunters just as truly as were their muscles. Fear and pugnacity alike saved life. The sex instinct created and perpetuated it. There was safety in numbers drawn together by sociability and gregarious tendencies. In modern culture, some of our industrial occupations, in contrast to the hunting life, apparently do not need such a rich and varied equipment of instincts for their requirements. Consider, for instance, the factory workers, or factory "hands" as they were classified in the enumerations of the earlier censuses. The requirements of factory work could be met by a much less varied and rich assortment of instincts than the human being possesses. Just as the factory extracts for its use from a wonderful muscular endowment only a portion of the muscles, so apparently the factory life requires not all of the instinctive tendencies and aptitudes. What is desired of them is that they become automatic like the machines, mere factory hands. Some types of modern cultural environment need only a part of the inheritance of instinctive tendencies. It has been found that in the case of muscles, to let them fall into disuse is detrimental to the organism. Does the parallel hold true in regard to the instincts? Is it harmful not to make use of the instincts?

The problem of the cave man and modern civilization raises the question as to whether only the partial use of man's equipment is a bad adaptation. Does the passive rôle or the lack of use of some of the instinctive tendencies result in harmful consequences to the individual, and is it thus a sign of lack of adjustment between human nature and culture? The problem as formulated above is plausible partly because of the analogy drawn between the situation with regard to the muscles and the situation in regard to the instincts. Analogies are often deceptive. For general analysis, what is needed is more light thrown on the nature of this psychological equipment, a significant portion of which is the instincts.

The nature of the instincts. The study of the instincts has a long history and much has been written on the subject, but we are interested in the matter only as it bears on the theory under discussion. That some of our behavior is instinctive is seen from our tendencies to fight, to love, to be afraid, and we speak of an instinct to fight, the sex instinct, and of an instinct of flight. Just how much of our behavior is instinctive is a matter of doubt, but that a very large portion is either simply instinctive, or the result of blends or conflicts of these original instinctive tendencies more or less modified by habit and learning, all will admit. Thus scientific research may receive its impulse in part from an instinct of curiosity and an explorative tendency. Some religious activity arises from fear and an instinctive tendency to abnegate self.

The instincts were at one time thought of as more or less mysterious entities residing in the body. This idea resembles somewhat the earlier notion of the feelings, called at that time humors. Thus when a person was in a bad humor, some such spirit or humor was in possession of the body. But it is now agreed that instinctive behavior is more in the nature of a reaction of the body or various parts of it to stimuli. Thus there is a recognition of a stimulus, an accompanying emotion, and a motor reaction. There are in all individuals these tendencies to action, functioning in response to stimuli. The external bodily behavior during emotion and instinctive action has been frequently described, particularly in the case of fear and anger. Recently physiological-psychologists have also learned a good deal about the internal changes that occur during certain emotional states. The ductless glands, particularly the thyroid, pituitary and the adrenals, pour out secretions which produce numerous internal modifications, promote activity and are probably related to the emotional states. We therefore conclude that the energy, drive and motivation necessary to that great portion of human activity originating from the instincts are inherent in the response of the various parts of the body to react to stimuli and we know that certain emotional states and desires or wishes accompany these responses.

All this mechanism of instinct is part of the original equipment of men, endowed by heredity, as truly as are the muscles. We think the whole of this equipment functioned in the primitive hunter. Is there a satisfactory functioning of these mechanisms in the life of the factory worker or the city dweller? Just as we may have ungratified desires, may we not have repression of the instincts? May not certain parts of our equipment need exercise in instinctive activity as truly as the muscles need exercise? Does modern civilization provide outlets for these desires, or exercise for this part of our equipment? We are chiefly interested in the nature of the instincts as they relate to these questions.

Variability in the stimuli to behavior. One problem of the nature of the instincts that bears directly on our theory concerns the nature of the stimuli that arouse our desires and set off this instinctive activity, particularly as to whether these stimuli are external or inside the body. Thus we might have the capacity for anger or for response to music, but unless we come in contact with these external stimuli we may feel no particular discomfort because of any lack of functioning of the pugnacious instinct or of our talent for music. There are really two questions here. One is whether the tendency to feel anger is dependent on some external stimulus. And the other is whether the failure of the equipment to function, in, say, a pugnacious manner, is a poor adaptation between culture and original nature. We shall consider now only the first question. If we consider hunger or sex rather than anger, the dependence of the desire on the external stimulus is not so clear. Hunger may be caused by internal bodily conditions as truly as by the smell or sight of food. The absence of food from the stomach, conditions affecting the secretion of gastric juice, contracting motions of the walls of the stomach, and perhaps other factors force the individual to desire food and to act to get it. There may be some connection here with an external stimulus but the bodily condition is a large factor in producing the activity.

The status of the seminal vesicles, the prostate gland, the distended bladder, the ovaries or the pituitary and thyroid glands may arouse sex excitement without the presence of the sexual object. Perhaps the status of the adrenals, of the liver, or of the thyroid may determine in part the threshold of the reaction to the anger stimulus. It is true in some cases that the bodily preparation is such as to make the slightest of external stimuli capable of setting off the train of instinctive activity. In such cases, desires may be thought of as arising from within the body. No doubt the different instinctive tendencies vary in their dependence on bodily status and external stimuli.

Where the variation in internal preparation is great and the dependence on bodily status is important, any failure to find an outlet or satisfaction for such instinctive craving would seem the poorer adaptation. On the other hand, if the dependence is largely on the external stimuli, the lack of functioning of the instinct may occasion no particular distress.

The variability in response to stimuli. The operation of the instinctive equipment in any culture depends upon the stimuli to arouse the activity. It should be observed that the arousing of an instinct is generally not confined to a particular stimulus, but it may be made active by a great variety of stimuli. Observe, for instance, the number of situations that will arouse fear. The ease with which an instinct mechanism may be conditioned to react solely to a secondary stimulus, which in the first instance had nothing to do with precipitating the reaction, is testimony to the great abundance of stimuli to instinctive behavior. In general, then, the fact that modern civilization is different from the hunting cultures does not imply necessarily that any lack of use of the human instinctive equipment is due to lack of stimuli. There are, it is observed, variations in the prevalence of stimuli for a particular type of activity in modern culture. Thus isolation removes many stimuli, whereas we say there is a great deal of stimulation and temptation in a city. But remembering the part bodily preparation may play in instinctive behavior, it does not appear probable that any lack of exercise of the instinctive equipment in modern culture would be due to lack of stimuli, save in exceptional situations.

What seems more probable is, not the lack of stimuli, but denial of the response. Instinctive behavior consists in the attention to the stimuli and also in the response in some motor reaction.

A natural response to stimuli that arouse pugnacity is fighting. The craving is not only aroused but there is also a satisfying of the desire. Desires may be satisfied sometimes in various ways and sometimes the demands are quite specific. An angry person gets some satisfaction in venting anger on various objects or persons rather than on the particular stimulus. Competitive games involving muscular exercise probably relieve somewhat the tension of anger and may mean also the utilization of glycogen poured into the blood during anger. Anxiety which contains an element of fear finds outlets in many different ways. The fact that neurotics express anxiety in the very safest of situations is an indication of the ease with which an outlet is found. There is a great variety of outlets possible for the instinct of curiosity. To the extent to which there are varieties of cultural responses to an instinctive tendency it is difficult to repress an instinct, and the lack of adaptation to culture due to the repression of instincts is less probable.

Nevertheless, there is such a thing as repression of instinctive tendencies; there are wants that are not satisfied. In fact, tendencies to react are inhibited by thousands every day. Such repression occurs whenever we have occasion to show self-control, make a choice, and whenever we concentrate or fix our attention. These many instances are relatively unimportant compared to the repression of strong motives, however. In the hunting cultures, the more powerful desires were repressed. Wherever there is group life such control must indeed take place. In primitive cultures, the rigidity of custom and the strength of taboos imply attempts to control the instincts. Outlets in particular directions are forbidden. But there are no comparative censuses of the repression of instincts in primitive culture and in modern culture.

The inhibition of natural response to stimuli. Another aspect of the nature of instincts that is of importance for the theory we are discussing is what happens when the natural completion of an instinctive act is prohibited, when a desire is aroused but not satisfied. The answer to this question by psychologists is not clear and positive. On the one hand, it is argued that certainly in some cases nothing of particular importance happens. As long as the stimulus is present there is a tension or feeling of unrest but with the removal of the stimulus the mechanism ceases to be active. In cases of inhibition involved in many minor instances of choice, or control or attention, this may be so. On the other hand, it is argued that in the case of certain stronger instincts the prohibition of the accompanying motor reaction may leave something like a more or less permanent tension, permanent until some discharge occurs. Therefore repressed desires though forgotten live on in the mechanism and continue to be sources of motivation, seeking other outlets, continuing the feeling of unrest and producing nervousness. There is some evidence, aside from psychoanalytic sources, that certain activities continue even after the removal of the stimulus, as in the frequently cited case of the hunting dog that has lost the scent. Also, though the external stimuli may be removed there may still exist certain internal stimuli. In cases where repressed instincts continue to be a disturbing factor, the repression of instincts is of more serious consequence than when the desire or activity simply ceases.

To organize these questions that arise from the nature of instinct in such way as to yield the answers demanded by our theory is difficult. Perhaps we may find in the prevalence of functional nervous diseases indices of the harmful extent to which repression of the instincts is carried in modern civilization. We shall, therefore, after summarizing the argument, take up for consideration neurosis and psychosis.

Summary of argument. We have in the preceding paragraphs formulated the problem of adjustment between modern culture and human nature as seen from the approach of social evolution and have made some critical observations on this theory of adjustment. The theory may be summarized as follows. For hundreds of thousands of years man lived as a primitive hunter in a crude culture. In a few hundred years culture has radically changed into an elaborate civilization. But man has not changed very much biologically within many thousands of years. A radically and recently changed culture and a constant human nature would therefore seem to indicate a lack of adjustment between the human nature of the cave people and artificial civilization. But our general analysis indicated that so simple a formulation should not be taken uncritically.

Although culture has become greatly different and although it is probably true that the original nature of man has not changed much in many thousands of years, it does not follow merely from these assumptions that there is unusual lack of adaptation, for several reasons. In the first place it is not necessarily true that human nature was perfectly adjusted to the culture of the cave people. The relatively short period of civilization may not be of special significance from the point of view of adaptation, because the adaptation need not be on the biological side alone, and because culture may be bent to fit human nature. The great difference between civilization and the culture of primitive hunters and food gatherers may be largely apparent; a difference in appearance between two cultures may exist yet human nature may function in somewhat the same manner and to the same degree. Furthermore, to state that human nature is constant or has not changed over a long period of time refers only to the original nature that is passed on by heredity. Human nature varies between individuals and may be changed greatly within a lifetime. And finally, although human nature, as thought of in terms of instinctive activities, may be somewhat imperative in its demands on culture for opportunities of outward expression, by virtue of the part the internal mechanism of the organism plays in creating desires, it does not follow that there is lack of adaptation. The fact that the external stimuli of action are almost unlimited in number and the fact that cultural expression of the instincts may find so many varied outlets reduce somewhat the chances of lack of adaptation implied in the original statement of the theory.

The foregoing theory of the adjustment of human nature and civilization from purely general considerations hardly justifies an uncritical reliance upon it. There may be a good deal of truth in it or there may not. It is hard to prove either way from general considerations. The theory does seem to form a very good background to problems of human nature. But it is so general as to be dangerous as a social philosophy or as a working principle if applied in a specific case without attention to the specific problem. It is somewhat like the principles of natural selection, struggle for existence, and survival of the fittest in biology. Such principles play their part in evolution; but, as a general philosophy of life, it is hard to tell just how applicable they are in a definite instance. Any general principle must undergo careful consideration in any specific application. It seems desirable, therefore, to make some observations on particular cases of lack of adaptation, and see whether such special analyses correspond to the theory.

2

EVIDENCE OF LACK OF ADJUSTMENT: NERVOUSNESS AND INSANITY

Evidences of lack of adaptation to environment on the part of physical man are found in death, disease, chronic fatigue, etc. Similarly we think evidences of lack of adjustment between culture and the psychological equipment of man are found in nervousness and insanity. Also a good many different social problems reveal a lack of harmony between psychological man and culture, but first we shall be concerned with neuroses and functional psychoses as indices of such maladjustment. Nervous symptoms we would naturally expect as evidence of psychological maladjustment.

Our inquiry is not concerned with accidental injury to, nor with the actual organic diseases of, the central nervous system, nor with the hereditary mental defects popularly known as feeble-mindedness. But after the foregoing types are subtracted there remain a number of kinds of nervous disorders such as hysteria, morbid compulsions, anxiety-neuroses, paranoia, melancholia, manic-depressive cases, where there may not be a permanent impairment of structure but where the difficulty seems to lie in the functioning of the structure. In any case, these so-called functional disorders appear to be occasioned or modified by the cultural environment and by psychological causes rather than, or in addition to, physical or physiological factors. Such an analysis does not necessarily rule out the hereditary factor in the functional disorders. In any group of persons, the susceptibility of inherited equipment to nervous disorders will vary. Tendencies or predispositions towards nervous instability are inherited. But the actual development of these disorders will also depend upon the cultural environment.

The nature of functional nervous disorders. Accepting, therefore, the point that many nervous disorders are evidences of psychological maladjustment occasioned by cultural influences operating psychologically rather than physically, we may next inquire into the nature of these nervous disorders. For our purposes it is not necessary to develop a systematic account of the theory of nervous diseases; it is desirable to utilize only such considerations as throw light on the problem of the adjustment of human nature and culture.

A trait common to the patients suffering from functional insanity is the strangeness of their mental outlook.[1] Their views of many phenomena appear unreal to the person in mental health. This trait is very notable in acute cases of neuroses and is perhaps present to greater or less extent in mild neuroses. A knowledge of the mental content of these patients reveals the fact that they live mentally in an essentially unreal or imaginary world. For instance, the persecutory and grandiose conceptions of the paranoiac and the morbid doubts of the compulsion neurosis are essentially fantasies. The conditions and situations of life which they see appear very diffcrent to them from what they do to well persons.

[1] Bernard Hart, *The Psychology of Insanity*.

Another trait that appears to be present or to have been present in these disorders is mental conflict, a fact of some significance for the theory under discussion. Such a mental conflict is more easily seen in the cases of neurotics and has been observed in the functional psychoses. The history of these cases frequently reveals the onset of the disorder at a period of conflicting desires, and an analysis of the mental content shows evidences of such a conflict. Thus one may have very strong libidinous desires, the gratification of which may be incompatible with certain other desires bound up with social standards and such conflicting impulses may lead to mental disease.

The trait of unreality and the trait of mental conflict are connected if it can be shown that one set of the cravings involved in the conflict finds expression in this play of imagination which makes the conceptions of unreality. It is true that the imaginative world is frequently so constructed as to furnish a partial fulfillment of desires involved in the conflict. Thus the unreal world of the neurotics becomes intelligible, especially, if we admit the use of a number of mental devices such as symbolism, rationalization, projection, compensation, displacement and various other distortion mechanisms. It would take us too far afield here to describe these mental traits. Descriptions may be found, however, in a number of books.[2] It is indeed quite conceivable that the world of the insane is the mental expression of the cravings involved in mental conflicts.

Factors in mental conflict. Our interest lies chiefly in the nature of these conflicts. What are the desires that are found in conflict in the functional nervous diseases? What instincts are involved? Can these conflicts be seen in terms of the original nature of man and culture? In the cases that Freud has studied he finds one element in the conflict practically always to be the sex desires.[3] Sex, however, is conceived by Freud to be a force, much more complex and given a much wider meaning than is understood by the average man; for instance, he designates as sex many manifestations of affection. He also sees sex closely bound up with fear, anger, display, art, religion, and various instinctive tendencies. Jung along with Freud calls one element in his conflict the libido, but Jung defines the libido as much more comprehensive even than Freud's sex.[4] It seems to be somewhat similar to what is ordinarily called the soul or spirit of man, a sort of life force. Adler sees the conflict as arising from the constitutional limita-

[2] Bernard Hart, *Psychology of Insanity*. H. W. Frink, *Morbid Fears and Compulsions*.
[3] Sigmund Freud, *A General Introduction to Psychoanalysis*.
[4] Carl G. Jung, *Collected Papers on Analytical Psychology*.

tions and defects of man's equipment along various lines and attempts to compensate psychologically for these defects as they are related to the various desires of life. [5] Hart, Rivers and various other writers think that sex has been stressed too much as a factor in the conflict or else that further research will show other instincts than sex as strong factors in the conflict. [6] Kempf's theory is that a conflict exists between the craving of various autonomic segments. Such a conflict results when access to the projicient motor apparatus is denied one portion of the stimulated autonomic apparatus by various other integrated parts of the autonomic system that dominate the neural paths. [7] We do not know just what the relationship is between the stimulation of the autonomic functions and the arousing of the instincts. The behavior that we call insane occurs when some autonomic segment hitherto prevented from access to certain nerve paths gets a control over the projicient motor apparatus. Kempf's theory of the autonomic functions is not apparently incompatible with the account of the instincts previously set forth.

The forces in the conflict most frequently discussed by the authors just mentioned are in the

[5] Alfred Adler, *The Neurotic Constitution.*
[6] Bernard Hart, *The Psychology of Insanity.* W. H. R. Rivers, *Instinct and the Unconscious.*
[7] Edward J. Kempf, *Psychopathology.*

nature of individual cravings and impulses, while the other factors in the conflict opposed to these cravings are forces that are like the desires to conform to social codes, seldom discussed by psychopathologists. These social forces in the conflict are quite important from the standpoint of culture, and we wish now to inquire into their nature. Freud speaks of the force opposing the sex as a censor. The censorship operates to make us conform to social standards. Kempf thinks of the cravings of an autonomic segment as being opposed by an integration of other autonomic segments that have a more complete control over the cerebro-spinal paths. These integrated autonomic segments slowly built up, he thinks, are the sources of one's personality, one's self that functions as an accepted social being. So it would seem that the opposing forces are certain tendencies that motivate social behavior, that respect and conform to social codes and moral standards. These tendencies may of course have certain springs of action in the gregarious instinct, in sociability or in the instinct of self-assertion. We do not know what the instinctive or mechanistic basis may be, but certainly they are the forces that make us conform to group life, that make us sensitive to the opinions of others. It follows, therefore, that the nature of social codes and group standards gives the particularistic direction to these forces. Just what accepted conduct is, cultural standards play a part in determining. So in a sense culture seems to be in part lined up against certain cravings that are rather close to what is thought of as original nature.

Comparison of the theory of original nature and culture and the theory of neuroses. The theory of neuroses that we have been discussing does seem to be in conformity with, and even supplements, the theory that artificial civilization produces maladjustments with the original nature of man. The theory of the primitive hunter in the modern factory sets forth the argument that the psychological equipment of man in the hunting cultures functioned fairly well, but that in modern factory life it is only partially used, resulting in overuse of some parts of the equipment and under-use of other parts, occasioning maladjustment. The theory of the neuroses we have discussed shows the great prevalence in neuroses of mental conflict between certain instinctive cravings strongly suggestive of original nature and forces that strive to conform to cultural standards. As far as I know these two theories have not been systematically compared, although Freud strongly suggests various implications of this nature in his *Reflections on War and Death,* and superficial connections have been obvious to several writers. To compare these two theories more fully necessitates a more detailed consideration of theories of the neuroses; and as one inquires into the details of the etiology of neuroses, the writers break up into rival groups with the claims of no one group substantiated.

There are, however, a good many who would agree that in so far as psychoneuroses and functional psychoses are not hereditary the foundations for them are frequently laid by the environmental influences affecting the life of the child and the infant. That the influences of childhood are powerful in shaping the adult should not appear strange; but ordinarily the full significance of influences at this time is not appreciated by adults and certainly not to the extent that some students of neuroses demand for them. The parents are agents that are particularly powerful in influencing the child; and probably the medium of their great influence is affection. According to Freud's theory the foundations are laid for future neuroses in childhood, although the precipitating agencies may be the strains occurring in adult life.

Closer analysis of the causes of neuroses shows that the sex instincts seem most frequently involved. According to Freud's evidence, at least, it is not the repression of the instincts in general or of any particular part of the original nature of man that is found in the etiology of neuroses, but quite specifically the repression of the sex instinct. For instance, Freud has somewhere said that whenever the sex life is functioning normally there is never a neurosis, or words to this effect, although he does not claim that when the sex instinct is not functioning normally there is necessarily a neurosis. There may be, however, some question as to just what the normal functioning of sex is. But the derangement that is claimed to occur in certain cases of conflict involving the sex motives does not follow, as would ordinarily be thought, because of sexual continence or particularly because of the failure to gratify the sexual desires with reference to the sexual object. The situation is much more complicated; there are various outlets to sex, and, strange to say, the trouble is frequently traced back to the sex life of childhood. While it is true that psychoanalytic evidence stresses the repression of only one part of man's psychological equipment, sex, nevertheless there seems to be a very close relationship of sex to such native tendencies as self-assertion, anger, fear, and various other motives. Other researches may show lack of adjustment of other instincts than sex. It is also to be remembered, that even if the non-hereditary influences that lay the foundation for neuroses, are effective in childhood, nevertheless the precipitating factors in adult life commonly associated with emotional shock, strain, overwork, etc., may involve a repression of various other parts of man's psychological equipment.

The cultural influences of child life. Another interest in comparing these two theories is to inquire what are the cultural conditions that make neuroses. Are the conditions found in the simpler cultures of the hunting peoples as likely to develop neuroses and psychoses as the modern social conditions? Unfortunately the psychopathologists do not answer these questions. There is still controversy as to the causes of mental disease. Psychopathologists are concerned as practicing physicians with helping the individual and not in altering the social system. There has been little development of preventive medicine in the field of mental disease. So it is naturally difficult to describe the cultural conditions that favor these disorders. From the foregoing analyses it would appear that the cultural conditions affecting neuroses are of two sorts. One is the conditions influencing early child life and supposedly laying the basis of any future nervous trouble that may develop. The other is the immediate specific situations that precipitate the outbreak of the disorders.

In regard to the conditions affecting child life, the theories are somewhat elaborate and by no means generally accepted or proved. These theories are set forth in the literature previously cited. In general they concern misdirected parental affection, including the much discussed Œdipus complex, lack of harmony in the family life of parents, bad personal habits in connection with the various openings to the body, the so-called erogenous zones, the lack of information or bad education in matters of sex, the over-accentuation of prudery, shame and disgust. It is also conceivable that such physical conditions as poverty, overcrowding, bad housing, school systems and general neglect of children may be factors. Some of these influences may appear to be prevalent in modern social conditions, but there seems to be no reason why many of them might not be found surrounding the child life in the hunting cultures. These factors do not seem to be correlated with the broad classifications of economic cultures, such as the hoe cultures, the domestication of cattle, land economy, the handicrafts or machine industry. It is possible that with some kinds of family life in modern times children may be thus adversely affected, but such conditions do not appear to be a necessary part of such great characteristics of modern civilization as the great increase in material culture and the adjustment thereto. About the life of children in the primitive cultures our knowledge is meagre, but the affection of parents and adults for children is frequently commented upon by the traveler, the missionary and the ethnologist. The period of nursing is usually long. Sex is taken more as a matter of course, and less attended by shame and prudery.

The cultural influences of adult life. Regarding the precipitation of neuroses and psychoses in adult life, it is commonly admitted that events and conditions of adult life play their part in causing functional nervous diseases, even granting that the groundwork may be found in heredity and early child life. That especial conditions surrounding adult life can bring on neuroses is seen from the great number of mental disorders that were brought on by the soldier's life. These cases were at first called shell shock, but were later shown to be functional nervous disorders, in which, by the way, the sex element is said to be not so obvious nor so impressive.

Another indication that cultural conditions are correlated with the frequency of mental disorders is seen from the fact that such frequencies are greater in urban than in rural districts. For instance, the rejections of drafted men with nervous diseases for military service in the recent war were greater for men from the urban districts as the following ratios show. The ratios are the percentages of rejections in rural districts divided by the percentages of rejections in urban districts, so that a ratio less than 1 indicates a greater prevalence in urban districts. Hysteria, 1.44; psychoses, 1.00; psychoneuroses, 0.95; constitutional psychopathic states, 0.81; neurasthenia, 0.81; dementia præcox, 0.76; general paralysis of the insane, 0.67.[8] The differences are even greater when the larger cities are compared. It should be remembered that much of the urban area consists of small towns and also that the population of cities is built up recently in part by migrations of adults from rural districts.

Evidence leading to the same general conclusion is presented in a survey of first admissions to hospitals for the insane in nine States of the United States in 1919 as shown in the following table.[9]

RATES OF FIRST ADMISSIONS FROM URBAN AND RURAL DISTRICTS

	Rates per 100,000 of population of same environment	
	Urban	Rural
Senile	7.2	5.4
With cerebral arteriosclerosis	3.3	1.4

[8] Love and Davenport, *Defects in Drafted Men*, pp. 351-2.
[9] Pollock and Furbush, "Mental Diseases in Twelve States, 1919," *Mental Hygiene,* Vol. V, April, 1921, No. 2, pp. 353–389.

	Rates per 100,000 of population of same environment	
	Urban	Rural
General paralysis	8.6	2.0
Alcoholic	2.8	0.6
Manic-depressive	10.5	6.8
Dementia præcox	19.4	9.5
All psychoses	68.2	36.0

One wonders whether the work in modern factories and mills brings on mental disorders. Long hours of monotonous work is the situation where one expects only a partial use of the psychological equipment. Numbers of psychopaths have been enumerated in industry but it is probable a number of such cases would be found in any random sample of the population. Of the rejections of drafted men, the eastern manufacturing sections showed high proportions of cases of neurasthenia, hysteria, neurosis, dementia præcox, psychasthenia and psychoneuroses, but there were other classes of mental disorders in not such high proportions. In such a classification there are other factors than occupations, that make comparisons not very trustworthy. If labor in factories and mills was a factor in producing such disorders, it would be expected that there would be greater proportions among men than among women, since there are much larger numbers of men working in industry than women, but the sex differences in total mental disorders as seen in hospital records are not great.

It is customary to think of strain as a condition favorable to the development of nervous breakdown. But one wonders what strain is in psychological terms. Is it due to overwork and does it imply the overuse of some instincts and the under-use of others? Is it due to the great stimulation of ambition to utilize the opportunities occurring in a competitive environment and in a changing culture? Is it the long-continued application to a single task? Or is it due to the restrictions and impositions of moral conduct in a stimulating atmosphere? Perhaps the strain arises from some crisis involving the affections?

Mental disease in primitive life. In regard to conditions affecting psychoses and neuroses among people living in simple cultures, we do not have much information. Cases of hysteria, insanity and homosexuality have been observed among these peoples, but we do not know in what proportions. The psychopathologists have not investigated cases among the primitive cultures, and the anthropologists are not psychopathologists. Freud, however, has a theoretical treatise, *Totem and Taboo,* dealing with primitive culture. One thinks from reading this book that Freud considers the various factors which he finds operating in neurotics also present among primitive peoples. That customs, taboos, extensive marriage regulations, do impose considerable restriction on the desires of peoples in the simpler cultures is certain. In fact, a familiarity with the different customs of primitive cultures impresses one with the remarkable adaptability of human nature to restrictions on conduct. In his *Totem and Taboo*, Freud tries to explain such primitive institutions as animism and exogamy in terms of the mechanisms operating in the neurosis. Even though strong repressions and motives interrelated as in neuroses are found among peoples with primitive cultures, it does not follow that they will work out into functional nervous disorders. These mental diseases are, it is generally admitted, frequently a matter of degree. That is, the types of conduct of the psychologically insane are also present in the so-called normal individual only to a less degree. There are also various outlets for the energies involved in mental conflict. The peoples with primitive cultures sometimes socialize tendencies that would be repressed in modern societies. Thus the shamans, the religious leaders among the American Indians, are in some tribes selected, for instance, because of the ability to experience hallucinations and because of their queer behavior.

Mental diseases in modern life. That nervous disorders exist in modern society to-day in large numbers is a fact. The third census of the National Committee for Mental Hygiene shows that on January 1, 1920, in the hospitals in the United States the number of patients with mental diseases was about 1 to every 450 of the population.[10] There are numbers of insane not in hospitals, as the States do not make adequate preparation for their care. New York and Massachusetts are foremost in the provision for their insane. In these two States there is one patient with mental disease in an institution for about every 275 of the general population. We do not know, unfortunately, how many of these patients are suffering from functional disorders.

The number of first admissions per year shows somewhat better the incidence of insanity than do figures showing the number in institutions at any one time. A survey of mental diseases in twelve States with a total population of about twenty-five million showed that there were 63.8 first admissions to institutions caring for mental disease to every 100,000 of the general population.[11] In other words, every year 1 in every 1600 is admitted to an institution for mental dis-

---

[10] Pollock and Furbush, "Patients with Mental Diseases, Mental Defect, Epilepsy, Alcoholism and Drug Addiction in Institutions in the United States, January 1, 1920," *Mental Hygiene*, Vol. V, No. 1, pp. 139–169.

[11] Pollock and Furbush, "Mental Diseases in Twelve States, 1919," *Mental Hygiene*, Vol. V, No. 2, pp. 353–389.

ease. But this rate is only for one year, whereas men and women in the United States live, on the average, about forty years. The average age at death in the United States in 1913 was 39.8 years.[12] Over a period of 40 years the number of first admissions would be about 1 to every 40 of the general population at any one year, on the basis of a constant population. These figures for first admissions include all types of mental disease, the organic and other classifications as well as the functional.

It would be important if we knew whether insanity were increasing or not. The number of patients with mental diseases in institutions in the United States has increased 469 per cent from 1880 to 1920, while the total population of the United States has increased only 111 per cent; but these figures may mean only that an increasing proportion of the insane are being cared for in institutions.[13]

Against the figures of the frequency of patients in institutions for the care of mental disease should be set the fact that not all cases are found in institutions. Also these figures include only a very small percentage of the neuroses. The

[12] *Mortality Statistics, 1913*, Department of Commerce, Bureau of Census.
[13] *Op. cit., Mental Hygiene,* Vol. V, No. 1, pp. 139–169.

number of cases of mild and acute neuroses must indeed be much larger. Neuroses occasion just as acute suffering if not more than do the various physical illnesses. Very probably the thing we call happiness is related to the state of the nerves more than to economic conditions or to material welfare. However closely paralleled the theory of the neuroses may be with the theory of original human nature and the artificiality of civilization, and however true an index nervous and mental disorders may be as a measure of lack of adjustment between culture and the original psychological nature of man, it is certainly true that neuroses and psychoses are serious social problems in modern society.

3

EVIDENCE OF LACK OF ADJUSTMENT: SOCIAL PROBLEMS

So far the evidence we have considered, of lack of adjustment between human nature and culture, has been the effects of a psychological nature on the individual, as neuroses and psychoses. But evidence may also be sought on the side of culture as well as on the side of the individual. Such evidence is found in social problems rather than individual problems, although such a line of demarcation is not clear-cut.

The current literature dealing with social problems is full of material concerning the behavior of human nature; and as the reader is familiar with modern social issues it will not be necessary to set forth many illustrations. Only a few such problems will be discussed and then only as types of analysis. Such a presentation can be made much more briefly than in the case of the neuroses.

Crime. A conspicuous instance of such a social problem showing evidence of lack of adjustment between human nature and culture is crime. Some crime is due to feeble-mindedness and to insanity, but a good deal of crime is due to social and economic conditions. For instance, social conditions may become so rigorous in their impositions or effects upon human nature that behavior we call crime will be resorted to. Under conditions of food shortage, looting may result. Slaves frequently steal. In periods of economic depression there is more temptation to violate laws regarding property. The amount of crime, particular'y against property, fluctuates with social and economic conditions, and such a fluctuation is thought to occur in lesser degree in crimes against the person, such as murder, assault, and sexual crimes.

In other words, the motives of the crime might not have caused crime if operating at another time or in another culture. Considered apart from the social consequences, such motives might have been quite normal biological desires. The cultural situation may be so framed that it becomes very difficult for the human desires to find satisfaction. A very good illustration is the increase in juvenile crimes that bring children before the juvenile courts in our cities. In the rural districts, the same motives found in the city juvenile delinquent might in many cases function without causing crime. The interests of the group must be protected, of course, against crime, and crime may be unjustifiable on moral grounds, but nevertheless the culture determines rules, the breaking of which is called crime. Crime is clearly evidence of lack of adjustment between human nature and culture.

Sex problems. Another illustration of such lack of satisfactory adjustment is sex problems. Adultery, prostitution and all sexual intercourse out of wedlock are seen as social problems, as is also divorce with the break which it causes in so important a social organization as the family. In these cases culture imposes a code in accordance with which human beings with strong desires often find it difficult to act. Even when there is conformity to the marriage code and when divorces are not granted, there may still be much unhappiness, a sign of unsatisfactory adjustment. The conflict of sex codes and human nature is a widespread and frequent cause of unhappiness. Sex, strong and variable, meets with difficulty in making adjustment to any rigid sex code, however moral it may be.

Selfishness. Perhaps the psychological factor underlying the largest number of social problems is selfishness. The fact that a great majority of individuals in most of the situations of life feel their own interests more strongly than the interests of others and act accordingly is fundamental in nearly all social problems. A large number of modern social problems flow from the unequal distribution of property; one reason why wealth is so unequally accumulated is the pursuit of one's selfish interests with not enough considerations for the interests of others, and another reason is the scarcity of social limitations upon such selfish actions. More or less unrestricted freedom to accumulate wealth may be legitimate, and culture may have grown more thereby; nevertheless a whole host of social problems follow because of this unequal distribution of income. Inequality in the distribution of wealth will be found a very significant factor in poverty, unemployment, disease, taxation, labor, government, war, and many other problems. If we were less selfish or more considerate, in some effective social manner, of the interests of others, many of our present-day social problems would be minor ones. A highly developed accumulation of material culture such as we have in modern society provides a wonderful opportunity for an apparently ruthless exploitation of selfish interests. In other words, the fundamental self-interest of our natures when functioning in a great wealth of material culture undergoing rapid change creates social problems in abundance which are evidence of a bad adjustment.

Many other social problems that show human nature and culture in a not altogether satisfactory adjustment might be cited. In fact, human nature is really a factor in all social problems, in the sense that if our human nature were different the social problems would either not exist or else would be different, because all social phenomena involve the two factors, human nature and culture. We are not in this paragraph concerned with whether these problems are due to the biological factor or to culture, but are interested in showing that social problems are indices of maladjustment. Social problems as well as neuroses, then, furnish evidence of lack of adaptation between human nature and culture.

4

CHANGING HUMAN NATURE VERSUS CONTROLLING SOCIAL EVOLUTION

So far we have shown that the adjustment between culture and human nature is not as satisfactory as is desired; and we have seen something of the theories as to why there is this lack of adjustment. To readers living in an age of so much social effort for improvement, the question naturally arises as to what can be done to bring about a better adjustment. This question, though stated in very large terms, seems appropriate, particularly since an effort to apply scientific methods to social questions is being made. Though we may not be able to answer definitely and scientifically the question of how best to adjust human nature and culture, yet some consideration of this question may be of value. To many, so general and simple a statement as the problem of adjustment between human nature and culture may be objectionable, since it may appear best to consider a series of special situations in detail. The value of such special studies of adjustment is realized and many excellent studies have been made and are being made. It is realized that not only is a good deal lost in attempting to make a general formulation, but generalizations are difficult to substantiate. Nevertheless there is a certain value in trying to look at the question in its broadest aspects.

Changing human nature. A harmonious relationship between culture and human nature may conceivably be attained by making the adaptations largely on the part of human nature or largely on the part of culture, or some adjustments on the part of both human nature and culture. We shall consider first the problem of changing human nature to fit the culture, the way the problem has been viewed, to a large extent, in the past, particularly from the point of view of religion and of morals. Such a method of adjustment seemed reasonable in the past when cultural growth was slow; not many changes occurred within a period of time so short as a few generations. To man with limitations to his knowledge of the past, culture appeared somewhat stationary. On the other hand, the adaptability of human nature through habit and will power appeared as a fact. The bad adaptations were labelled as evil and the approved adaptations were called good. And the problem of adaptation was to seek the good and eschew the evil. Such a method of controlling or modifying human nature within a lifetime has been of great practical value.

Changing the hereditary basis of human nature. With the rise of the science of biology a good deal of emphasis was placed upon the process of biological adaptation. The changing of species was seen in terms of adaptation to environment. Those organisms not adapted, unfit to survive in the struggle for existence, died. The changing that was done in order to establish adaptation was on the side of the organism rather than environment. That is, nature did not bend the environment to fit the organism. Casual readers of biology, therefore, have naturally thought of the problem of adapting man to environment a good deal in terms of changing man. The programme of eugenics is a programme which attempts to achieve desirable changes in biological man. But with the passing of the theory of the inheritance of acquired characteristics and the appreciation of the infrequency of mutations, the process of biological change for purposes of adaptation to culture is seen to be very slow. This point is of considerable importance because it emphasizes a stable biological nature. Of course selection may be made within the limits of variation, and some better adaptation may thereby be achieved, in so far as those at one end of the curve are better adapted than those at the other end. Such a selective process is difficult to realize practically. Careful readers of biology, therefore, realize that any idea of changing the biological nature of man is a very ambitious one, and are impressed with the slowness of biological change. We do not know what the researches of biology may discover, but at present the knowledge necessary for the control desired in eugenics is meagre. Practically, therefore, a rapid, controlled change in the inherited biological nature of man seems almost impossible for the present.

Changing human nature for a lifetime. This conclusion does not mean that the inherited nature of man may not be highly adaptable within a lifetime. In fact, a great variety of adaptations have been made this way in the past, and such has been the approved programme of statecraft, religion and morals, and justified to a great extent by experience. But with the rise of abnormal psychology some skepticism arises in regard to a whole-hearted approval of this method of adjustment. The point of the difficulty lies in the fact that a good deal of the bending of human nature to fit the cultural environment means a repression of quite normal biological processes and denial in many cases of the normal expression of some instinctive tendencies. This repression, in some cases, as was observed in the etiology of neuroses, causes strain, unhappiness, mental conflict and neuroses.

It is difficult to generalize as to the extent of such harmful repression as a method of adaptation, and such an estimate involves, as was pointed out, more knowledge as to the extent and causes of neuroses than we now have. But for those whose programme calls for a bending of human nature to fit the culture, it should be recognized that the lesson of recent researches in abnormal psychology indicates that there are limits to which human nature may be bent in the process of adjustment to social conditions. But the goal of those seeking adjustments between culture and human nature is not only to avoid the danger limits, but to seek the best possible adjustments. For such a goal, it is not possible to indicate how much or how little repression is desired or what the nature of such repression should be. These points should be taken up in detail. Of course, the practical and psychological value of self-control is appreciated. There must be a very large amount of such repression each day. The point is that in such repression one should endeavor to avoid the kind that leads to serious mental conflict.

Changing culture. When it is realized that there is slight prospect of changing the hereditary traits of biological man to fit culture, and when it is seen that it is not the happiest solution to bend human nature far within a lifetime, in making adjustments to culture, we naturally turn to the attractive idea of modifying culture to fit human nature. This theme has been very interestingly presented by Graham Wallas in his *The Great Society*. He there discusses the unsatisfactoriness of the "balked" instinct and suggests a way out through changes in the social environment. Such a possibility will occur to one when the vast amount of cultural change that is taking place today is observed in comparison with the great stability of biological man. It is the stream of culture that is undergoing rapid change and not the biological stock. Therefore why attempt to change the biological stock to fit culture? Why not direct the changes that are occurring in culture to fit man, and so reach a better adjustment? The fact that such a plan will be welcomed emotionally by most of us who have felt the annoyance of unsatisfied desires, should put us on guard against uncritically putting our faith in such a programme.

While it is true that the changes occurring today are preponderantly in the culture rather than in biological man, it does not follow that these cultural changes are controlled and purposively directed by man. Despite the fact that man appears as an active agent in these changes, cultural factors such as social forces and economic processes play quite a determining part in these changes. It is not true that man creates culture freely as he wills. The extent to which man is a freely determining agent in directing social evolution is one of the fundamental questions in sociology. This question is very similar to the old philosophical and psychological question of freedom of the will. It is also at the root of the question of the influence of the great man in history. An understanding of this problem of freedom and power of the will and of social determinism in cultural change is of far-reaching significance, extending beyond the purpose for which we are now considering it. But we must not omit some important observations which will throw a good deal of light on it.

Social forces. The material presented in the previous sections shows that culture grows because of purely cultural factors, despite the fact that this growth occurs through the medium of human beings. Thus the nature of the inventions that will be made depends in large part upon the existing plane of culture, and there is a relationship between the number of inventions and the amount of the existing material culture out of which to make the inventions. In other words, the nature of the growth of culture depends upon past development and accumulations. Cultural growth and change in a particular locality result from adopting elements from other cultures as a result of contacts. If a culture is isolated changes take place very slowly indeed. But if lines of communication are opened between a hitherto isolated culture and various other different cultures, changes will occur because of cultural diffusion. In other words, by taking thought or through the power of the will, man in isolated cultures does not produce the changes that come through cultural processes like diffusion. The growth of culture within a particular locality is to a much less degree due to inventions within that locality than to diffusions from other cultures.

The deterministic nature of cultural change. Also, there is a good deal of evidence to indicate that the accumulation or growth of culture reaches a stage where certain inventions if not inevitable are certainly to a high degree probable, given a certain level of mental ability. The fact that an invention is independently made in several localities suggests such a cultural preparation. This probability of an invention due to cultural preparations is more noticeable perhaps in later cultures than in earlier cultures. In earlier cultures the accidental element may have been more frequent. Observation of such processes diminishes somewhat one's faith in man's ability to create or change culture howsoever he wills.

The unpredictable social effects of inventions. Furthermore, it should be remembered, that although man may invent because of purpose or desires or will, the cultural effects of such changes thus started are far more than can be seen at the time of the invention. The consequences of some inventions cannot be foreseen, much less controlled. In fact a good many inventions in the material culture, instead of being purposively directed for control of culture, rather introduce a good many new problems of control. This is especially true of certain very important changes such as the domestication of cattle, the use of the plow, or the use of steam. In fact, recently so many and such significant changes have been occurring in the material culture, that man appears hard put to it to keep up with the changes, rather than appearing in the supreme rôle of planning, controlling and directing them.

The great man and social change. It is understandable how the social or cultural forces as causes of changes are obscured and how they are seen in terms of man's ability, will, and purpose. In the first place, man always appears as an active agent in any social change, in the sense that none of these changes could take place without man. The invention, however inevitable, is made by man and social movements proceed through the instrumentality of leaders. Human nature with its interest in personalities, its hero-worshipping tendencies, its appreciation of leadership, is more interested in giving recognition of achievement to a human being than to some abstract conception of some social force. Besides, these social forces are not easily seen nor their nature readily known. James J. Hill is given due credit for having built the Great Northern and the Northern Pacific railroads. But if James J. Hill had never lived the railroad lines would have been built across this great northwestern area to the Pacific Ocean. The fact that Hill built the railroads meant a great deal to a particular financial group; and the particular great man is often of utmost significance to a particular social, economic or political group in the competition for control and rewards. Perhaps the great man is a more decisive factor in political groups, in setting national boundary lines, in war, or in other forms of culture such as art or religion, than in material culture. To the extent that social forces are causes of development rather than leaders and great men, to that extent will it be difficult to modify the culture of the future for the purpose of making it better adapted to human nature.

Regarding the relative influence of the great man and of social forces, which it is difficult to measure and in the absence of data is so much a matter of interpretation, there is always a strong subjective element in one's attitude. Thus men of great self-assertiveness, of potency, of great hope and faith, active in effort and eager for achievement, probably have a strong subjective bias in giving recognition to men's power over culture. Such subjective elements are sure to distort the truth until the facts to prove the case one way or another are known. There has been enough discussion to show that the difficulties of controlling the cultural stream or directing its course according to our will are very easy to underestimate. In fact, if the analysis be true, it appears like a grandiose dream to think of controlling according to the will of man the course of social evolution. Our conclusions indicate indeed that to change man to fit culture or to change culture to fit man is each so difficult a task as to be almost impossible.

5

SUGGESTIONS FOR BETTER ADJUSTMENTS

While it does seem true at the present stage of development of man and of culture that it is futile to think of man's ability freely to control cultural changes as he wills, still it is thinkable that a more harmonious adaptation of culture to man may be made without any such deity-like power over culture as a whole. In other words, to make a more desirable adjustment, it is not necessary to have all power or even to make wholesale changes in culture. Indeed it is conceivable that by making certain changes in culture, relatively minor compared to the plan of directing culture as a whole, a more harmonious adjustment may be attained. For instance, the acuteness of the lack of adjustment between culture and human nature is manifested in certain spots or areas like neuroses and social problems. To bring about better adjustment the attention should be focused chiefly on the particular fields where the maladjustment is most serious. The achievement of better adaptation even in such problems may be very difficult to make. Yet such a programme would appear to be much more practicable than the larger plan of directing the course of civilization. In the growth of culture there are probably limits to the lack of harmony with human nature, since in adopting new cultural forms human desires play some part. The bringing about of a more harmonious relationship, then, concerns certain special fields rather than culture or human nature as a whole.

This Part is not concerned primarily with amelioration. There are readers who are fired with so great a zeal for making the world more livable that plans of change for the better are to them the only things worth while. Such an attitude cannot be praised too highly. These individuals furnish the drive that results in making the world a better place to live in. Such readers will feel the inadequacy of the space given to constructive plans and the fragmentary nature of what are merely suggestions for better adjustment. In answer it may be said that there is a value to preliminary analysis, which characterizes the present and the preceding chapters. Plans may be worked out more fully after certain fundamentals are clear. Furthermore, there are a great number of individuals doing most excellent work on important practical programmes. It is because there is so much constructive work done on practical programmes that the following suggestions are made less extensive and with less regard for emphasis and relative importance.

Nervous disorders. In so far as psychoses and neuroses are evidences of lack of adaptation, attention should be concentrated on preventing these functional nervous disorders. A very important group of psychopathologists claim that neuroses have a sexual origin and that disturbances of a somewhat sexual nature are found in psychoses. If the sexual theories of many mental and nervous disorders should prove true, then the problem of better adaptation would concern primarily the adjustment in regard to this complex sex instinct. It is not certain now just how this could be done. It might concern a more intelligent expression of parental affection. It might involve a wiser sexual education, particularly in very early life. Or it might involve certain changes in the general social attitude towards sex. Such social programmes would be more or less difficult to attain. In some cases serious mental conflicts are, it seems, impossible to prevent. Some form of therapeutic or prophylactic treatment might be devised so as to be widely accessible.

Sublimation. Some attention has been paid to a process known as sublimation as a happy solution of the sexual situation. There is a good deal of lack of agreement as to what the process is and some psychologists deny that there is such a phenomenon. Since there is so little agreement as to what sublimation is, we might be pardoned for passing it by. But if there is such a process its importance is quite great and some comment is desirable. According to most writers on sublimation the energy of the libido can be drawn into channels other than customary sexual channels. Thus the libido may be turned to social, religious, artistic or scientific aims. One would therefore expect better adjustments to be made by a general development of social, religious, artistic or scientific aspects of culture. There is some evidence to indicate that if this sublimation of the sex instinct occurs it takes place chiefly in very early life. Much sublimation in childhood, while it might make the individual more religious or more artistic, does not appear to be a guarantee against mental conflict. And, indeed, there are limits to the extent of sublimation. From certain ethical and social standards a high degree of sublimation appears to be desirable; and perhaps it may be desirable biologically and psychologically. We know very little about how sublimation may purposively and practically be brought about.

Strain. It is probable that neuroses and functional psychoses may be precipitated in adult life as a result of general strain, despite the fact that some individuals appear to stand strain remarkably well. But it is borne with only fair success by others. In any case, the severity with which mental strains affect individuals indicates a lack of adjustment. We may therefore consider what can be done to lessen the tension of life in modern civilization. The overuse of some instincts and the under-use of others may theoretically produce a very uncomfortable state which leads to great restlessness and nervousness. Whether such a state be a strain or whether it helps to precipitate a neurosis, it is frequently not a very satisfactory psychological state of being for an individual, particularly when persisting over a long time. It seems to be true that the division of labor and the social differentiation accompanying modern civilization do lead to a life where some types of response to stimuli occur very frequently and monotonously. The specialization of modern life means for some an extensive use of only a part of the varied and wonderful equipment of man. Just how serious this unequal functioning is we do not know. The more normal adaptation would appear ideally to be one where all parts of man's equipment would function perhaps not exactly as it did in the days of the cave people, but nevertheless to a degree which would correspond to some normal biological standard. It may not be possible to define such a standard, and the human system may show a high degree of variability in this respect, but some such goal is desirable.

Obstacles to the use of our psychological equipment. Assuming on the part of some groups an unsatisfactory emotional and instinctive life, how can more normal functioning be attained? Prominent obstacles are long hours of labor, specialization of labor and social codes. There are also other obstacles. Our codes of conduct frequently show a certain rigidity apparently not suited to the variation due to change nor to the variability due to heterogeneity. There seems to be something akin to survivals in our codes. Perhaps well suited to earlier conditions, they have not changed to meet the changed material conditions. Also, no doubt, the great development of science reacts on our morals. Codes of conduct are undergoing, nevertheless, much change. However, there will always be social pressure to conform in conduct. There will always be a code of morals, resulting in repression of desires, even though they may be changed greatly in the interest of better adjustments.

With regard to specialization, the trend appears to be towards more rather than less of it. Specialization, particularly among the manual workers in modern industry, means less variety in occupation and an activity during working hours somewhat machine-like. Specialization plus the long working day, particularly at uninteresting tasks, does not give a picture of well balanced activity. The shortcomings of specialization in labor may be counterbalanced by fewer hours of labor. The movement is still in the direction of fewer working hours per day. But to maintain production, probably for some time to come, a fairly large number of hours of labor per day will have to be worked. Under either socialism or capitalism, we shall have specialization. And we shall always have moral codes. So no doubt there will be tendencies to an unbalanced use of man's original equipment. There will always be repression of desires. What shall be done in the face of specialization, social pressure, morality, ambition, repression, necessary hours of labor, and the inherent inevitability of conflicting interests and motives?

Substitution. The idea of substitutive activities arises as a solution. It is suggested from the partial use of man's physical equipment. Individuals following sedentary occupations do not in the course of their work use their muscles as fully as did the primitive hunter. To meet such a situation we have invented the gymnasium and devised various athletic activities. What seems to be needed is some invention that will do for the mechanisms of instinct what the gymnasium does for the muscles. That is, certain instinctive tendencies, certain desires, certain mechanisms of psychological reactions that do not find expression in the daily routine of life, need the use of substitutive devices that would provide the desired activity and yet be in accord with moral and social conduct. The urgency of such substitutions depends upon the harmfulness and extent of repression and upon the nature of instinct, matters previously discussed. But that such substitutions are desirable is unquestionable.

Recreation. While there is no such single institution as a gymnasium for the functioning of the instincts, nevertheless it is thought that such services are performed by certain activities which may generally be grouped under the term, recreation. We shall be interested in inquiring concerning recreation as an institution for the functioning of emotional and instinctive activities, particularly those not active during the daily routine. Such a possibility exists because of the fact that the same emotion or instinctive tendency may be incited by many different stimuli and there are many different motor outlets possible for the same instinctive tendency. Thus, self-assertion or acquisitiveness or anger may be aroused by many different stimuli and their manifestations may be various. In recreation a special set of stimuli are formed and special motor outlets are created. Recreation, as the term is here used, is seen as a possible substitute for certain functionings of human nature which are prohibited through the daily tasks of many occupations or through the prohibitions of the moral code or for other reasons. May not some substitute outlet for many of these tendencies be provided in recreation? Modern life provides a great many stimuli to desires which are not gratified. Such stimuli are the multitudinous advertising displays, the behavior of others, the various incidents that appeal to hope and ambition, types of recreation, and pleasures possibly beyond our economic means. Some of these stimuli are popularly called temptations.

Modern life arouses many desires and longings that are not satisfied. Is it not possible that recreation may furnish an outlet for some of these instinctive tendencies?

Psychological aspects of recreation. Obviously emotions and specific instinctive drives are found in recreations. In games, for instance, are seen fear, anxiety, anger, the desire for mastery, self-assertiveness, leadership, sociability. It is possible indeed, if the instincts were listed and the many types of recreation analyzed, that all the instincts would be found operating in one recreation or another. It is therefore quite feasible to provide for the functioning of instincts. Thus in the case of a factory "hand," recreation will enable certain instincts to function which find little opportunity to do so within the factory walls. But in the case where instincts are aroused in the course of daily life but do not complete their expression it is not quite so obvious that recreation will provide the desired outlets. It is a question of the time element between stimulation and expression. Can there be a delay between the beginning and ending of an act of instinctive behavior? One's tendency to self-assertion may be aroused in a committee meeting and not find expression there, but, our point is, can the self-assertion thus aroused find expression in a later meeting of the committee, or in a game of tennis?

That the aroused state may hold for a time is true, as previously instanced, but perhaps the more immediate the completion of the response the more satisfactory it is. The efficacy of delayed substitution will vary with the different desires and in different situations. Much more definite information can be known by a study of particular situations. Generally, however, the use of substitution seems to be rather widely applicable.

Much substitution may occur through activities other than what is customarily known as recreation, as, for instance, in religion or in the pursuit of hobbies. Recreation is, though, a broad and fertile field for utilizing such substitutes.

The idea of substitution is thus seen to be a very fruitful one. It is not to be confused with sublimation. In sublimation an internal change of a more or less permanent character is supposed to occur; whereas in the substitution we are speaking of, manipulation is largely of external situations with no fundamental change in the personality. In substitution, the instincts as they exist in an individual are aroused, or their functioning completed, or both, by substituting stimuli and outlets in the place of others, or in providing them where they do not exist.

The primitive nature of recreation. Concerning recreation, Patrick in his *Psychology of Re-*

laxation has compared the recreation of modern man to the serious activities of our primitive ancestors. This comparison is quite impressive, for instance, in the case of hunting, fishing, and camping. In bull-fighting, in boxing and in football the resemblances are very close. Perhaps he pushes the analogy a little far in the case of baseball, where he says that there are three sets of motions preëminent in baseball that were of survival value in the business of living of the primitive hunter, namely, hitting, throwing and running. This conception of sports conforms to the theory that we are cave men trying to live in an artificial civilization. Of course, in so far as modern sports are objectively the same as the business activities of primitive hunters, presumably somewhat the same instincts would come into play. But also the instincts of the primitive hunter may function in activities where the objective resemblance to the business activities of primitive hunters is very slight. In interpreting recreation in this light one should remember that cultural traits, as, for instance, the learned traits of a primitive hunter, are not inherited. An understanding of this theory of sports is dependent upon an understanding of the theory that we are cave people living in an artificial culture.

Stimulation and expression. The place of recreation in the problem of adjustment under consideration is, in a general way, clear. Some more detailed observations should be made, however, on the nature of recreation. There are really two different kinds of recreation in regard to the functioning of the instincts. One kind stimulates the instincts but makes poor provision for what we have been calling their outlet. Others do not make such provision. It is recalled that there are several distinct parts to an instinctive act. There is the perception or the awareness of the stimuli; the feeling or the emotion is a distinct part; and there is motor expression, or outlet. A complete instinctive act has these three features. In certain types of recreation, there is a satisfactory stimulation of the feelings but apparently very little provision for any motor expression; at least, the drive does not work out through much bodily activity. Where an individual participates in a boxing match or a football game or in various athletic contests, such is not the case, for there is abundant provision for motor outlet. This does not appear on the surface to be so true of a recreation such as attending the theatre, except as there is expression in tears, laughter, or applause. The theatre is a wonderful invention for arousing the emotions. As one identifies oneself with the different characters of the play, one feels love, hate, ambition, rivalry, fear, passion, etc. We do not know very much about the motor outlet in connection with many of these emotions; it is conceivable that there may be outlets or expression with little bodily activity. Activity may occur in various glands during these emotions which may be somewhat similar to the frequently referred-to motor outlet. Again, some muscular activities, like shivering though not massive are distinctly motor and fulfill profound needs. We are not, however, in a position to speak positively concerning the recreations involving little movement. There are, of course, many other types of recreation which are similar to the theatre in that the motor outlet is not impressively recognized.

Observers and participants. Recreations may also be classified according to whether we are observers or participants. It is easier to believe that the instinctive behavior is more complete in the case of the participant than of the observer. The observer at a game is in the same position as an observer at the theatre. There is evidence of emotion but not very much evidence of the activity that is supposed to follow some emotions. Our information is meagre concerning the motor aspect of instinctive behavior; but there is clearly a difference between the arousing of a desire and its gratification. Some types of recreation, such as, for instance, those that appeal to the sex instinct, apparently arouse the instinct but do not provide for the completion of the act. The observer, in contrast to the participant, may have his emotions aroused, but find insufficient outlet. An inventory of the recreations further reveals many such as dancing, card-playing, gambling and talking, concerning which it is not very clear what happens psychologically when one takes part in them.

The importance of recreation. Human behavior does not consist wholly of simple unrelated tendencies such as the instincts. There exist certain desires more general, complex, and flexible and more bound up with the conception of self than the stereotyped tendencies described as instinct in studies of animal behavior. Instinctive tendencies are built up into what McDougall calls the sentiments. In man memory and experience play a great part in determining the nature of the operation of our drives. The mind, the soul and the spirit are other terms used for less specific tendencies. The importance of recreation will presumably be greater, the greater the importance accorded to the more specific tendencies. Recreation will hardly cure a troubled soul, nor will it cure a neurosis. No doubt there are many failures in adjustment to culture that involve a less specific tendency than what we think of as simple instinct, and the value of recreation in such situations is not so great. The importance of recreation in the problem of adjustment also depends upon the extent to which modern culture "balks" the instincts. It is very easy to overemphasize the "balking" of the instincts, for the reason that there are so many different cultural stimuli and cultural outlets for instinctive desires.

We have argued that recreation is a device of considerable value in making adaptation between human nature and culture. It is claimed that the significance of recreation for social theory has not been sufficiently appreciated; nor has it been accorded the place it deserves in sociological literature.

We regret that our investigation does not lead to a more definite formulation. But it should be remembered that human motives are a very tangled web. Their mysteries have been probed by poets, novelists, psychologists and leaders. No one at this time could be so presumptuous as to expect a reduction of the many diverse problems of human nature to a simple formula. Under any form or organization of culture, there will be problems of human nature as long as we live together in groups, which will be always. Still it is thought that a consideration of the instincts, the libido, neuroses, sex problems, substitution and recreation do point to very distinct possibilities of a better adjustment between our modern culture and human nature.

Cultural change involved in social problems. As to the evidence of lack of proper adjustment between culture and human nature as seen in sociological problems such as crime, sex problems and unequal distribution of wealth, it would seem that the modification of the particular cultural features concerned would in general be more practicable than further attempts to change the original nature of man, and somewhat better results would be expected from such a procedure. It was observed that a great many of these social problems flow from the dominance of what is called selfishness and the lack of the power and scope of what is known as altruism. This is of course a profound question and deserves very full and careful consideration at the hands of sociologists. But from the biological consideration of human nature we have been discussing, there is no occasion to depart from the position already taken that to change culture to make the better adjustments is somewhat more practicable than to change human nature. There are, in connection with the problem of selfishness in social probblems, a great many opportunities for arranging cultural situations, not necessarily to diminish or repress selfishness and increase altruism, but rather to keep selfishness in bounds.

Perhaps we should discuss plans of changing the economic order, such as are involved in such extensive programmes as socialism, and the more specific schemes for dealing with particular problems. Each such programme must be studied on its own merits. Much attention has indeed been devoted to these issues. There are no doubt many merits in socialism, and surely we can imagine a better economic order which would be accompanied by less injustice; but even assuming a fundamental change in the economic order to have occurred, social problems would not have disappeared; there would still be inequalities in the rate of cultural change, and many problems involving human nature would remain. This is not the place to pass rapid judgment on so fundamental a programme as changing the economic order.

SUMMARY

In the discussion of the adjustment of human nature and modern culture we have examined first the theory that we are cave people trying to live in an artificial culture, a theory that is rather readily suggested from the contents of Part II. This theory as popularly conceived is partly erroneous and misleading for several reasons. Foremost among these reasons is the fact that the term, cave man, is a deceptive and an inadequate description of the original nature of man. Furthermore, while our modern culture is recent and objectively different from any culture that has preceded, it does not necessarily, for this reason, cause maladjustment. Although human nature may be stable over a great number of generations, it is quite adaptable and flexible within a lifetime and also culture, by virtue of its rapid changes in recent years, may display considerable adaptability.

However, there is evidence of a lack of harmonious adjustment between modern culture and human nature, as seen particularly in the extent of neuroses and functional psychoses, and in certain social problems. In the more acute cases of maladjustment the more probable solution of the difficulty lies not in attempts to change human nature but rather in attempts to change culture; for the reason that in such acute instances further efforts at changing human nature result in repression of instincts which is followed by objectionable consequences to the individual and aggravations of the social problems. On the other hand the nature of cultural growth and change shows that it is futile to plan any wholesale and powerful control of the course of social evolution. Directing the change of culture is much more difficult than is customarily conceived. It is, however, not necessary to change culture as a whole, for relatively minor changes may result in much better adjustments. These changes, though difficult, may be looked forward to as feasible, if not now, certainly in time. They concern influences affecting the life of children and parental affection, sex education, modification of social codes, shorter hours of labor, recognition of boundaries to selfishness, specific social programmes, and finally it is thought that possibilities of better adjustment lie in the wise development of substitutive activities such as recreation.

PART VI

SOCIAL EVOLUTION, RECONSIDERED

I

When this book, *Social Change,* was first published, fifty years of writing and discussion of "social evolution" was coming to a close. The interest in social evolution was stimulated greatly by the discoveries in biological evolution, and it was hoped that the theory of social evolution would explain the origin and development of civilization as the theory of biological evolution had explained the origin and development of man. Darwin had reduced the evolution of species to three causal factors: variation, natural selection, and heredity. Of the variations of a species, say, in color, in muscular tissue, or in temperature, nature selects for survival those variations which fit it better for adaptation and allows the less well adapted, the weaker, to perish. When heredity passes on any new variation valuable for survival, we see how apes could evolve into Homo sapiens provided new hereditary variations occurred. This discovery was an explanation of a process—a change from one species to another—and not a description. The species had been previously described by a long succession of naturalists such as Linnaeus.

The broad outline of how one species evolves into another as drawn by Darwin is remarkably simple, easily grasped by a person of average education; but its significance was tremendous in a religious age to a people who believed literally in the Bible and that man, the noblest work of God, was created by God himself in the Garden of Eden.

It was natural then that the anthropologists and the sociologists would want an equally satisfactory and significant explanation of how our society evolved. There had been descriptions in world histories of society since the origin of writing, and also descriptions of preliterate societies. What was wanted was explanation rather than description.

Why these attempts were not early successful need not be discussed here except to say that many investigators were too slavish in copying the biological account in terms of selection, adaptation, survival of the fittest, variation, survival, recapitulation, and successive stages of development. Then, too, some of the writers confused evolution with progress, without quite realizing that progress was merely the moral evaluation of evolution. Also, some writers sought to see in both biological and social evolution the guiding force of some supreme being in charting and carrying out the great orderly process of evolution for good, and thus to demonstrate that there was a God behind the process of evolution, both social and biological.

The point of diminishing returns seemed to have been reached by these writers, and the reaction was to abandon the term "social evolution." It was about this time that this book was written, not under the title "Social Evolution," but under "Social Change." Even though the term "social evolution" has come to be used less, the problem still remains; namely, how does society evolve and how did our civilization [1] come to be. As our progenitors came down out of the trees, their society was simple and crude as compared to our own. They had little society; we have a truly magnificent one. How did it come to be?

The common assumption seems to have been that the reason society evolved was because man, who made society, evolved. In other words, men who had not evolved very far would have a crude culture, while men who were fully evolved, such as the people of Western Europe, would have an advanced society. Society was seen as social behavior, and behavior was a function of biological

[1] The word "civilization" has many different uses, such as any set of higher moral qualities of society, varying from author to author; as any of the superior virtues of any large, orderly state; as the social organization based upon civil status rather than kinship status; as synonymous with culture whether preliterate or modern; and as the tail end of cultural development which began many hundred thousand years ago. It is in this latter sense that the word is here used.

structure. A duck had webbed feet and swam. A chicken did not have webbed feet and could not swim. The animals of the farm, horses, pigs, sheep, and dogs, behaved differently because they had different structures. As we behave differently from the apes, so we have of course a different structure, particularly in our ability to speak a language. A European behaves differently from a Melanesian—hence he is supposed to have a different structure. The outstanding characteristic of man is his large brain, more than twice as large as that of the largest living anthropoids. Hence it was readily assumed that superior civilizations were the result of superior brains.

But since the size of the heads of some races with less capable cultures was not greatly different from that of Western Europeans, it was assumed that brains differed not only in size but somehow in quality of organic matter. Though writers of the late nineteenth century said they were seeking the cause of the evolution of society, they spoke and wrote as if men created civilization rather than as if it evolved. Since society was created by man, the men with the more complex and elaborate civilizations were *ipso facto* men with greater mental abilities and hence with superior brains.

So axiomatic did this seem that a superior culture was considered as genuine evidence of superior hereditary brains. Higher cultures occurred therefore because men with better brains occurred. This assumption of how we got our civilization was considered about as obvious as that God created man. The Garden-of-Eden story, though, was more widely held, for not so many were concerned with the origins of civilizations as with the Book of Genesis. The identification of civilization with behavior and the correlation of behavior with organic structure were great stumbling blocks in the scientific inquiry of the causes of social evolution, for civilization was seen as society and society as social behavior dependent upon organic structure. This was the obstacle which led to the point of diminishing returns in the early writings. Civilization was not seen as an accumulation of culture or as a conditioning environment in which inadequately organized infants were born.

A mighty blow was delivered against this explanation by anthropologists, particularly Franz Boas in his work on the mind of primitive man and on the mental ability of races. He made an excellent demonstration that peoples with primitive cultures could have just as much inherited mental ability as modern man with his advanced civilizations; and that levels of culture of different peoples were not indexes of their inherited abilities.

Then, too, telling was the challenge, stated in this book, that there was no evidence that the genetic capacity for brain function of the whole population of Europe had changed any at all during the past twenty-five thousand years, for the brain cases of men were as large then as now. That the texture of the brains of modern man is superior now to what it was then was charged but really was merely a claim without any data at all to support it.

This demonstration was a purely negative one. It was like showing that the Garden-of-Eden story of the creation of man was false without telling how man was created. So destruction of the belief that culture evolved only as biological man evolved did not provide an explanation of how culture did evolve.

However, on re-reading the section on social evolution in *Social Change* it is thought that the essential factors that explain social evolution are there to be found. They are there set forth quite modestly, with apologies for the scarcity of evidence. Nor are they drawn sharply and with emphasis. Since the first printing of this book, there have been additional researches which strengthen and confirm those there stated. Also, there has been little criticism of these theories of social evolution in the years since their first publication.[2]

This reconsideration of the problem of social

[2] The only part of the theory that has been criticized is the concept of cultural lag—criticisms based, I think, upon distortions and misunderstandings. However, the concept of cultural lag is not a fundamental part of the theory of social evolution.

evolution is to appraise it in the light of the experience since *Social Change* was published, to outline the problem and the theory more sharply, and to integrate the factors more tightly. The presentation is made brief and with little reference to evidence, purposely, to make the factors stand out without being obscured by detail. It is desired to see the forests without attention to particular trees.

To argue that the problem of social evolution has been solved refers only to the essentials of the problem; that is, essentials that are demanded by a general curiosity concerned with the larger aspects of the problem. For instance, those who want to know the general processes whereby modern civilization became what it is are not, for this reason, concerned in the details of why the Mohammedan civilization arose or differed from that of the Hindus. Nor are those who are interested in the general processes whereby the apes evolved into men concerned for that reason in the evolution of the wasps. The evolution of wasps and of Mohammedan culture should of course follow these general processes. But the general processes do not explain the details of any particular culture or species.[3]

Nor does the argument that the problem of

[3] Anthropologists who have done such excellent work on social evolution have, I think, not defined the problem properly. In general they abandoned the explanation of culture for the attempt to explain cultures.

social evolution has been solved mean that no further researches are needed. Quite the contrary. Science grows by refining and by accretion. For instance, in biology the factors of variation, selection, and heredity were set forth as one explanation of the origin of species. But we have since learned much about heredity, and there is much we want to know about reproductive isolation and the causes of variation. Indeed, research on the explanatory factors of biological evolution has been accelerated. So, even though we should know the main factors that have developed our civilization, further researches on social change are expected to be accelerated rather than to be stopped.

Before we consider the factors that explain social evolution we may ask the question: What is it that is evolving? [4] The answer is usually: Society. But insofar as society is inherited biological behavior, then we have no evidence that the biological element in society has been evolving during the

---

[4] There is considerable variation in what the different writers in this field are discussing. Toynbee seems to be discussing culture areas whose boundaries are largely determined by the spread of a particular religion or moral system. Sorokin is concerned with the variation in an attitude across history. Spengler deals with a creative spirit that is tied in with an effective and expanding state. Brooks Adams, when he uses the term "civilization," is talking about an effective and large politically and economically organized state. None of these writers is discussing culture as the anthropologists and sociologists use the term.

past twenty-five thousand years.[5]   That part of society that has evolved is some other element than the biological.

To the anthropologists, particularly to Robert H. Lowie and to Alfred Kroeber, in 1917, we are indebted for the clearest conception of what this other element is.   It is culture.   Social evolution becomes then cultural evolution; and the evolution of groups since glacial times is part of the evolution of culture.

2

What then are the factors that explain cultural evolution?   They are four: invention, accumulation, diffusion, and adjustment.[6]

[5] Up until the brain case of the anthropoid that was to become man had reached its present size and until the ability to use a language was developed, there was a correlation between social evolution and biological evolution.

A species may remain for a long time without any evolutionary change. Such is the case with modern Europeans over the past thousand years (and perhaps over seventy-five thousand years or longer). Since a change cannot be explained by a constant, the change over the last thousand years or longer in Western Europe cannot be explained biologically.

[6] Of these four factors, the central one is invention, as the central factor in biological evolution is mutation; viz., a new variation that is inherited. Accumulation, diffusion, and adjustment all lead to further invention, but they do more. Each is a significant and special process, irrespective of their stimulation of new inventions.

1. Invention as here used is not confined to mechanical invention but includes social inventions, such as the League of Nations, and innovations in other parts of culture, as, for instance, the invention of a religious ritual or of an alphabet. It also comprises scientific discoveries. Invention is defined as a combination of existing and known elements of culture, material and/or non-material, or a modification of one to form a new one. The modification of an invention is often little more than an improvement. The vast number of patents granted to inventors are for quite minor improvements on some basic invention. By inventions we do not mean only the basic or important inventions, but the minor ones and the improvements. Inventions, then, are the evidence on which we base our observations of social evolution.

The crucial position of inventions in cultural evolution precipitates the question as to how they are made. They result from the operation of three factors: mental ability, demand, and the existence of other cultural elements out of which inventions are fashioned, sometimes called the cultural base.

A current theory of inventions is an heroic one. Inventors are geniuses. Inventors, it is true, may have superior mental ability as compared with others in the same group at the same time. But over time the proportion of superior inherited mental ability in a group would be the same if there had been no biological evolution. There would be more inherited mental ability in modern Europe than there was when it was peopled by Cro-Magnon man only because there are more people in Europe now than then. Insofar as mental ability is learned, then there would be a much larger proportion of men of such ability in Europe than in Cro-Magnon times, owing to the fact that there is more to learn.

The demand for invention, the second factor in the inventional process, does not always meet with success; but extreme demand, sometimes called necessity, is said to be the mother of invention. Many inventions and discoveries are made accidentally while working on something else; for these demand did not direct the invention. Such are many discoveries in pure science. The use of an invention, however, implies a demand. This demand may vary over time and is a cultural variable rather than a biological one. Thus there may have been much more demand for inventions during the past hundred years than formerly. At any one time it is selective; some are demanded and some are not. In prehistoric times there may not have been much variation in demand. Social demand now directs the learning process and may be much greater in one sector of culture than in another.

The third factor in the inventing process, which is the number of existing elements, takes us to the second factor in the explanation of social evolution, namely, accumulation.

2. Accumulation occurs when more new elements are added to the cultural base than are lost. In general the loss is greater the smaller the area. For the earth as a whole the accumulation of inventions [7] is inconceivably vast at the present time. Presumably inventions accumulate for the same reason they are made: they have utility. But there is replacement of the more efficient by the less efficient, so there may be much loss, particularly in a small area. The loss may also be great in a non-material culture, such as religion, where the subtractions might be greater than the additions. In science, culture is very accumulative. The accumulation process was speeded first by the development of speech and then by writing.

Societies in action are an accumulation of learned ways of behaving. To say that societies are an accumulation has advantages, in studying change, over the customary statement that society is behavior. Society is both behavior and an accumula-

[7] Counting one invention only once, no matter what the extent of duplication.

tion. But the emphasis in behavior is often associated with biological behavior, which is for man a constant over the time under consideration for a population. It is the learned behavior that has varied with time and is accumulative.

The advantage in studying social evolution or emphasizing accumulation is seen in that it destroys the ethnocentric myth and egotistical fantasy that man created his civilization. Much truer is the idea that he inherited it.

Different peoples are born into different accumulations of culture. Though they have the same inherited mental abilities, their operating mental abilities may vary enormously, according to the pile of culture into which they are born. A baby born of a woman but reared in the meager culture of wolves will probably create not a single element of culture that is different from the culture of wolves, and the child can do only what the wolves do, even though the child were the offspring of an Isaac Newton. So also a child picked at random from the public schools of Greece to-day can do operations in mathematics that Aristotle could not do. The accumulation of mathematics is much greater today than it was in 350 B.C.

This accumulation tends to be exponential because an invention is a combination of existing elements, and these elements are accumulative. As the amount of interest paid an investor is a function of the size of the capital he has invested, so the number of inventions is a function of the size of the cultural base; that is, the number of existing elements in the culture. In compound interest the principal accumulates, as does the "principal" of culture. There are more inventions in the United States to-day (per unit of population and per unit of time) then among the Eskimo, not because the people of the United States have any more inherent mental ability, but for the reason that we have a larger cultural base; that is, more with which to invent.

Put in figures, this argument would mean that if a cultural base of a hundred thousand elements yielded one invention, then a cultural base of a million elements would yield a thousand inventions, even if the inherent mental ability of the peoples of the two cultural bases were the same. But in reality the yield of the second cultural base would be more than a thousand inventions. The reason lies in the definition of an invention as a combination of existing elements; and as the existing elements increase, the number of combinations increases faster than by a fixed ratio. Thus three elements can be combined by twos in three different ways, four elements in six different ways, and five elements in ten different ways. Even though only a microscopic fraction of combinations will result in a useful invention, the principle of an increasing rate holds.

So exponential accumulation means acceleration, a phenomenon borne out by the curves of Hornell Hart and Harvey C. Lehman of recent years and by the data of Darmstadter.

Exponential growth seldom exists for long in reality, for the increments quickly become too large for reality, as is obviously the case with compound interest and with population growth. The accumulation of culture has then only a tendency to grow exponentially. Reality lessens the slope or flattens it out eventually, perhaps to begin growing exponentially again for a time. Exponential growth may work out to be irregular—now popularly called cyclical.

This numerical analysis has been proceeding as if all elements were the same, much as the statistics of population are all of the same units; viz., human beings. Actually there is the greatest variety in inventions even in the same part of a culture. A steam engine or a dynamo can be fitted into many more combinations than a windmill or a sailing ship. Some inventions are prolific in their stimulation of other inventions, others hardly at all; hence more irregularities in growth. When we say that the British and the Americans are very inventive, what should be said is that the inventions of the steam engine, of steel-making processes, the discoveries in electricity, have led to an unprecedented number of other inventions. A burst of creativeness may be explained in terms of a fortuitous combination of a few inventions, significant in proliferating others.

There can also be declines in the rate of inventiveness without an actual loss of inventions. Those who deal with the qualities of culture as in philosophy and art often report a decline, a decline which is analogous to a lessening of patents on a particular invention. Immediately after a big invention is made, a plow, a locomotive, or some other, the improvements as shown in patents are very numerous, but they lessen as the years go by until some other fundamental change is made.

If a people happens to be the carrier of a culture that is evolving rapidly, it is given approbation as a creative people. On the other hand, if a people with the same inherent abilities is the possessor of a culture that is changing very slowly, as in isolated islands or mountains, it is spoken of as a backward people. Whereas the difference would be better described by saying that with one people the culture is changing rapidly; with the other it is changing slowly. A people is the carrier of a culture that is growing either rapidly or slowly.

In prehistoric times cultural evolution was very slow; perhaps so slow as to be invisible over four or five generations. Such societies are referred to as stationary. Even so the change could be exponential, but the rate would be very low over a large unit of time. A people in such a slowly changing culture would be far out-distanced by a people in a culture that was accelerating rapidly.

The functional relationship between the size of the cultural base and the number of new inventions plus the tendency for cultural elements to accumulate helps to explain how our civilization came from simple beginnings to what it is today. The view of culture as a growing accumulation is more realistic than the conception of it as behavior or as the creation of peoples.

3. Diffusion, the third factor in the process of social evolution, is an expression used by anthropologists in referring to the spread of inventions from one area to others, usually from the area of their origin. The spread of inventions is promoted by the various communication and transportation inventions. We have been speaking in preceding paragraphs as if the only way a culture of a people grew was through an invention made by the people out of existing culture elements. But the people of a culture area may acquire inventions without making them, by importing them from elsewhere. In fact most of the inventions of a limited area are acquired by diffusion, as has been shown in the long literature on independent origin versus

diffusion. Diffusion may then be viewed as simply one source of invention in a particular area, in contrast to another region; namely, that dependent upon the three factors of mental ability, demand, and the existing elements. But diffusion is also more than the source of invention. It is a process of bringing many different inventions from various sources together in a common cultural base. It becomes then a very important factor in explaining some particular culture as well as an explanatory factor in the growth of culture as a whole. By diffusion a people profits by the inventional contributions from many different parts of the world. The evolution of culture is more rapid because of diffusion. Thus the growth of culture in any one area arises not so much from the functional relationship between the number of inventions and the cultural base as from importation. But, of course, the faster acquisition of inventions from elsewhere adds to the cultural base and hence increases the rate of inventiveness.

Bursts of creativeness of a people sometimes occur because of the diffusion of significant inventions or of large numbers of them. Thus the creativeness of the Renaissance period in Italy seems to have been due in part to infiltration of inventions (ideational) from the heritage of antiquity long buried.

One of the puzzling questions about social evolution has been the unequal levels of culture among different peoples and in different areas. Formerly it was attributed to racial abilities, but since this is highly improbable, then the question of why a culture is complex and efficient among one people and simple and crude among another still remains. The answer is to be sought in the rate of accumulation. Still we want to know why the accumulation has gone further in one place than another. Unequal rates of acceleration partly explain the phenomenon. But location plus diffusion appears to be the better explanation for most comparisons. For inventions to be diffused they must travel. Hence isolated spots benefit less by diffusion than do locations at crossroads. What is a barrier to travel at one time, high mountains and oceans, for instance, may not be at another time, when travel inventions exist to surmount the barriers, as, for instance, the airplane and the steamboat.

As an illustration, at one time the culture of the eastern Mediterranean was at the crossroads, a focus for diffusion. Just at this time there was an unusual number of significant inventions to be diffused into this favored spot: the domesticated horse, the improved seagoing boat, metal-working, the wheel, cattle, the alphabet, writing, ceramics, and a variety of customs and ideas. It is not surprising therefore that the cultural advance at this time and in this place received such a great push forward. The advance is usually credited to the genius of the Greek people, as was claimed by Francis Galton, whereas, according to the theory here advanced, there is no reason to think that the great push to culture at this time in this region favorable for the diffusion of new inventions might not have occurred if the Greeks had been Negroes.

With all these important inventions diffused, the culture accumulation accelerated more than it did behind the barriers of the deserts and the jungles and took a commanding lead over other cultures.

Diffusion is therefore a factor in the growth of world culture as a whole, especially in very early times, and particularly is it an important explanation of cultural growth in a smaller area.

4. Adjustment of one part of society to another is important in understanding the evolution of culture, for the parts of culture are intertwined in varying degrees. For instance, government is related to economic institutions; the economic institutions are related to the family; the family is related to education; education is related to science; science is related to religion, and so on. In some cases the connection may be very close, as, for instance, between highway and automobile. In others, the connection is more remote, as between poetry and the steam engine. This interrelationship is the organization of culture.

Because of this interrelationship an invention occurring in one part and producing a change therein will also occasion a change in a part closely correlated. Thus the invention of the factory with machinery driven by steam produced a change in the family by taking occupations out of the home, especially those of women, and putting them in factories. Hence an invention in one part of a culture may produce many changes in other differing parts of a culture.

These changes are often inventions in the nonmaterial part of culture, as for instance the factory led to the invention of workmen's compensation. We may speak of this new social invention as an adjustment to a change in the material culture, namely, the factory.

Inventions in one part of culture may occur then as an adjustment to an invention in a related part of culture, as well as by diffusion from another culture area and as well as by independent origin.

The adjustment of one part of culture to a change in another part is then a source of invention, but we treat it as a new factor in social evolution, along with invention, accumulation, and diffusion, because of its very great potentiality in producing changes in culture.

These adjustments do not take place instantaneously but are made after a delay and are called cultural lags. Over the long course of social evolution measured in thousands of years cultural lags are invisible. At any particular moment, however, they may be numerous and acute.

A society long stationary without any social changes is in equilibrium. The various parts, through trial and error, have become adjusted to one another. There is a harmonious relationship of the various culture trains. There is no social evolution. But when a significant invention occurs in one part of culture, the balance is disturbed, change is set up in the other related parts as a process of adjustment to the new invention. Thus social evolution goes forward by inventions which produce a disequilibrium in society, which in turn sets up forces which seek a new equilibrium.

Some parts of culture have been observed to be particularly influential in favoring invention in other parts, at least in modern historical times. A stable and efficient governmental organization appears to be one such condition. Government is intertwined with many other parts of a culture. A disorganized government torn by civil strife and inadequately supported by taxes does not seem favorable to invention in the arts. Again, a densely populated area such as a city seems to be one in which change takes place more readily than in small communities of one hundred or more persons. Certainly the number and variety of social inventions in a community of twenty families is more limited than in a metropolis of five million inhabitants. Perhaps back of the advantages of such social organization lies an economic factor. Economic institutions are also correlated with many other social institutions. Thus it takes wealth to support a large capable government, and a big city rests upon at least high productivity. Indeed, in modern times variations in economic conditions produce changes that are widely spread over the different parts of a culture. One more of these empirical observations of significant interrelationships may be noted. It is the potentiality of technological and scientific changes to produce changes elsewhere in the culture. The multiplier factor for a mechanical invention or a discovery in applied science is exceptionally large in our modern civilization.

The difficulty of adjustment, as here defined, may be quite great, involving as it may the creation of new social inventions. For a simple and crude culture with an influx of new inventions by diffusion the problem of adjustment may be too difficult and may be accompanied by great disorganization, as has been the case with some groups of American Indians.

The adjustment of the respective parts of a culture to one another in the inventional process is evidently an important factor in explaining social evolution.

3

The problem of social evolution, in conclusion, is seen as the problem of explaining how society changes and of answering our curiosity as to how our modern civilization came to be. The traditional explanation has been in terms of the evolution of inherited mental ability. This explanation may be largely valid for that long period before the brain of the animal that was to be man had attained its present size and before he attained the free command over language which he now has. For a period of many thousands of years, however, this explanation is not valid, for there is no evidence that the inherited mental ability of man has changed and there is much evidence to indicate that it has not. Inherited mental ability is a factor in our civilization, of course, but over time it cannot be a factor in the changing of civilization unless inherited mental ability has changed. A change cannot be explained by a constant.

With the traditional explanation of inherited mental ability inadequate, what are the factors that have caused the great evolution of our culture from crude and simple beginnings to the magnificence it has now attained? The explanation lies in four factors: invention, accumulation, diffusion, and adjustment. An understanding of these four factors makes it clear how our civilization has come to be what it is. These four factors offer also a general explanation of any one culture, such as that of China, or India, or Greece. This understanding is one of broad perspective, much as is Darwin's explanation of biological evolution in terms of variation, natural selection, and heredity.